Americans Together

Americans Together

STRUCTURED DIVERSITY IN A MIDWESTERN TOWN

Hervé Varenne

*Qu'est-ce qu'un mythe, aujourd'hui?
Je donnerai tout de suite une première réponse très
simple qui a'accorde parfaitement avec l'étymologie:
le mythe est une parole.*
—Roland Barthes, *Mythologies*

Teachers College Press
Teachers College, Columbia University
New York and London

Library of Congress Cataloging in Publication Data

Varenne, Hervé, 1948-
      Americans together, structured diversity in a midwestern town.

      Originally presented as the author's thesis, University of Chicago.
      Bibliography: p.
      1. Middle West—Social conditions—Case studies. 2. Middle classes—Middle West. I. Title.
HN79.A14V37 1978   309.1'77'03   77-10109
ISBN 0-8077-2519-6

Manufactured in the United States of America

92 91 90 89   4 5 6

To my father and mother

Contents

List of Tables

Preface

The work of American social scientists on their own culture has often been conceived as a search for the "reality" behind the "myths" of America. It is only proper for native intellectuals to criticize the actualization of the ideology that is the basis for their cultural identification. Foreign students of this ideology do not, however, have the same responsibility. Their responsibility lies elsewhere.

By necessity, foreign observers are placed in a position different from that occupied by native philosophers. Their personal and intellectual experience of everyday life in the foreign country is different. They are not involved in quite the same way, and thus they must write in a different mode. This has not traditionally been a serious issue for anthropologists, since they have usually addressed audiences who could be assumed to be in essentially the same situation in relation to the culture studied as they themselves were. The goal was to present a picture of an alternate life-style, and to fulfill this goal it was enough for them to do what they are best equipped to do; that is, to present a nonevaluative picture of a system in its own terms. The task is more delicate when the observer addresses himself to the very people whose culture he is reporting on, for how useful the type of knowledge an outsider has to offer is not obvious.

I am a native of France and was raised in a closely related, though different, cultural atmosphere. It is as a Frenchman that I have attempted to understand American ideology as it is lived, or at least talked, in a small Midwestern town. I have lived in the United States for nine years now, four in Chicago while I was attending the University of Chicago, one in the small town, which I will call Appleton, where I conducted the fieldwork on which this book is based, and four in New York as assistant professor at Teachers College, Columbia University. These experiences have proved complementary in the development of my understanding and appreciation of America. The specific character of this understanding is, of course, the result of my own development as an individual with a certain history. Some of the American teachers and friends who have read this work have honored me by saying that they sometimes recognized themselves in these pages. They have also told me that they recognized the point of view from which I looked, that my French and Catholic background came through.

What, then, can I say to Americans? What I can say, I believe, is that there is a coherence to their culture that they may lose sight of as they get involved with the inevitable flaws that mar the picture. From a distance, the flaws disappear or even become harmonious parts of the canvas.

What I have tried to do, then, is outline a certain cultural ideology in its own terms and not in terms of an idealized picture that the natives may cherish or in comparison with my own idealized culture. I believe I have done this faithfully, and I hope that this work will be an apt return gift to all those—friends, teachers, informants, colleagues, acquaintances, and foundations—who have given me so much in so many different ways.

It is not without some trepidation that I offer these pages. For I know what my informants, friends, and, I am sure, readers from similar backgrounds value most. And thus I know that some of the things I will say will strike them as at least implicit criticism of their way of life. I note repeatedly disunity, stress, and lack of love in families and in the town. These things, though they are acknowledged to exist in private, are not thought to be appropriate matter for public display. Conversely, I believe that Appleton is as good an example as any of American democratic life. I believe I saw there the best and truest America, which will be for another part of my audience quite as constroversial a thing to say.

I realize these things. I hope that they will not lead the reader to reject outright an effort that is trying to do something other than justify or denigrate America. I hope that readers will be able to withhold temporarily their habitual responses to the realities I explore and perhaps get a new perspective on them that might even help them operate more consciously and deliberately in their own culture.

I thus offer this work in exchange for the gifts I received in

Appleton, and I hope it will be accepted not because it always flatters the sensibilities of the persons involved but because it is an honest attempt to assume the responsibilities of a foreigner talking to the people who have commissioned him to hold a mirror up to them. With all this in mind, I want to thank all the people and institutions who have helped me, at one stage or another, in one way or another, with the creation of this work.

I want to thank, first, the Wenner-Gren Foundation for Anthropological Research, which provided most of the funds that made this fieldwork possible, and the Department of Anthropology of the University of Chicago for supplementing these funds and supporting me financially throughout my years of graduate work. I want to thank the many students and friends who have contributed to and criticized my ideas about America, particularly Marilyn Blackmon, James Boon, David Buchdahl, Marian Eaton, Elizabeth Haggens, Anthony Seeger, Richard Weber, and the participants in Professor Milton Singer's Workshop in American Culture. I also want to thank the faculty and staff of the department for the challenging atmosphere and opportunities offered me. In particular, I want to thank Professors Lloyd A. Fallers, A. K. Ramanujan, and David M. Schneider, who have read and criticized the dissertation on which the present work is based and have encouraged me on my way. Professor Singer must receive special notice here, since he read the bulk of my early papers and drafts and supported me with continued expressions of interest. It has always been a pleasure and a challenge to work with him.

Since I joined the faculty at Teachers College, many other persons have helped with the work. I would like to mention Patricia Caesar, Lawrence Cremin, Clifford Hill, Francis Ianni, Marge Kelly, Leslie Kiss, and particularly Professor Hope Leichter, without whom this work might never have gone through its final mutation from manuscript to printed page.

Special reference must be made to my parents, to whom my debts, in all areas, are too great for me ever to repay. My mother typed parts of the original draft; my father contributed philosophical commentaries. Both sacrificed personal comfort to support me financially through the years of graduate study. But it is their moral support that is irreplaceable and that I acknowledge in offering them this, my first book.

Finally, this book would not have been the same without the loving presence of my wife, Susan, during the months of final composition and revision. I want to thank her especially for having typed the final copy of the manuscript when it was a dissertation and for having retyped it for publication, for having helped bring my English closer to the norm, for having given me new insights into American life. But most of all, it is because I love her that I close this Preface with this expression of gratitude to her.

Hervé Varenne

Chicago and New York,
September 1971–June 1976

Introduction

Since we have been a conversation—man has learnt much and named many of the heavenly ones. Since language really became actual as conversation, the gods have acquired names and a world has appeared. But again it should be noticed: the presence of the gods and the appearance of the world are not merely a consequence of the actualization of language, they are contemporaneous with it. And this to the extent that it is precisely in the naming of the gods, and in the transmutation of the world into word, that the real conversation, which we ourselves are, consists.
—Martin Heidegger, "Hölderlin and the Essence of Poetry"

This is a book about people. It is about some people who live in a town in the Midwest of the United States somewhere between Peoria and Dubuque.

Why should their lives—personal, social, and cultural—interest us? What can we learn from them? Most of the people who appear in this book are white, middle class, and Protestant. For many readers, such people will not have the quality of exoticism that South American Indians, African Pygmies, Appalachian whites, the blacks of Harlem, or even the Irish and Italians of South Boston may have. For many, Midwestern whites are "us." They are "us" in a most immediate and mythic sense. Hated or loved, they seem easy to understand. There appears to be no need for translation in order to apprehend their reality.

For some, these Midwestern whites are still the envied citizens of romantic small towns where one knows everybody and is known by them, where society is on a human scale, where the pace is slow, where one can watch the seasons of the year and the seasons of life come and go. The image is of white-frame churches and the shrill voices of children in the quiet streets under the drooping elms. It becomes all the more a romantic and nostalgic image with the realization that the elms are dying, that beneath the quiet is the dull, persistent rumbling of the trucks on the interstate highway that bypasses the town, and that often the stillness is broken by the roar of a pack of motorcycles, snowmobiles, or hot rods leaving in their tracks empty beer cans and whiffs of marijuana smoke. Mass society has touched the small town, some say, and they mourn.

For others, small towns are Main Streets, environments of petty gripes, rigid ideologies, intolerance, and prejudice deadening to those without courage or the opportunity to escape into the cosmopolitanism and real life of the urban centers. For these critics, small towns are closed societies, stuffy, oppressive; they are places to run away from.

For both advocates and critics, small towns are considered simple societies, one-dimensional cultures of conformity removed from the complexities of mass urban society. Conflicts have been solved, moral dilemmas are absent. One can raise happy children there who will remain sheltered from the evils of society until they have the strength to withstand them as adults.

This image is susceptible to a positive or negative evaluation. The perception of the nature of small-town life that underlies each evaluation is the same, and it is problematic. Can there really be societies quite so one-dimensional as the small towns of popular sociology? Whether Americans live in the cities, congratulating themselves on a narrow escape *from* small towns or yearning for the opportunity to escape *to* small towns, whether they live in small towns and talk about their experience to themselves and to outsiders, they are prone to view small towns as something that I believe they neither are nor could be.

I lived for one year in such a town. It is not quite so small nor quite so remote from metropolitan centers one imagines when conjuring up the image of such a town. It is a town, though, that its inhabitants and visitors would consider small. And yet what I found was not simplicity, conformity, lack of conflict, or dilemma. There was, rather, an intensity of life, a depth of feeling for the tragic element in the human situation that none of my reading in the academic (and nonacademic) literature on small towns had led me to expect.

We have learned that neither poverty of means nor primitiveness of technology nor isolation from the major centers of civilization means poverty of imagination, primitiveness of expression, or isolation from the central problems posed to *all* men by the nature of their relationships with the world around them and each other. We know this applied to the thinkers whose wisdom has grounded the greatness of our civilization: Socrates, Jesus, Shakespeare, Pascal, Marx. We have come to accept as somehow worthwhile the wisdom of truly foreign sages like the Dogon Ogotemmeli or the Yaqui "Don Juan." But this should not be accompanied by the kind of reverse snobbism that scorns the no less wise world view that underlies the nonextraordinary lives of the middle class.

To find wisdom only in the most foreign forms bespeaks a false humility that can lead only to more radical degrees of ethnocentrism. We, French or Americans, are no less exotic to each other and to the rest of the world that looks at us than are those at whom we look. The traditional goal of the social sciences in general, and anthropology in particular, has been the attempt to demonstrate that "out there" they are not savages (free from the convention of civilization or subjugated by ignorance, disease, and feebleness of mind) but men with all the qualities and potentialities that we recognize in ourselves. This demonstration has gone hand in hand with a constant reiteration that what is strange to "us" is familiar, ordinary, to "them"—*l'exotisme est quotidien* as Georges Condominas puts it.

The other side of the coin is that our everday life is exotic, too, and one of the main goals of this book is to try to make the familiar strange. The simple awareness that there are other ways of life than our own may be enough to make us realize that we do not know ourselves quite so fully as our empathic understanding of our situation may lead us to believe we do. But becoming aware of the exotic qualities of our everyday life is a complex process, and we do not have many models showing how to go about it. Claude Lévi-Strauss has argued that most of our cultural ideas, like those most "others" have about themselves, are the product of wild thinking—*la pensée sauvage*—rather than of a rational discovery of the logic of nature. We may agree that this has intuitive validity, but the demonstration has not really been made.

What I want to do is surprise readers into a reevaluation of what they thought they knew about small towns, the Midwest, the middle class, whites,—maybe themselves. Throughout the book I will stress everyday life and everyday interpretations of the world. At times I will refer to the more esoteric knowledge that cultural specialists possess, but more as a way of staking a claim than as a central argument. I want to demonstrate that everyday life is internally structured in a complex fashion. That this structure should look like the structure of the great tradition of America is interesting and probably not surprising. But the discovery of correspondences between great and small traditions is not the central point of this book. In fact, at the time I was in Appleton, and even while I was writing the main body of the book, my knowledge of the great tradition was very limited. Except for what I gleaned from a few works written by sociologists and anthropologists about small towns, I was essentially ignorant of America, and what I have come to know of it derives mainly from my encounter with the everyday life of my informants.

I am an anthropologist, and as an anthropologist I went to Appleton and am now reporting on its natives (many of whom were not born there!). In a Postface to the body of the book, I will detail my theoretical position for those who would like to go into these questions at greater depth. But what can anthropology contribute?

Traditionally anthropology has demonstrated from still another angle what disciplines such as sociology and social psychology also demonstrated: that our nature as human beings is but the product of our position in a certain historical process. To attain an analytical understanding of "who we are" it is necessary to become aware of our total context, what we might refer to as "the world." At the most general, there is us, and there is the world, a world given to—indeed, imposed upon—us. It is a world that we must react to, but also one that we can operate on, and thus change. The outcome of our operations then becomes a part of that very world "outside" to which we must react anew, on which we must operate, and so on in an infinite and ever-expanding spiral.

The process of our intervention in the world is oftentimes mechanical and essentially unconscious. In these situations we have no real "choice." In other situations the pressure of the historical situation is indeterminate. While boundaries are set, they are very broad and allow for much variation. Choices must be made. And insofar as these are "conscious"—that is, insofar as we have verbalized the unconscious—we translate the world into a language, a *culture* that interprets it and organizes how it is to be perceived. Human beings in all situations possess enough freedom from unconscious determinisms to have developed everywhere such structures of interpretation and in the process to have submitted themselves to new forms of determinism that must also be analyzed if we are to understand fully who we are.

Franz Boas wrote that anthropology is dedicated to expanding our knowledge of "how we are conditioned by [our civilization], how our bodies, our language, our modes of thinking and acting are determined by limits imposed upon us by our environment." This is done through an exploration of "the life process and behavior of man under conditions fundamentally different from our own."[1] From the beginning, anthropologists have refused to be confined to the intellectual ghetto of curiosity-seekers and have insisted on the relevance of their insights to an understanding of the culture that produced them, and have, indeed, shown the way along which further research ought to proceed. Anthropology has probably contributed most to the analysis of these processes, processes that are also at work in our societies as anthropologists have long agreed.

Margaret Mead, for example, is famous for her brilliant attempts at relating her work among "strange" societies to issues of immediate interest to her readers. She has commented extensively on such questions as: Is a crisis at adolescence a necessary part of the process of growing up? Is the division of labor between the sexes as we know it a "natural" thing? What is the relationship between early socialization and adult character? A. R. Radcliffe-Brown through his students W. Lloyd Warner, Alfred L. Kroeber, and Claude Lévi-Strauss have all commented more or less formally on our own culture. This is a great tradition, and it is not without trepidation that I attempt to place my work in it. My work would not have taken the shape it developed had it not been for their contributions.

And yet the major efforts of these anthropologists in this area have quite a different quality from those they made in other areas. Take Margaret Mead, for example. She studied the Samoans or the Arapesh from the point of view of ignorance, as an outsider. She wrote about Americans in her book *And Keep Your Powder Dry* from the point of view of intuitive knowledge, as an insider. We must, of course, take into account the context of Mead's book: she wrote it as a conscious attempt to raise the morale of Americans as they entered World War II. As she was writing, other researchers were taking a more strictly anthropological route—for example, W. Lloyd Warner in his work on social structure, and Geoffrey Gorer in his work on national character, two authors representative of the main approaches to the study of America at the time. A few years earlier, Robert and Helen Lynd had written two books about Muncie, Indiana, often considered to be the first examples of the application of anthropological techniques to the study of America.

The Lynds were already conscious of the danger, "never wholly avoidable, of not being completely objective in viewing a culture in which one's life is imbedded, of falling into the old error of starting out, despite oneself, with emotionally weighted presuppositions and consequently failing even to get outside the field one set out so bravely to objectify and study."[2] But in fact what limited their insights was not so much their emotions as the mode of thinking they had adopted. They agreed with the functionalist tradition that there are, "despite infinite variations in detail, not so many major things that people do,"[3] and they adopted the list of things set forth by W. H. R. Rivers, a list he had used to deal with his ethnographic descriptions of primitive cultures. In the process the Lynds transformed what, though not so obviously, were in fact cultural categories into natural ones of universal validity. It took anthropologists many more years to recognize this mistake than for the Lynds to "accept" the validity of the foreign experiences they observed.

When anthropologists are away from home, their temptation to use their own categories to organize their data is not quite so crippling, since the data itself obliges them to transcend the boundaries. To say that in most primitive societies kinship is the foundation of social organization is to criticize implicitly our thinking about the family as solely an agency of early socialization. In many societies the family is much more, and, indeed, in ours it is also more. As Hope Leichter has recently argued, it is very much an *educative* institution.[4] As David Schneider has pointed out, the symbols that structure the definitions of the family, ethnicity, and religion are essentially the same.[5] From a different angle, Lawrence Cremin makes the same point when he says that education is not something that takes place solely in the schools, but that churches, libraries, newspapers, and so forth have a distinctively educational function.[6]

To criticize the Lynds, Mead, Warner, or Geoffrey Gorer for implicit ethnocentrism should not, however, be taken as a denigration of their findings. I am convinced that my work, too, is ethnocentric in some of its most basic assumptions, those of which I am not conscious. Only outsiders to my frame of reference will be able to perceive these assumptions, just as I am now able to perceive some of the assumptions behind the Lynds' organization of their book. In 1929 they could not have done much else than what they did, and that was pioneering. In their context, they *were* objective. In *my* context, which is different from theirs if only because their work itself is part of it, my attempt to be "objective" about our own society, a goal that I share with them, must be based on a criticism of their work. To be part of a tradition is not to duplicate the works of the founding fathers.

Progress is being made. We are becoming more critically aware of the exact nature of these "cultural prejudices," which the early writers knew existed, even though they could not exactly locate them. We are discovering that culture does not operate simply at the level of manifest values but at the deeper levels of the semantic constraints built into language that prevent the speaker of any language from easily describing any other way of perceiving the world than the one the language itself provides. In other words, a shift is occurring in the perception of what it is exactly that anthropology must objectify. It is because I intend this book to participate in the exploration of this new way that it does not look like a traditional community study. I did not use the traditional categories to organize my material, though all the data that could have fit under them are there, but spread throughout the book in an effort to make a different point.

I ask the same question social scientists ask: What is the reality of American culture? My answers, however, proceed along a different line from the one they generally follow. I am not interested so much in how Americans do certain things as in how they say these things, not so much in their actions as in their verbalized perceptions. To this extent I see my task not as one of demythologizing commonsense interpretations by demonstrating how distant they are from action, but as one of exploring these interpretations to understand with more precision their exact structure. I will not ask: Is America democratic? Not only does this way of asking the question ensure a negative phrasing of the answer—how could America "be" democratic, since cultural interpretations are by definition *not* equivalent to the world with which they deal?—it also prevents the researcher from confronting the very notion of democracy as a problematic area in its own right.

Democracy at the level that interests me is a complex symbol or rather a metasymbol—a summary symbol for a host of more limited symbolic practices and definitions. So are notions like "community," "individualism" "love," and "freedom." My work could be seen essentially as an attempt to understand these notions as they are lived in Appleton. I did not, however, go to the field to explore them, and they do not provide the principle behind the organization of the book. But as I explored the everyday life of my informants, I was led inevitably to remark on questions that are often asked of Americans: Are Americans individualistic or are they conformist? Do they (generally) do their own thing or are they mostly occupied with keeping up with the Joneses?

Many answers have been given. Max Weber's ideas on the relationship between Protestantism and capitalism have been used to argue for the primacy of individualism among Americans and their belief in the "Protestant ethic." On the other side is David Riesman's insistence that "inner-directedness"—a concept not so far removed from individualism—was only a stage in the development of the American character, which then shifted to "other-directedness," where the clue to success is external to the person rather than internal. According to Riesman, most people acquiesce to this insidious form of dictatorship and thus become conformists, probably without realizing they are doing so.

Riesman's book *The Lonely Crowd* appeared in 1950. Ten years later the children of these other-directed parents exploded into the dual celebration of "doing one's own thing" and of communal ideals such as "caring." While some broke old values with a vengeance, others like Philip Slater lamented what he called the "pursuit of loneliness."

It is not my intention to pursue variations on the theme of the incompatibility between individualism and community, for I believe the problem is not well posed in this formulation. The attempt to measure America, or Americans, against a scale—be it democracy, individualism, or any other one might come up with—implies the belief, even if only operational, that these concepts have a fundamental and transcendental meaning that can be specified outside the context of actual use. "Democracy" is a universal in this perspective, and one can rate the United States as "more democratic" than Russia but "less" than the ideal. I do not believe that such a popularized Platonism is warranted. I would like to challenge this Platonism by raising a question that is ignored in all these discussions: What is the systemic meaning of the concepts of "individualism" and "community" as used by Americans? In other words, in what context do Americans use these concepts and what can we learn from recognizing that they do use *both*? They gain their meaning only within the context of their occurrences. The major consequence of this epistemological decision is to make this meaning problematic. We, as participants in a society, do not fully know what we mean when we use such terms, since we do not have access to many of the contexts in which they are used, nor can we control the utterances of others around us.

I went to Appleton to listen, not to evaluate or classify. My study is not so much an effort to discover the "real" behind the "ideal" as it is an attempt to make the familiar strange and, in so doing, to discover the unsuspected relationships that structure American interpretations of the world that both limit the American imagination and yet continually generate cultural performances of a human quality as high as any. I remember well the feeling of elation that came over me one Sunday morning in a glorious Indian summer. As I was walking in my best suit to the Methodist church for the eleven o'clock service after a week spent at Farm Bureau meetings, in classes at the high school, cruising the country roads, and drinking with the hippies the night before, it dawned on me that I was living a sort of improvised baroque concerto with various instruments playing the theme and answering each other. It seemed to me that all the miscellaneous activities I had experienced proceeded from the same fundamental source and exhibited a wholeness that did not consist in simple repetition or the quantitative totality of my apprehension of Appleton.

I also remember other times, sobering times, when I realized that what I perceived as the thematic tensions that an author builds into his work, if only to dazzle the audience with his skill at resolving them, tensions that made Appleton interesting and, indeed, beautiful, were tensions that individuals *lived*. There is no author to a culture. Its unity comes from the self-regulation of feedback mechanisms. The process, however, works through individuals, and as it works through them, they suffer, for they cannot see the eventual purpose of a local tragedy. It is their son or their husband in the immediate present. My informants were actors in a play they did not write, but one they had to live existentially.

I hope the intensity of this life will come through in the following pages, and that I have been successful at expressing the beauty and romance and irony in the life of the people I met and am reporting on. I will be talking about structures and regularities in pattern. The task is probably drier and less rewarding than a simple immersion into the gestalt of the culture in pursuit of an intuitive understanding. It is not that I see culture as a static and unchanging crystal. I am convinced. on the contrary, that it is in constant recreation and transformation. It is, indeed, a process. And yet to understand this process, to appreciate it, and maybe even to intervene in it, we must know the mechanisms that make it work.

A Note on the Organization of This Book

In this book I have not followed the order of presentation of data that is traditional for community studies. I have indicated briefly why I believe it is time to renew the genre so as to make more apparent the exoticism of our everyday life and its structure. For readers interested in a more theoretical presentation of my point of view, I have included a Postface where I address myself to some of the issues that I may have raised in the body of the work, particularly issues relating to structuralism and to the theory of culture. Certain issues must, however, be dealt with at the outset in order to guide the reader through the body of the work.

As Lévi-Strauss has emphasized many times, no analysis of human phenomena can ever be finished and closed. Life goes on, and continually offers new material that could modify the analysis as it was left dangling when the analyst stopped collecting the odds and ends of phenomena that he encountered during his fieldwork. What I will offer in the conclusion to this work will thus not be one structure but rather the temporary product of the stage my analysis has reached.

This form of analysis does not allow easily for the detailed exploration of domains into which one may still wish to categorize human life. In fact, it is a good method for people who do not believe that it is very fruitful for social science to collect butterflies and then pigeonhole them, in Edmund Leach's colorful metaphor, and for those who believe that most of our categories— for example, that most hallowed category of all, kinship[7]—have no reality in the real world, except the rarefied "real world" of sociological theory. Some may not wish to go this far. For the latter, the main interest of the method, and of this book, may lie in what it tells them about linkages, correspondences, and congruences between domains.

This book is organized from the point of view of these correspondences in structure. Data about family life are, for example, spread throughout the book in chapters 1, 2, 8, 9, and 10. Data about politics appear in chapters 1, 4, and 6. Reference is made to religious doctrine or organization in chapters 3, 5, 6, and 10. This means that in Chapter 1 readers will find discussions of family relationships, political organization, and political ideology. In Chapter 2 they will find more discussions of family life and some brief discussions of education, general ideology, and social structure.

There is another way in which this book is a departure from traditional community studies. The units of study of most social anthropologists or sociologists are "integral entities," in the words of Robert Redfield, "a person . . . , a people . . . , a nation . . . , a civilization . . . , [or a] small community."[8] As Redfield says, this may be more of a commonsensical view than an empirically defensible one. The point is that the categories of inquiry remain exterior to any category the culture may have. They may be categories that have common sense validity, such as the category of community, or categories that have theoretical validity, like the category of social class. In both cases they are categories that are defined a priori and that one explores as if they were integral, discrete entities on the model of isolated islands.

My task is precisely to investigate the commonsense categories that our culture uses to structure its perception of the world. I must thus work outside them. Theoretically constructed categories *are* useful for scholars interested in going beyond native interpretations. They can be used as a check against getting to see the world as the natives see it. I, on the other hand, am interested in these very native interpretations. My units of study must thus be drawn so as to give me access to them.

They must also be, insofar as I want my statement to be scientific, directly observable and recordable events. What kind of events? Generally, spoken utterances and, more broadly, texts. I will explain in more detail in the Postface some of the implications of this approach. Let it just be said that a text, as I understand the notion, is a sequence of verbal, or verbally interpretable, behavior. I see these texts as concrete, empirical events-in-the-world that can be studied with no attention paid to their relationship to any other "more real" level, except in attempts to separate what is necessary (in most cases, the content of the utterance) from what is contingent (the cultural style of the utterance).

Whatever I may say about texts, I have no way of knowing whether I am saying this about the people who create, perform, or utter them. Who created the Pledge of Allegiance or a certain way of telling one's life history? The individual who recites or performs the text? An individual who once upon a time "invented" it? Culture? The question remains unanswered. Insofar as these texts are performed by people who call themselves American, we may consider them examples of American culture. I will expand on this point in the Postface. But we cannot assume in any simpleminded way that any text refers to anything other than itself. An example might make this point clearer. A few years ago the Catholic Church rephrased the Creed, in which the basic tenets of the faith are enunciated, from "*I* believe in one God" (first-person singular) to "*We* believe in one God" (first-person plural). This was congruent with a general reordering of certain points of dogma. All Catholics now recite the new formula, in public rituals at least. Does this mean that they as individuals have changed their beliefs? A simple examination of the Creed would not tell. It remains, however, that the faithful have no choice, that a mode of interpretation is given to them by the tradition and that their personal lives are lived in the context of this tradition whether they like it or not, whether they "believe" in it or not.

A tradition may not be imposed quite so autocratically or be so consciously enforced as the Catholic tradition is to be effective in framing the perception of participants. For example, Americans are prone to deal at length with their emotional states at particular times. The third part of this book will thus deal in detail with the discussion of these states and their place in the ideological structure. The importance of these states was great for many of my informants. And yet it was generally impossible for me to decide whether my informants were really happy, in love, having fun, depressed, or whatever it was they were telling me they were feeling at the time. I just did not have the techniques to measure the reality of these states.

They *were* able to tell me that they were feeling something; they had different words for the different feelings, and clear patterns in the usage of these words could be discovered, as I will try to demonstrate. To this extent, their accounts of their personal impressions in a particular situation are texts, real events that can be the starting points of a scientific analysis.

Thus this book is organized around texts reconstructed from my field notes. I have chosen them more because of my greater familiarity with the events in the lives of the people involved than because of any belief in the typicality of the situations. These texts are of different types; they are life histories, descriptions of reunions of a small group of friends, the position taken by four people during the unfolding of a love story. Analysis of these main texts is complemented by consideration of shorter texts or of long texts in less detail.

The first text, for example, consists of two life histories that I recorded in intensive, though diffuse, interviews over the year I spent in Appleton. The text is thus an aggregation of statements rather than a complete statement made at one sitting. Mr. and Mrs. Mark Howard were two of my best informants. I ate with them many times, spent a few days living in their house, and generally developed a very satisfying relationship with them. Compared with everything I got to know about them, these life histories remain only very sketchy outlines, a skeleton list of events and the ideological comments that were made on these events. In all cases the material was psychologically much richer, and I have often been sorry that it wasn't a novel I wanted to write so that I could have given more human justice to the reality that I was allowed to share. Yet I believe that I have reported quite faithfully the experience of two Americans as they themselves saw it. In all the pages where I tell the history of the Howards directly, my own analytical interventions have been kept to a minimum. Even in passages where I am not quoting verbatim, the ideological interpretations are Mr. and Mrs. Howard's.

At the end of the first chapter, I will begin the process of generalization by juxtaposing the long description of these two lives to a very short text, the creed of an institution that played a large role during a part of their lives: the Farm Bureau. This creed was composed by persons sociologically, demographically, and economically very close to the Howards, and it offers a concise summary of some of the principles that governed their lives.

The book will then continue to unfold in a manner inspired by the organization of Lévi-Strauss's *Mythologiques*. The Farm Bureau Creed will not be analyzed as a complete explanation of the Howards, but simply as one possible way of looking at them and of discovering relations and meanings not directly perceivable at an initial stage. Similarly, I will not argue that the Howards or the Farm Bureau Creed can be explained by reference to an educational system, a kinship system, or even a set of religious ideas. Rather I hope that each new set of evidence will somehow illuminate, and be illuminated by, the other evidence that I will already have presented or will present later. In this sense the Howards' history should appear much richer, even in my watered-down account, at the end of the book than it probably will seem to be at first.

I realize that there may still be some confusion about my stance in individual passages. I have tried to be as careful as possible about distinguishing the different points of view that I must use to conduct my demonstration. At the simplest level, there will be reports of what an informant told me he had done. However, informants often were very long-winded or told me about certain things over several sessions. In most cases my reports are summaries. I cannot even say that I myself worked on the verbatim statements, since in most cases I was not able to record conversations that were either too private and would not have occurred if I had barged in with a tape recorder or else too public (during a car ride with a group, or a church service, in the lobby of a movie theater, and so forth) to give me a chance.

Also, on many occasions I was told about other people in the speaker's network. I have generally used this as evidence for the speaker's mode of interpretation. I have also used it as a way of collecting information about the simple occurrence or nonoccurrence of an event.

I will also refer to what I "saw" or "observed," but generally as a counterpoint to what I was told and as a way of discovering the implicit structure that generates the statements informants make. "What I observed" is not *the* reality. In most cases I was not able to record the event in a way that would allow me to validate my own statements about what I saw. The usefulness of "what I saw" is that is represents another mode of interpretation to which the informants' mode can be compared. My references to "how it is in France" have the same sort of usefulness. I am a native Frenchman, but I am not an expert on France; I have not done intensive fieldwork there. However, I became aware of many of the things I saw in Appleton because they shocked me by their difference.

My rationale for the many references to other analysts of American life throughout this book is the same. I have used them during the process of analysis to build my conclusion. I am using them in this book to express and communicate these conclusions stylistically. Furthermore, these authors have written about other times, other places, with other interests and points of view, and they can help readers, if they are aware of these works, to tie my own to some that may be more familiar to them. My presentation may be strange, but the facts themselves are familiar, and most readers will have experienced situations similar to at least some of those I discuss. I hope they will use these clues to criticize my analyses.

In the preceding pages I have often used the pronoun "we" when I wished to emphasize that I and the reader shared certain things, particularly an interest in self-discovery or a position in relation to the world. In the body of the work, as I am doing now, I will use mostly "I" as a marker for the times when I, as analyst, am intervening: I recorded this, I saw this, I have seen this done in such a way in France, and this is what I make of it. I hope this will not be taken as self-aggrandizement but rather as the humility of the researcher assuming responsibility for his work. I am part of a tradition. And this tradition is working through me. However, as I write these lines I stand alone, and it is only through the reaction of the audience that they will come to be accepted, or rejected, by that tradition.

PART

Individualism

I perceive that I am apt to speak in the singular number, though our partnership still continued; it may be that in fact the whole management of the business lay upon me. Meredith was no compositor, a poor pressman, and seldom sober. My friends lamented my connection with him, but I was to make the best of it.
—Benjamin Franklin, Autobiography

CHAPTER 1
Living in Appleton

*Anthropologists don't study villages . . . . They
study in villages.*
—*C. Geertz, The Interpretation of Cultures*

Since I was looking for no more than a group of persons referring
to themselves as "American," my specifications for the demographic and social characteristics of the town I would study were
minimal. It had to be of a size that could be encompassed by one
investigator. It had also to be somewhat diverse to maximize the
possibility for internal comparison. I interpreted the first requirement as meaning less than ten thousand inhabitants, and the second as implying that the town be someplace in the middle of the
continuum of farm to industrial town and rural to urban (or suburban) town. Finally, I did not want the town to lie in an area that
has been historically considered to be "different," like the South or
the hill regions. This left many towns as possible candidates, particularly in the Midwest. Eventually I chose the town I will call
Appleton. I will now briefly introduce it.

Appleton, a Sociological Sketch

Appleton is a few hours' drive from Chicago and situated in a
very densely populated region of the Midwest. The 1970 Census
reported that the population of the town was 3,160, and the population of the township, 5,645. The county had 56,173 people, and

the state, 8,875,083, most of whom lived in the general area where Appleton is located. The town has maintained its geographical integrity insofar as it is surrounded by farmlands and is thus physically distinct from the nearby towns.

Appleton is almost indistinguishable from hundreds of other such Midwestern towns. A traveler straying from the interstate highway that passes it would probably not be able to differentiate it in his memory from the string of other towns lying within a radius of five to ten miles. But it is unique, and a more experienced traveler waking up suddenly on the bus as it entered the town would recognize it immediately by the long, narrow lake that borders it on one side and by the fact that the courthouse is relegated to a side street of the town and does not stand at its center. The visitor might also notice the wineries that denote the presence and importance of Italians in the social and political structure of the town.

Sociologically there is nothing very extraordinary about Appleton. The town was studied briefly, a few years before I did my work, by an Indian anthropologist, Surajit Sinha, who published a short article on its religious organization. He called it "Mapletown," which I persist in considering somewhat inappropriate, since the town remains associated in my mind with apple growing, one of its important economic activities.

No group or income level dominates the town either statistically or ideologically to the point of significantly influencing the general impression it makes. Nor can it be said to be "typical," if anything can be said to be. There is first the relatively large ethnic population and the fact of its rather complete integration into the life of the town. There is also the rapid transformation it seems to be going through at the present time from a purely service town for farmers in the surrounding area into an upper-middle-class residential suburb of the middle-sized industrial and university town of La Crosse that lies only twenty minutes away from Appleton on the interstate highway. The land around the town is not among the best in the Midwest, but it is not bad, either. Many small, independent farms still exist beside larger, quasi-industrial complexes. The discovery that the land is suitable for fruit and grape growing has resulted in its maintaining a high cash value. Contributing to this value, too, is the development in the area of small-scale industry, trailer parks, and private homes. The area is still too far from the surburban area around La Crosse to have seen large-scale development of housing. It is being developed at present mostly by individuals who buy a plot of land a build a house on it.

The region is also known as a resort area. It is dotted with lakes, all of which are edged by houses, often the summer and weekend retreats of the people living in the surrounding towns and the metropolitan areas of Chicago and Detroit. The area was a popular one for retirement until Florida became more accessible. There is now a movement toward transforming the summer houses into year-round residences, which has inflated the price of land by the lakes or even simply close to them. For many informants, this area is ideal because it combines a rural/recreational environment with easy access to large urban centers with their sprawling shopping malls, colleges, and jobs.

Many people see Appleton as a refuge and would like to keep it the way they perceive it. By means of severe and well-enforced building-code restrictions, the town itself succeeds in general in keeping extreme poverty outside its boundaries and in maintaining a neat, respectable, middle-class atmosphere. But its relatively well-developed industries need cheap labor who cannot afford to live in the town, and they are simply pushed into hidden places on back country roads where they are all but forgotten. They are not often seen, except when exhibiting food stamps at the local supermarket checkout counters, but they are there. There are twenty-two blacks living in the town itself, but several hundred in the surrounding rural townships. They are generally to be found in geographically well-defined areas, dating from the time when active segregation of housing was enforced. Many of the blacks, the descendants of escaped slaves, have lived in the area for many generations, and some are thoroughly integrated into the local society. Others are retired doctors, dentists, lawyers, and other professionals who used to live in Chicago. There are also more recently immigrated, and much poorer, blacks who were attracted by the apparent availability of jobs in the area, and who compete for them with Southern whites and Mexican migratory workers.

Thus the area around Appleton reveals a social diversity that the town itself may not possess. My informants were necessarily drawn from the surrounding areas, rather than the town narrowly defined, since the town is a very artificial unit in terms of social organization and I was necessarily drawn outside its administrative boundaries. But what the town may have lacked in terms of social diversity, although it *was,* in fact, quite diverse socially, it made up for in terms of ideological and—as my informants sometimes called it—"cultural" diversity. From traditional "Puritan ethic" farmers, to Birchites, to radical, long-haired hippies, to liberal intellectuals, to mild, middle-aged, middle-income, middle-management, middle-class persons, every shade of political and religious ideology that one can find in the wider United States could certainly be found in Appleton. The only experience that one probably would not know there would be that of being with a large group of people sharing the same ideological background in every respect. The anxious search for consensus that I will later describe at length may have been exacerbated by this constant diversity of opinion.

I stress the essential diversity in social background and ideology of my informants to prevent the urban reader of this book from assuming that Appleton is in any way a socially and ideologically homogeneous unit. This assumption is probably one of the most common, and fondest, myths that urban Americans entertain about rural Midwestern towns, myths frequently restated by urban journalists reporting on localities where they have spent a few hours. The people of those localities probably did greet them with a rhetoric of unanimity appropriate to the development of the myth. Such rhetoric is used regularly on the appropriate occasions. But to take it at face value is as deceptive in a small town like Appleton as it would be in Chicago or New York. The only general, sweeping statement that one can make about Appleton is that no general, sweeping statement can be made about it. And to this extent, at least, Appleton is a true microcosm of the United States.

Marc Howard

I first became aware of the town when I met James Howard, a native of Appleton, in Chicago. He invited me to visit his parents, whose farm was situated a few miles from town. It was from him that I received my introduction to Appleton and to a family whom I would come to know very well, and to appreciate even more, as great human personalities.

While we were driving to Appleton, James Howard delivered a long monologue on his parents, particularly his father. He had a very high opinion of his father, and he gave me the idea that he was a very wise patriarch, honored and heeded by the whole family. However, I got the wrong impression from his remarks. When I met Mr. Howard, I saw at once that his role in the family was anything but patriarchal.

Marc Howard was born in 1908 in Esmond, a small town ten miles north of Appleton township. His parents were farmers of Scottish and English descent who had moved from southern Wisconsin to Esmond at the turn of the century. Mr. Howard's grandfather was a small farmer in Wisconsin, but there were tensions between him and his son, apparently for economic reasons. The father did not want to let the son share in the management and profit of the farm because, according to Mr. Howard, the farm was too small to sustain two families. But Mr. Howard also remembers that his grandfather was talked about in his family as a fierce, cold man who would not help his children in any way, even when he could. Mr. Howard does not seem to know exactly why, but he remembers clearly the bitter tone of his parents' remarks about his grandfather. Thus, after Mr. Howard's father married, he decided to buy a farm away from his father's. He could not stay in Wisconsin, apparently because land was already too expensive; eventually he settled in Esmond, where he bought a farm and raised his four children, one boy and three girls.

Twenty years later, when Mr. Howard finished high school, he confronted the same situation his father had years before. Mr. Howard very rarely speaks of his parents, and it is hard to judge whether there were strong personal tensions between them, though there are many signs of such tensions. Once an adult, Mr. Howard did not start working full-time on the farm. He had, of course, worked on it as an extra hand early in his life but had never had any say in the way it was run. So for two years, in 1931 and 1932, he left Esmond to work in the steel mills of Chicago, an experience that marked him deeply and of which he talked readily.

For the first time in his life, as he told it, he lived in a large urban center, and for the first time he met Catholics, recent immigrants to America, people who swore, drank, and behaved freely and without feelings of guilt in ways that he had always been taught and had always believed to be evil and sinful.

"One of my best friends was a big fat Irishman who took a fancy to me. It was the first time I saw someone get dead drunk, and what surprised me most was that he did it as if it were natural—he did not consider it a sin. And besides, he was a real nice guy who taught me that Catholics were not necessarily an incarnation of evil, as I had been told they were in Sunday school.

My stay in Chicago was a tremendous eye-opener. I went to the bars with my friend, and I had the best time just watching what was going on. I did not drink; I did not feel I needed it. I got drunk only once, but got so sick I decided I would not do it anymore."

Mr. Howard would speak of his stay in Chicago as of a conversion experience, the first of the two periods he mentioned as turning points in his life. In Chicago, he "realized," as he himself put it, that life was more complex than he had thought, that he needed more education to understand it and to make an intelligent contribution to progress in whatever field he would eventually choose. So he went back home to go to college. For two years he attended La Crosse College, a small but relatively good private institution in La Crosse. He never finished, apparently because of his marriage to Elaine Tyler, also of Esmond.

Elaine Howard

Elaine Tyler was the eldest of two daughters of one of the most prominent men in Esmond. Both her father and her mother had gone through college, and her father was a "self-made man" who had started with "nothing," put himself through college, and ended up as a salesman for a drugstore chain earning twenty-five thousand dollars per year ("in 1920!"). They had a very large house and the first car in Esmond. (This is the way she remembers it. Local history attributes the first car in town to a different family.)

Elaine Howard talked about her childhood with pleasure and pride. She told fondly of the pranks she used to play, of the musical atmosphere of the house—how her family owned a grand piano and how everybody in the family could play an instrument (she herself played the violin regularly in local ensembles until about ten years ago). She was proud of her parents and their achievements. ("It was very rare at that time for women to have gone through college, but my mother had!") The ever-present implication in her recollection was: "But we (my husband and I) have never reached that level." It came out clearest in periods of tension with her husband, though she did try to check this at other times. But this feeling of dissatisfaction with her status as a farmer's wife was avowedly the reason she went back to school later in her life, got an M.A. degree, and, after a few years of elementary-school teaching, got a job in the English Department of the State University in La

Crosse. Yet now, even with two incomes, the Howards barely matched the twenty-five thousand dollars Elaine Howard's father had made in 1920.

Mr. and Mrs. Howard: A Family Biography

When they were married in 1932, the financial and social contrast between the penniless farmer's son and the sophisticated daughter of one of the most well-to-do men in town must have been quite great. The Howards did not spontaneously analyze their difficulties on such grounds, at least to someone like me. But difficulties there were. In fact the Howards were married for six months before they told their parents.

They knew very hard times at first. With the aid of federal loans, they bought two hundred acres of land in Appleton township, a few miles from Esmond, and remembered moving into the old, rundown frame house without furniture or any amenities. As Mrs. Howard tells it: "The yard was covered with junk, there was not a bit of shade, and the first summer we thought we would die from the heat." It was fifteen years before they could remodel the house into the "proper" model, as it was nationally advertised. During these fifteen years their first two children were born, and Elaine Howard worked on the farm driving the horse teams, then the first tractors. They put all the money they made back into the farm for capital improvement, and it was only after another fifteen years that they finally owned their farm totally, having at last paid all the mortgages and loans.

During these thirty years or so, the Howards led a life very close to what is considered the typical life of an intelligent, conservative, individualistic farm couple with a definite puritanical bent. Neither of them drank or smoked. They worked hard for themselves and for their community (a group of a dozen farmers owning land in the northwest corner of Appleton township). They gave a good education to their three children, who all finished high school and went on to college. Some did not finish college, to the despair of their parents.

The Howards were exceptionally generous to the poor around them and went to great lengths to help their hired hands "get up in life." They spent a lot of "time and effort"—money, too—on such efforts, often with indifferent results, something they still cannot understand. "How could these people refuse to follow our example when we tried so hard to understand them, when we were so sincere in our efforts?" they mused. Politically, they almost always voted the straight Republican ticket—at the local level because they often knew the candidate personally, at the national level because they appreciated the political rhetoric of Republican candidates.

The two most important aspects of this period of their life were certainly their fight for their farm and their involvement with community affairs, two types of activity that they still consider to possess a high moral value. (It must be said that nowadays their outlook on the world has very much broadened. They do not take excessive pride in the fact that they successfully performed both sets of required activities, but they still value this type of life highly when they detect it in others.) Another of their all-important life goals was to give as good an education as possible to their children. This was not because they believed in education for its own sake, or because they thought it would allow their children to rise in the social hierarchy, but because they believed that it is only through a good education that one can become a worthy individual—that is, one who contributes to the welfare of his fellowmen. Education can thus be said to be a means toward the two goals the Howards valued above all: self-reliance and community involvement.

In my first interview with Mr. Howard, when our relationship was at its most formal, he was particularly vocal in emphasizing his apparently unshakable belief in self-reliance. I had led him into explaining to me the opportunities that agriculture in his state could offer to a young man who wanted to become a farmer but was starting with nothing. Mr. Howard believed that if a young man already knew, or was willing to learn about, modern agriculture (he might need an apprenticeship of two or three years) so that he could convince the board of local farmers who were in charge of determining his eligibility for a government loan that he was a good risk, he could get a loan for close to one hundred percent of the price of a farm and machinery. If the young man were willing to put all the profits he might make on the farm into capital improvement during the first years, if he were willing to live on a minimum income for several years, and if he were wise, intelligent, and hardworking, there was no doubt in Mr. Howard's mind that he could make it, provided no catastrophe intervened. He remarked regretfully that very few people accepted this type of life anymore, but he did not believe that the main reason was that it had become impossible. For Mr. Howard, it was simply that most of the young people he had talked to would much rather take a job that paid three or four hundred dollars a week immediately so that they could buy a house, two cars, a boat, and a snowmobile. "Some of them ask me about becoming farmers. But when I tell them that it would mean forfeiting their standard of living in the present to build for the future, they just cannot do it."

By Oneself and with a Little Help from One's Friends

Mr. Howard's interpretation of his society, when he talked in less formal or less stereotyped situations, was, in fact, much more complex. However, it is now possible to make some interpretative comments about the preceding life histories. One might be tempted to refer the reader first to Max Weber's study of the Protestant ethic. Indeed, Mr. and Mrs. Howard's approach to life and morality corresponded closely to that of the traditional Puritan farmers and industrialists who seem to have formed the backbone of the development of capitalism in the eighteenth and nineteenth centuries. One might refer the reader then to David Riesman's study of the "lonely crowd"—America at mid-twentieth century—and to his hypotheses regarding the disappearance of "inner-directedness."

If both interpretations were accepted as historically accurate descriptions of historical, or even demographic, processes, one would have to conclude that the Howards represent only a survival of an old and now irrelevant value pattern, and that to start an examination of present-day American behavior with them would be a dangerous enterprise.

I believe, however, that they are a very good place to begin for a demonstration intended to cast doubt on the validity of Weber's and Riesman's interpretations. Beyond the fact that Weber's account is often read as an apology for Protestantism, while Riesman's is a critique of contemporary American life, both their hypotheses are flawed by their insistence on a single determinant for cultural behavior, be it rugged individualism or mindless gregariousness. It is as if in the nineteenth century people remained consistently alone and withdrawn and as if later they had become interested only in the impressions they made on others. And yet small-town insistence on conformity is not something recent in

America. Nor did it prevent the development of varied—and nonconforming—life-styles, divergent political and religious sects, and so on, not only up to World War I but also afterward, as the 1960s recently demonstrated.

It would also be an ethnographic mistake for me to stop my investigation of the Howards' ideology at their opinions on the prerequisites for success in life, or on the nature of this success, and at their interpretation of their life history along these lines. The Howards readily acknowledged that their statements on these subjects were a matter of opinion and that other people might dissent. Mr. Howard felt he was right; he felt that a life led according to such principles was morally better than another one. He believed strongly that he had followed those principles himself, but he also recognized that they were not a complete description of the life that he had led. It had not been purely toil in the fields, alone and cut off from the rest of society, with little fun or enjoyment.

Mr. Howard, as he told me his story, did not stress the contribution of any outside help to his success, which is consistent with the traditional Protestant values. He attributed his success solely to his own work. Two other sets of characters appeared consistently in his accounts: his parents and his children. The interesting thing about Mr. Howard's relationship with his parents is his emphasis on an essential discontinuity between them and himself. He would say that his parents were "good people," that they gave him a good education, and that he loved them. And yet he established his farm away from theirs, and he did not recognize their practical help, if there was any, which seems doubtful. In particular, he never talked of the distribution of his parents' material possessions at their death. His parents were not completely penniless, and Mr. Howard's share of his inheritance may have contributed to his own success, but Mr. Howard kept no symbolic mementos of his parents. Their farm in Esmond had been sold, and the children had dispersed all over the area.

Mr. Howard's relations with one of his sisters and her husband, who farmed only a few miles away, are particularly interesting in this context. At the time I was there, relations between the two families as a group were minimal. There was not one family reunion that year. Mrs. Howard and her children were polite to the others when they met, but they did not try to multiply these meetings. Mr. Howard, on the contrary, did go to see his sister regularly, on business most of the time. He lent and was lent tools, and there

was some sharing of summer work—events that could have served
as the groundwork for an ideology of family unity. Such an ideology was not present. It was not a matter of personal likes or
dislikes—my experiences in France have shown me many times
that the use of a rhetoric of family corporateness generally does not
imply that the members of the group all truly like each other. On
the contrary, Mr. Howard seemed to genuinely like his sister, which
did not prevent him from leaving her completely out when telling a
stranger about his life. The help he received from his sister was not
part of his life; it belonged to a different realm.

Mr. Howard was not really alone. He helped, and was helped
by, not only his sister, not only a few poor people with whom he
came in contact in his search for hired hands, but also a group of
neighboring farmers very similar to him in ethnic origin,
socioeconomic status, and political ideology. Participation in the
activity of this group was an important part of the Howards' life
and certainly contributed to their success, as they also acknowledged in the appropriate contexts.

The Farm Bureau: Two Creation Myths

Mr. and Mrs. Howard were active in the Farm Bureau for
more than twenty-five years. At the time I met them they were not
active anymore but still had close ties with the organization, and
they introduced me to other members. I went to several meetings
of the association and its multiple committees (county commission,
local community group, women's committee, board of directors).
From various people I obtained a sort of oral history of the development of the Farm Bureau in the area. I cannot vouch for its
accurateness because it necessarily must leave out many elements,
but it is of great interest structurally, since it contains two "creation
myths" (if I may refer in this manner to the stories of the original
founding of the association and then of its reorganization).

The Farm Bureau was founded in 1919 by a group of farmers
dissatisfied with the way things were going for them. Their idea
was to defend farm interests through political power. In this insistence on working through the political system, the new organization differed from the older defense groups, which insisted on
moral action, on a strengthening of the individual with the idea
that moral superiority would necessarily mean economic superior-

ity or at least prosperity. Beginning in about 1910, this approach had been judged ineffective by younger farmers in the area. Small farmers had more problems than they had ever had, and small farms were disappearing. The farmers also had the example of industrial workers who appeared to gain excessive privileges through political action backed by the numerical power of large unions, and they decided to follow suit.

At the beginning, the Farm Bureau was purely a trade association formed to further the economic welfare of its members through lobbying efforts at the national level. Gaining political power did not mean an attempt to transform the political system into something else. It meant a desire for a larger share of the national wealth within a given system that these farmers accepted unquestioningly and, in fact, actively supported, as they still do. At the local level, the Farm Bureau was also a trade association insofar as to belong, one had to show a definite interest in farming. This requirement has been interpreted more and more loosely in recent years, and people whose main source of revenue lies in areas outside farming may now belong. But in those early years the members were active farmers who worked their own farms on a family basis.

What this says, then, is that a group of farmers—a group of individuals—gained the same consciousness of the nature of their position in the economic system and evolved similar ideas about a plausible solution to what they conceived to be their problem. They arrived at this solution essentially on their own as individuals, and it was only *after* this process that they looked around for similar-minded individuals to create a new association.

The essence of their problem was their perceived inability, in spite of all their efforts, to be successful at their chosen occupation. It was not a case, as it had been for earlier settlers, of fighting a tough physical environment not particularly suitable for agricultural exploitation, but of fighting the adverse economic and political environment. Like their predecessors, these men and women were not ready to pool their resources to defend their ability to survive *as a group* in a particular place. They were individuals who had chosen this occupation, this place to live their own lives and raise their own families, but who realized that they could not do so without the help of other people in a similar condition. The environmental pressures that demanded they seek help from friends had changed. In earlier times, since a man and his wife could not raise a barn or build a house by themselves, "building parties" during which all the neighbors congregated and helped a young couple who wanted to start a farm were traditional. As the economic environment was transformed, it became more convenient to borrow money from a bank and hire a contractor to do these types of jobs. But the same forces that helped the farmers become less directly dependent upon their neighbors in the original direct manner, pressured individual farmers in new ways and triggered new patterns of mutual help as they continued in their search for survival as independent agents.

The Farm Bureau started as a loose organization that had more formal reality at the national than at the local level. By the 1930s it was powerful enough to be asked to participate in the discussions of the New Deal under President Franklin D. Roosevelt. In this first period the organization had many members in rural areas but no formal organization, which probably meant a very heavy burden on the local leaders as well as accusations that they were cliquish and unrepresentative as the organization expanded. Indeed, the national delegates' policy of accepting government involvement and controls soon began to be contested in favor of a return toward traditional individual self-help and local self-determination. The result was a reorganization of the Farm Bureau, which was intended to formalize it as a grass-roots association in which all levels of the administrative hierarchy receive their legitimacy from the local community group. The area to be considered a "community" is left to be defined by the members themselves and is not to be necessarily based on local or state administrative boundaries.

Nowadays, each of these groups meets once a month to discuss and vote on current issues. The votes are tabulated nationally and, theoretically, must guide the leaders. The local groups elect delegates to the county organization, which chooses state delegates at an annual mass meeting. National delegates are chosen by the state board. Once a year a countywide plenary session is held, and the activities of the county organization are reviewed and accepted or corrected. There are also state and national conventions with representatives from all county organizations reviewing the activities of the state and national officers. The formal structure is thus a mix of participatory and representative democracy.

I attended two or three of the meetings of one of these local groups that form the official grass roots of the Farm Bureau. Both husbands and wives were invited and both participated fully. The evenings began with a pot-luck supper, an important affair for which every woman brought as sumptuous a dish as she dared and everybody congregated around a table overladen with food. Too much food was customary; not enough food, or even not enough of a particular dish for people to have seconds, would have been embarrassing for the whole group and considered bad planning. In such a case a conference would have been held at once among the women to ensure that it would not happen again. Stories about the day when "everybody brought salads and there were no main dishes" are often swapped in such situations.

The meal was opened with a prayer for "those who have prepared this food." A festive atmosphere was maintained throughout, no controversial subjects were touched on, and no strong dissenting opinions were expressed. After the meal, the men moved to the living room, the women cleared away the dishes, and it was only after they had finished that the business meeting itself began.

The business meeting opened with an invitation by the president to recite the Pledge of Allegiance and ended with a motion to adjourn. The group followed parliamentary procedure very strictly. At the end, five or six patriotic, religious, or traditional folk songs were sung. Less than the meal, but more than the business meeting, this was a moment for laughing and joking, for enjoying the fact of being together.

The times I was present, no substantial issues arose and the meetings were poorly attended. Only twenty came, out of the more than two hundred people who could have participated. This was a long-standing pattern, as was corroborated by the fact that the meetings were held in private homes that could not have accommodated a larger crowd than the one that actually came. The people who came were the original founders, now in their sixties to eighties. No young adult attended the meetings. In this context it is not surprising that the business meeting appeared to me—and from what I could observe, to most of the participants, too, I suspect—to be the dreariest part of the whole affair. Discussion was weak, superficial, uninvolved. The leader had to force and cajole people into taking positions, something that they did only after ensuring that unanimity would not be destroyed by their decision. The business meeting was quickly adjourned. It is also interesting to note that while the votes taken were supposed to ensure that the national leadership would maintain its ties to the grass roots, it was the national leadership itself that decided which issues were to be considered and that provided background material. The local group was thus both powerless and at present all but irrelevant.

Younger farmers did make their voices heard, sometimes rather loudly, but they did so behind the scenes in committee sessions of the county organization and in informal meetings with the leadership.

The split between the leadership and the rank-and-file was not solved by the Farm Bureau's reorganization. The national leadership is still closely involved with political figures and handles large sums of money. It has a grasp, however ideologically tainted, of the broad socioeconomic problems of the nation. The local group has none of the above. Even between the two lower levels of the organization, the community group and the county organization, this split could be recognized. On one occasion I was told, "It is only at the level of the state organization that one can do something." The actual powers of the community groups are minimal. They can, of course, vote all incumbents out of office in the case of a strong deviation from the accepted political line; but this rarely happens, because the state and national levels have become very good at telling the rank-and-file what it wants to hear and at doing what they think is good for it. In recent years they have been rather successful and thus have not made anybody in Appleton township mad enough for serious controversy.

All this does not mean, however, that the structure adopted by the Farm Bureau is meaningless. It is, on the contrary, the only structure that is meaningful to most people. A meeting of the local community group may be no more than a ritualization of a creation myth perceived as history, but it is a ritual that is a direct transformation of the myth, and thus inevitable.

The Farm Bureau Creed

Printed in all issues of the national Farm Bureau newsletter and mimeographed at the beginning of the program schedules for local conventions or the bylaws of such suborganizations as the Farm Bureau Women is a Farm Bureau Creed in which members of the organization are supposed to believe. It runs like this:

I have united with these friends and neighbors to enjoy a special hour, to study our common problems, to support through the Farm Bureau the organized effort which is essential to the welfare and prosperity of agriculture, to the end that such cooperation may provide a comfortable liv-

ing for my family, education for my children, and independence for my old age.

I have no way of knowing how seriously members of the Farm
Bureau took this Creed or how much meaning it had for them. It is
obvious, however, that as a text this Creed is heavily structured.
Interestingly, this structure is the same, transformed into a different mode, as the one that underlay both the Howards' autobiographies and the telling of the creation and recreation of the Farm
Bureau.

According to the Creed, it is an individual, *I*, who has united
with friends and neighbors. Not with all of them, however, but only
"with *these* friends and neighbors"—those, we can assume, who also
belong to the organization. Indeed, the community group whose
activity I observed comprised people from all over the township
and no actual neighbors. Neither theoretically nor empirically is a
community territorially based; it is a matter of choice on the part of
the "I."

I come now to the practical results expected from this union. A
person joins a special-interest group because it will *do* something
for him. Results in the Farm Bureau are for "*my* family . . . *my*
children . . . *my* old age." The way to achieve all this is "to study *our*
common problems, to support through the Farm Bureau the *organized effort* which is essential to the welfare and prosperity of
agriculture." The union is intended to be beneficial to me as an
individual. The goals have nothing to say about the welfare of the
group as a group. It only mentions individuals (I's) and an activity
(agriculture). The desire for independence is central. It consists of
an attempt to remain an autonomous unit even when physical conditions, such as old age, make it more difficult for the ideal to be
realized. The creation of a union such as the Farm Bureau is not
intended to create a framework in which old people fit by virtue of
their age, but rather one in which they can continue to operate as
individuals, alone and independent *in spite of* their old age.

Here again is found the dichotomy between the "I" and the
"we" that underlay Mr. Howard's statements. It is not that the
individual must remain consistently alone and never seek the help
of friends, but rather than individualism and cooperation belong to
different aspects of human existence and that they have different
attributes. Just as the hierarchical reciprocity between castes in
India does not destroy, but on the contrary reinforces or at least is a
statement of the distinct uniqueness of the caste as a group defined

against other groups, the egalitarian reciprocity of services between individuals that the Farm Bureau attempts to channel formally does not destroy the individualism of the men and women in it. It is, on the contrary and very clearly, a formal and quasi-ritual recognition of their nature as individuals and of the practical means by which they can survive as such.

The dual aspects of Mr. Howard's expectations, his stress on self-help and at the same time his acceptance and offer of cooperation, is thus but another, less formal statement of the same structure. The Farm Bureau Creed was written by a cultural specialist; Mr. Howard did not plan his life to conform with the structure. And I cannot judge whether it actually did. The fact that his perception of his life is structured in a way similar to the Creed is an indication of the relevance of this Creed to an understanding of the processes of interpretation involved.

I will now try to make the same point through an analysis of a process that is the reverse of the one I have just investigated. If I am right in stressing the importance of the voluntary decision of an individual to cooperate with others, it should be possible to find examples of cases where it is the refusal to cooperate that stands out. This refusal should hinge, like the acceptance of it, on a perceived lack of agreement between the persons involved as to the means necessary to achieve the goal of self-realization.

Mr. and Mrs. Howard and Their Children: Conversion and Change of Life

During the first twenty-five years of their married life, the Howards believed strongly enough in the idea that the means stated in the Creed were appropriate to reach the ends they pursued, to participate actively at all levels of the Farm Bureau. Mr. Howard held most of the administrative positions on the local and county boards at one time or another, and his capabilities and devotion to the organization led him to be considered a likely member for the state board as soon as an opening appeared. For a long time he also participated in a research program sponsored by the state university that was intended to study the organization of a farm and how to make its management more rational. This meant complex bookkeeping procedures, long hours spent after work in the field to record when and how each crop was planted or harvested, how many hours the machinery had been used, how many man-hours were needed to do a particular job, and so on. Mrs. Howard volunteered for many social activities, was secretary of the county organization for a while, edited the paper, and helped her husband in management tasks and in the tricky job of deciding which experiments suggested by professional agronomists were worth trying. Indeed, all of this helped him to become successful, to repay all his loans and pay for his machinery, and to see the yield of his intensively worked fields increase fourfold in thirty years.

All of this also meant hard work and long hours; in fact, a few years ago Mr. Howard became seriously ill, had to stay in the hospital for some time, and was told by his physician to slow down. Mr. Howard had the choice of abandoning either the dairy part of his farm or most of his outside activities, which cut deeply into his nights. This illness gave him time to think, and he perceived it as the last step in the second "conversion" he experienced during his life. He saw that his economic achievements were fragile, that the world outside the northwest corner of Appleton township was in turmoil, a world that his children brought home to him and that he could not really understand despite his desire to and his feeling that something important *was* happening there. It became clear to him that the local Farm Bureau had even less understanding of all these things than he did and that it had adopted an ostrichlike attitude about them. He also felt that even if he could explain the seriousness of the situation to his friends and convince them of it, the Farm Bureau was not an appropriate channel for his new convictions. One other event in this change of life was his wife's decision to go back to school.

At the time, the end of the 1950s, the Howards were in their early fifties, comfortably established on a medium-sized farm, and highly respected by their neighbors, most of whom were in the same general economic position. They had achieved what they had started out to achieve, and one could have expected them to relish their success and await retirement with a routine continuation of the life they had led until then. This is what several of their friends did, and during the year I spent in Appleton I learned how popular it was for retired farmers to spend the winter months in Florida enjoying themselves.

The Howards did not follow this path. As soon as the farm was more or less safely on its feet, Mrs. Howard found that she was deeply dissatisfied with her life. She had enjoyed participating in the struggle to build the farm, but as soon as the challenge disappeared, she decided that she could not end her life as a farmer's wife interested only in the preparation of the next Farm Bureau dinner or the health of her grandchildren. She started teaching in elementary schools in the area, went back to college herself, earned an M.A., and was eventually hired by the state university, first on a three-year contract and then as a tenured full professor in the English Department. Her salary suddenly permitted her and her family to afford many luxuries they had never had before, such as new dresses, new furniture in the living room, and an expensive car.

She dropped most of her ties with the farming community in which she had been so active; she stopped going to the Methodist church because the pastors were "too dull" and frequented the Presbyterian church for a while, first in Appleton and then in La Crosse, "because they are more intellectual there." Eventually she stopped going to church altogether, because "I just cannot believe anymore in what they say, it is too illogical, and so many people are just so hypocritical. I might go again if I found a pastor who was both sincere and intelligent. But it might not even be sufficient because not everybody in the congregation would be like this, probably." She considered the decision to go back to school the move that most changed her life; it permitted her to develop all her potentialities, it "liberated" her (though generally conservative in her political outlook, she is a vocal proponent of women's liberation).

At the same time, the Howards' two eldest children were coming of college age, and they decided they would have nothing to do with farming. The eldest son, John, appeared to have disappointed his father most. Mr. Howard clearly expected his son to succeed him on the farm and continue the process of making it grow into a successful enterprise. But the son resisted, felt constricted, had dreams about changing the world, and making it a better place to be in through education and religion.

The other son followed the same track, though he was more intellectual than his brother, who chose a mystical path. The house suddenly filled with books. The first time we talked at length, Mr. Howard showed them to me with more pride than he exhibited over the farm machinery. He himself started reading Camus, Mailer, and all the popular contemporary philosophers his children thought somewhat relevant to being a "better person" and to building a "better world." Mr. Howard recognized that he did not always understand the points these books tried to make, though he admitted that the goals he had pursued through farming and an involvement in the rational development of agriculture had more chances of being achieved through education and teaching. He was not totally enthusiastic about this new development but very singlemindedly held to the ideas that his wife and children planted in him.

He had, in fact, good reasons to be dissatisfied with farming and with the Farm Bureau. Through the constant efforts of the first groups, membership in the association had risen to several hundred in the county and its political power had grown proportionately, at least locally. A candidate for the state legislature or even the U.S. House of Representatives would not succeed in the district if he were not endorsed by the Farm Bureau. But the character of the organization had changed. It was less and less a group of friends uniting together, and more a purely abstract association from which new members expected concrete benefits but in which they rarely participated. What is more, many new members did not farm as a way of life but with the avowed means of making money; they were no longer committed to farming per se and often had other, sometimes more flourishing, businesses, which made the traditional farmers suspect that their farms were only a means of evading some taxes. This split inside the Farm Bureau was apparently related to a generation gap. The older people—the bulk of my informants—regarded the younger group with suspicion and were ready to accuse them of deeds or motives they would never dare attribute to their own friends.

Mr. Howard also found that it was harder and harder to survive as a farmer, that small family farms were going out of business at a faster rate then ever, that the fifty acres a family could live on in the 1920s had become two hundred acres for him, and that his son would have needed at least five hundred acres to make a comfortable living. Mr. Howard discovered that he had to go back into debt after thirty years of hard work to get out of it. He felt he was barely subsisting. In the previous five years, the farm had produced almost no revenue, all household items having been purchased from his wife's salary. In spite of the long hours he put in—twelve to fourteen daily in the summer—the farm could be considered almost a luxury for his private enjoyment.

This was probably one of the major disappointments of Mr. Howard's life. Like Jefferson's ideal yeoman farmer, he had consciously chosen farming as an activity in which one can best develop personal moral qualities. He still considered the individual farming of one's own land a privileged business, not so much for itself but rather because it is conducive to a well-rounded life, a practical solution to a spiritual problem. He had come to think that it could no longer be considered such a solution. Farming as he liked it was disappearing, and even though he was not completely conscious—as few farmers were—of the economic reasons that made this movement away from small farms necessary in an industrial and capitalistic society, he recognized that little could be done about it.

He did not change his belief in the goals he had held all his life, goals that are partly summarized in the Farm Bureau Creed, but he could no longer agree with the definition of the means stated in this creed, and, using his illness as an excuse, he suddenly stopped all participation in the Farm Bureau. During the year I spent in Appleton, neither he nor his wife attended a single meeting or participated in a single activity planned by the community group of which he was still officially a member.

This action can be considered a reverse proof of our analysis of the Creed and of individualism as it was lived in Appleton. In its ritual meetings the community group appeared to be a closed, enduring, tight-knit society. And in many ways it was such a society to a greater degree than many more "natural" and longer-lasting small communities, to the extent that the participants were very much *personally* involved in its survival. By the same token, it remained an artificial creation, sociologically speaking, and thus fragile. The people who had joined the Farm Bureau, like those who continued to participate in it for however long a period of time, did so freely. Freedom in this instance meant the perception that participation is based on a personal recognition of the validity of the positions taken by the organization. This decision may be rationalized with reference to its rational efficacy. But the determination of this efficacy remains a personal matter. And thus any shift of opinion must necessarily involve a withdrawal from participation when one decides that one is no longer in agreement with the majority of the people in the group or, more precisely, with the positions verbalized publicly during the meetings; there can be a wide variation between the public and the private stance. "Majority" is a rhetorical word; in such a small group no vote is ever taken that is not unanimous.

This example is particularly interesting from our point of view because there was no compelling reason for Mr. Howard's decision to abandon the Farm Bureau. He was not the only member of the group to be facing economic hardship, nor was he the only one to see his children leave the farm. Most members felt that the world outside had become threatening, though many did not understand the situation at all and preferred to take refuge in an extremely closed-minded political conservatism. However, at least one other member of the community group to whom I spoke had been confronted with the same problems as Mr. Howard, had understood them as Mr. Howard had, and had decided that the answer was an even deeper involvement in Farm Bureau affairs, for which he more or less sacrificed his farm, as I was told.

Individualism: An Initial Statement

Neither Mr. nor Mrs. Howard was an "individualist" in the strict sense. Their individualism could be understood only *in the context of* their involvement with different groups of relatives or friends, different "communities." I will argue that any understanding of American culture must proceed from such a contextualization of individualism and, of course, also of conformism. The individualism of America is but one pole in a complex structure, a piece of the whole. It consists of an emphasis on the material and spiritual welfare of the individual as the constitutive element of society. But if there are no societies outside the individuals who participate in them, neither are there individuals outside of societies. This is a philosophic point, of course (though one that seems of more significance to American than European philosophers), but it is also one that structures the commonsense perceptions of the world held by my informants.

In other words, individualism implies community. All my references to the concept must be taken in this way. What I have done in the last pages was try to delimit *one* element within a wider pattern or structure that my informants in Appleton used to organize their world. They used it to explain this world to outsiders, they used it to reconstruct their history, to orient themselves for future action, and to deal with each other. I have done this through an analysis of occasions, treated as "texts," in which the same element within the structure reappeared. These situations were sociologically and psychologically varied, and their reality may have been quite different from the verbalizations that were made. But these verbalizations *are* real *as* verbalizations, and they possess an internal logic that makes them amenable to scientific analysis.

This structure was summarized in the most pristine form in the few lines of the Farm Bureau Creed. It was also present, as I have tried to demonstrate, in the two autobiographies. The Howards were totally oriented toward their own welfare, and their involvement with the Farm Bureau was the product of their desire to succeed in a chosen occupation, farming, rather than the result of a predefined social situation. They were members of the Farm Bureau not *because* they were farmers but because they thought that participation in its activities would be useful for them. As soon as it appeared that it wasn't, they abandoned the organization. The reasons that led them to this change of mind were rather vague. In the statements they made during the many interviews I had with them on this subject, they could not describe an overriding cataclysmic cause. Their reasons were put in terms of likes and dislikes, opinions, personal idiosyncrasies rather than sociological pressures. Whether these were the only objective reasons, I do not know, but I am convinced that these were the only ways they perceived their reasons, and this is why I took them as the basis for my analysis.

Similar principles are at work in domains other than those I have just explored. I will not go into so much detail as before because this would entail endless repetitions. Indeed, the domains I am going to explore have been studied over and over again from many different angles, and their relationships with an idealized individualism have been established. My contribution will not consist in showing once again that American Protestantism is individualist, for example, but in showing that its individualism is best understood in the context of the set of culturally defined principles that are spontaneously lived by the people who practice it and is not necessarily a direct reflection of a philosophically defined individualism or a scientific definition of the human condition. I will explore, first, education and the use of psychology from my own data, and then I will talk briefly of marriage in the light of Schneider's work on American kinship. I will end this first part of the book with a consideration of the place of individualism in religion and politics.

CHAPTER 2
Individuality, Humanity, and the Person

Anthropologists in the tradition of the "culture-and-personality" school often regarded educational processes as a privileged domain for the understanding of cultural attitudes. Some authors sound as if they believe in a direct causal relationship between educational techniques (such as swaddling) and religion, social structure, or intellectual history. Even if these are rare extremes, I must stress here more than they did that the type of education given by members of a society to their children is culturally determined—in other words, that education is shaped by sociocultural choices. This is the position that will be taken in this book, not because of any a priori decision on the order of the causal relationship in this "chicken-and-egg" business, if there is any, but because of a methodological choice: my research is oriented rather toward a synchronic understanding of adult positions and a study of some of the consequences of these positions than toward a more diachronic or processual analysis of the life histories of persons going through the system. This, indeed, is the meaning of the very plan of this book. Also important in approaching education from the educator's point of view rather than from that of the educated is that in America adults have been very conscious of the importance of education. They have been the source of many philosophic and intellectual statements about what education is and should be. And this consciousness of purpose belongs not only to intellectuals or even professional educators but to most of the people I have talked to on the subject in Appleton.

Education

Definitions of the nature of the educational process and of the manner in which children should be educated abound in Appleton and are very well summarized in the following two statements that I reproduce almost verbatim. The first statement, more conservative and philosophic, was made by a judge:

> "We can do only one thing in our schools and in our homes, and it is to explain to our children why we have made the choices we made in our life, moral and otherwise, give them both sides of the question and all the reasons that have made us decide for one way rather than for the other. If we are good parents, and if we have good teachers, we should be able to make our children understand us and follow our tracks."

The second statement, more liberal and technical, was made by a schoolteacher:

> "The students nowadays do not want and should not be taught as they used to be taught with a lecture from me one day and a quiz the following day to find out whether they can regurgitate what I told them the day before. They should express their opinions and teach themselves."

I heard variations on these statements many times, even from parents who disapproved of the liberal methods of education that had completely invaded the public school curriculum and were starting to be used in the Catholic parochial school too. I rarely heard statements denying the first statement directly or by implication. This was particularly true among the most educated and reflective informants. The only homes in which I was told that education should be merely a process of indoctrinating children with a set of undiscussed truths were those of informants whose European background still pervaded all their other attitudes.

The Catholic school was a fortress of such sentiments until recently, when it began to give in to more orthodox—that is, "liberal"—attitudes. European influences were fading away with the disappearance of the immigrants who had dominated the parish until they were replaced in positions of responsibility by their children or grandchildren. Indeed, it was striking to see that many recent and not-so-recent graduates of the parochial school had finally been almost totally enculturated into mainstream Americanism.

Implicit in the statements I quoted is the idea that the child is already a fully formed person who can make choices based on rational and intellectual premises, a person who possesses the inner wisdom to "teach himself," to discern truthful, or at least useful, statements of fact from other statements that might be appealing for purely emotional reasons. The second quote is reminiscent of Plato's idea that truth is inherent in every human being or at least that anybody may be led to discover the truth for himself. Indeed, when a teacher is very good at the Socratic method, real teaching may take place in the classrooms where spontaneous methods are used. If not, it is clear that no teaching is possible—teaching as distinct from education, which should be considered a more general process from which no child can escape, whatever method is used. Many students in Appleton had so well accepted the idea that they were free agents as far as being taught is concerned, that it was becoming more and more difficult for parents and teachers to retreat from the extreme position they had reached, as some said they would like to do. It was all the more difficult because this freedom of children to develop according to their own personality was not restricted to the classroom.

Among my informants in Appleton, the children were left essentially free to choose their own life-styles in their early teens in many families, and certainly in all of them by the time they entered their junior year in high school. In the context of other aspects of American culture, this meant that children differentiated themselves from their parents very early; indeed, that they were more or less *expected* and educated to do so. Differentiation has been institutionalized; the generation gap is a necessary by-product of the structure.

The pervasiveness of the push toward differentiation between children and their parents is amazing, and it is difficult to realize that there is nothing "natural" about it. When the thirteen-year-old daughter of the Methodist minister stuck a Joe Namath poster on the ceiling of her otherwise very conservative bedroom with the amused tolerance of her parents, one can measure the extent of the acceptance of the idea that a child is a full person, an individual who should be left free to develop through his or her own whims and desires. Both parents and children would say that there are limits to this freedom. They meant that though the parents expect and prod their children into significant variations from their own pattern, this variation can become too great and trigger negative responses by the parents. The children may persist and then break away from the parents, abandoning the community they used to form with their parents in much the same way Mr. Howard broke from the Farm Bureau. The child may also desist and come back to a safe level of variation. Some parents may allow a wider range of variation than others, and some children may be more adept at minimizing overt conflict; in all cases, the process remains the same.

Another way of measuring the institutionalization of this definition of the nature of a child as an individual is through the observation that even among the most educated informants, who were not professionally involved in the field of education, few would quote the libertarian educators of the past fifty years: John Dewey, Margaret Mead, or Dr. Benjamin Spock. Furthermore, many informants who classified themselves as politically conservative gave a great amount of freedom to their children, while some liberals held a tighter rein and showed more interest in their development.

A corollary to this view of the child as an autonomous human being very early in its life can be found in what is often called the lack of interest displayed by many parents concerning the actions of their children. But this should not be seen purely in these terms, for it is also closely linked to the idea that children cannot be interested in the business of adults and thus would not want to participate in many activities or even be present. This was not expressed solely in negative terms—parents refusing the presence of their children at social functions. It was also stated positively as the need for children to have interactions with other children rather than with adults, since the absence of such interactions would endanger the full development of the child. The refusal to systematically involve children with adults was thus often a sign of positive interest in the child's welfare.

This was translated into action in many ways. Very young children would be left at home with a babysitter instead of being taken to the activity the parents were attending; nurseries were provided during church services and on other social occasions; and so on. When they were older, children would be left at home, sometimes alone, more often with their own friends. Very soon, they discovered that they were not "wanted," that they were special and different from their parents, that they might, and even had to, have their own activities. By the time they reached their teens, they generally had come to prefer their own company to that of adults. From time to time a church group would remark that this break was too sharp, that parents and children should be together during church family dinners to prove their solidarity. I never observed any success in such attempts at intergenerational solidarity. The older children resisted being seated with their parents and ended up at a table by themselves; the younger children might successfully be forced to eat with their parents but were always moved to the nursery as soon as the meal ended and before the program started. The same distinction is revealed in this statement by a woman about her daughter: "When Grace turns sixteen next year, we will buy her a car if we can. It is so much more convenient. I have my clubs, and she has her activities. Our time schedules do not coincide, and it is a lot of trouble for me to go and pick her up or for her to wait for me."

Some adults, like the church group mentioned above, are distressed by this dichotomy between the two worlds and talk about "bringing families back together." Many more, particularly the less reflective, protested vocally and somewhat aimlessly that "young people are given too much freedom nowadays." Very few adults were conscious of the relationship between designing special activities for children and the children eventually designing their own special activities with little consideration given to whether their parents approved of them or not.

Parents considered their young children to be different from them; older children came to believe this, too, and they expressed it. This resulted in the often paradoxical spectacle of an otherwise totally respectable and conservative youth antagonizing his or her respectable and conservative parents on very minor points rendered all-important at the time of the exchange for no apparent purpose other than an affirmation of freedom on the part of the youth.

The revolt of children in their middle and late teens is culturally necessary. It does not have to be very radical, but it must be communicated verbally and otherwise to the parents or to an authority representing adult society (the police, the dominant political parties) in such a way as to create a dramatic tension, even in the many cases where the positions of the parent and child are not so far apart. This is indeed what happens, and why it soon becomes very hard for adults to realize that they, too, revolted. But they were looking from a different side of the generation gap, to use an anachronistic term, and they do not recognize the landscape from their point of view. They remember that, apart from a few pranks, they were nice kids, and now they see their children turning "wild," or they are made to believe that this is what is happening; but if they could look at their children without passion, they would see that, apart from a few pranks, like getting drunk on strawberry wine or high on pot, their children possess a system of values very close to their own. Their children are just as individualistic and understand the need to build a feeling of community just as much as their parents.

Sociology as Psychology

Appleton High School did not have classes in personal hygiene or the modern world, but it had a class in sociology, which turned out to have a very similar purpose: to discuss and explain the modern world to the students before they confronted the world outside after their graduation. This language reveals the generally accepted idea that upon graduation from high school, the child, who has reached the age of sixteen to eighteen, becomes socially autonomous and morally responsible. If there is to be a sharp break between a child and parents, it is at this time that it occurs; and even when the break is more latent than open, all signs point to the importance of this period: the first dates, the first unsupervised parties (the first time one gets drunk or high), the first time that church youth groups are considered autonomous. Senior year in high school is thus the last formal occasion when the adults can try to influence their children. Informal communication may have ceased before that time, or it may continue afterward; the formal break occurs at graduation from high school, and indeed the first real change in the life of a young man or woman does occur then (I should note here that the percentage of children finishing high school in Appleton is high—in 1960 more than 50 percent of the adults had a high school education or more; in the 1968–69 school year, the dropout rate was only 5 percent), whether he or she is going on to college, getting a job, or marrying.

The high school sociology class was an attempt to verbally communicate a certain view of society to the soon-to-be-graduated students. By this time, the students had been totally enculturated. They had organized their own private lives according to rules they had abstracted from the actions and statements of their parents. The most enlightened teachers did not even attempt to impose their personal viewpoint on the students. But while they perceived their intervention as consisting solely in the elicitation and clarification of each student's viewpoint, they *were* imposing a *cultural* viewpoint, the viewpoint that moral decisions are a matter of individual rather than group responsibility. Some students, among the most thoughtful, were disturbed by such a relativization of values, which they perceived as a hostile challenge to their more absolute beliefs.

In Appleton the relativistic argument was, however, fully accepted by most teachers and students. The class in sociology concentrated more on a presentation of the problems that certain moral decisions may create than on the dogmatic enunciation of a comprehensive system. There was a system, of course, but it was implicit rather than explicit, which is interesting in itself. The class was *explicitly* about morals but only *implicitly* about a particular system of morals (American). When it became explicit, as sometimes happened, what was stressed was the way in which the individual person gives morals meaning and how dissent is permissible.

Nine topics were discussed in class: (1) personality (self-concept), (2) sex education, (3) marriage and the family, (4) religion and the new morality, (5) drugs, (6) crime and delinquency, (7) mental health, (8) black–white relationships, and (9) demography. All were dealt with similarly. A movie would be shown or an oral report would be given by a group of students. It would set up a situation, and a discussion would develop on the proper response. The situations were considered as given from the outside. The consequences that might be attached to the various solutions were also often considered as given. But the process of situation-to-consequence was not considered given because it depended on an individual decision. Would *you*/should *you* have sex before marriage? What are the consequences for the individuals involved in getting married and having children? What are the dangers of drugs? And so on.

In the discussions, dominated by the students' perceptions but chaired by the teacher, no consideration was given to the forces, sociological or cultural, that shape individual action. They were not denied, just forgotten. What was stressed was that action is shaped through the mental constitution of the individual and that this form of shaping is of overriding importance. Society is active only through a reinterpretation of its pressures by the individual. Maybe it is the environment that makes people commit crimes, but through either will, psychological treatment, or salvation, they can transcend this environment. The individual dominates society, and if he is weak, another individual (therapist, preacher) can help him. This was not presented as an act of faith, as in the Farm Bureau Creed, but as the result of scientific inquiry into the nature of human action.

I have emphasized that this perspective on human action must be seen as cultural and "arbitrary" to the world in the Saussurian sense, and not in any simpleminded way scientific or necessary. It may *also* be scientific, or at least useful for the development of our understanding of the individual psyche, but it was not its scientific quality that made the approach possess what Geertz has called, in reference to religion, "compelling facticity." It is something that was much more pervasive, an approach to the interpretation of social life that sprang out wherever there was a need to talk about human action, be it in the conscious declaration of one's faith, the unconscious patterning of one's way of telling one's history, or the search for a proper answer to questions posed to all adolescents in any culture as they grow up biologically and culturally. And at the same time as it is a perspective useful for the development of the discipline of psychology, it is one that may be fundamentally at odds with the sociological mind, which may explain why the "sociology" taught by the teacher I observed had such a "psychological" quality.

Kinship and Marriage

American kinship was recently, and brilliantly, studied by David M. Schneider.[1] I did not go to Appleton to check on his analysis, nor did I see myself as building on his work. That I ended doing just this is interesting in itself. Thus, I will not explore the domain of kinship in any great detail. What I would like to do is to give a brief indication of the way Schneider's conclusions fit with the argument I am making.

To do so, I will first return to the text provided by the life history of the Howards and their children. They never told me anything to make me believe that their definitions of the units of kinship were any different from those that Schneider collected. For the Howards, like all other people I talked to in Appleton, a family is, first, the unit composed of a husband, his wife, and their children. Only secondarily is it the unit of all the living relatives. Husbands and wives are together because they love each other. This is symbolized by sexual intercourse. There is a difference in the social world between people to whom one is related and those to whom one is not. The former are one's kin. A further differentiation is made among these according to whether the relationship is by blood; that is, the result of a marriage contracted by the speaker or one of his blood relatives.

These are some of the features used by my informants to distinguish a certain type of people from other people—what Schneider calls "the distinctive features which define the person as a relative." Those features are rarely discussed as such; they are thought to be grounded in a scientific analysis of the world and thus to be unchallengeable. They can be assumed and taken for granted. When one tries to explain to an informant that in some societies people make a distinction between patrilateral and matrilateral cousins, this is generally greeted by a blank stare, a shrug of the shoulders, and a comment to the effect that "of course" those people "do not know" the facts of life, that "really" cousins are all the same whether they are born of the father's siblings or of the mother's. What cannot be assumed is the way relatives ought to conduct themselves toward each other, and references to cross-cultural variation in the code of conduct expected from relatives can lead to lively discussions. How women should be treated by men, children by their parents, how one should treat the children of one's son's wife by her first husband—all this is problematic and is constantly being renegotiated.

The only requirement is that relatives, particularly the closer ones, "love" each other or, at the very least, "be nice" to each other. These specifications, however, remain very vague indeed. They cannot be taken as a guide for everyday behavior toward relatives. At most they are a yardstick against which to measure whether one's practical actions are appropriate. As I will mention later, natives can recognize whether love is present, but they do not define it. Love, liking, being nice to, are relations, not formally spelled-out contents. Biological fathering, on the other hand, is purely a content because one remains a father to one's children even if, whether through death, divorce, or abandonment, one never relates to them. Children, of course, are in a problematic position, for they participate in both content—or "substance," as Schneider calls it—and code of conduct. One is expected to take care of one's progeny, physically at least (as through child-support payments), until their majority. After that, children lose their substance, and any further help is voluntary—an expression of love, not of biologically based necessity.

People do relate to their kin. They are simply entitled to relate to them in whatever way they please—with great warmth, or bare politeness, or not at all. One may deal differently with relatives of the same type. One may even, within one family group, consider one's relatives in a different way from other members of the group. The relationship between Mr. Howard and his sister is a case in point. He felt somewhat close to her but was not able to make his own family participate in this relationship. In fact, it is not only relationships between family units or between somewhat distant relatives that remain unspecified; relationships between spouses or between parents and grown-up children are just as vague and dependent on the persons involved.

Schneider deals at great length with this lack of definiteness of the code of conduct. He shows that the specific code of conduct chosen by two relatives in their relationship depends solely on a decision made by these people. For those two people, for certain families, for certain subgroups, the code of conduct may be very specific indeed, involving strict rules as to gift giving, greeting-card exchange, regular invitations, and so on. But even among those who demand a rigid code of conduct, it will be insisted that specific acts are only symbols of the love that is supposed to bind family members, that they express and reinforce their love and should not be considered an end in themselves.

As Schneider says, a relative is a person, and in one's dealings with one's relatives, one must always take this into consideration. The vagueness of the code of conduct is thus not a matter of statistical variation. It is not a result of the fact that in no society do people consistently follow the rules dictated by that culture. The vagueness or, to be more precise, the possibility of choice between different codes of conduct and the resulting variations that can be observed in such an outwardly well-integrated community as Appleton are built-in structural factors in American culture.

Thus it can be understood why the impression I got from my initial talk with Jim Howard (see page 22) was mistaken. Mr. Howard was not a patriarch, nor could he be because patriarchy is outside the American cultural structure. When Jim talked of his father as a good man, a better man than his mother, he was not implying anything about his authority or the special rights and responsibilities of fathers in general. Indeed, Jim was not talking about a father so much as he was talking about a unique individual, a person to whom he happened to be related as son but who could be evaluated comparatively in much the same manner as any other person he may have met. The point of reference was not fatherhood. Jim might have said the same thing about his mother. The point of reference was the more general humanity of the person as expressed in a unique psychological makeup.

Individualism and Social Structure

My analysis of the Farm Bureau showed that it was an organization whose membership was open to (1) anyone who could call himself a farmer, and (2) anyone who accepted a certain set of means to reach a more widely desired goal. I have just shown that a family is a group open to (1) anyone who can prove relationship to the group by blood or by law, and (2) anyone from that set of people who accepts a certain code of conduct that is, in fact, a set of practical steps toward a more general goal. The parallelism in structure is evident.

Farming, like being related, is an objective thing. One cannot declare oneself a farmer if one cannot demonstrate that one actually farms. Joining the Farm Bureau is like marriage: the act is unequivocal, but it is a matter of personal choice initially and a matter of maintaining unanimity of purpose, or at least the pretense of it, during the tenure of the association. Marrying and joining the Farm Bureau are both "forever," though this aspect of the relationship is ritually stressed much more in marriage. Yet joining the Farm Bureau is never considered a temporary move, and there is no formal limit to it; indeed, most Farm Bureau memberships, like most marriages, *are* forever.

Conversely, divorce is permissible and relatively frequent. (The rate of divorce in Appleton is slightly lower than in the United States as a whole. In 1970 it was 44 percent.) Why does one divorce in Appleton? Sometimes because of what could be considered a strong breach of the code of behavior, such as when one's wife or husband becomes an alcoholic or heroin addict, though much more often it is for more elusive reasons. ("We just could not stand each other anymore. I did not know her when we got married, and she turned out to be a bitch.") In some cases, the fact that the husband or wife has been found "going out with" other women or men may be called the "last straw," but if one investigates further, it is found that the real breach is explained as having occurred before and as being basically of a personal and psychological nature.

The cultural perception of interpersonal relations remains structurally similar in all the domains, kinship and otherwise, that I have explored. In fact, it is possible to go further and argue, following the lead offered by Schneider, that it would be a mistake to interpret the view Americans have of their society as involving several domains that would be "structurally similar." It might be said that there is really but one system of principles regulating interpersonal relationships, which applies to all the situations confronting Americans. This system involves what I have called "individualism"; that is, the necessity to deal with other persons in a way that is negotiated on an ad hoc basis.

In other words, the social structure of a town like Appleton—the term "social structure" being understood as the system that Americans have created to direct their interpersonal, social intercourse—is not made up of different groups considered to be in a symbiotic relationship, but rather of different individuals who come together to do something. Appleton is not divided into "wife-givers" and "wife-receivers." Nor is it divided, as Indo-European societies were, into a system of merchants, farmers, warriors, and priests. Nor is it dichotomized between a working proletariat and a group of capitalist entrepreneurs—between a *peuple* and a *bourgeoisie*. It is divided into as many individuals as there are people in the town.

I said that these individuals are considered to come together to do things. What are these things? I mentioned farming and farmers, procreating and relatives. There are, of course, many other such categories of people: doctors, merchants, factory workers, Italians, blacks, and so on. A complete listing of all these categories would not mean much because they are, culturally speaking, indefinite. They describe what people do, not how they relate to each other. A person can be a member of several of these categories: he can be an Italian, and also an industrialist, and a grandfather, and a husband; he may play different roles, but he is still considered to remain the same person, "himself," within these roles. This allows him to refuse participation in a trade association, to divorce his wife, to refuse to help his children financially, to dissociate himself from his ethnicity, or, conversely, to claim ethnicity when the blood claims are very weak.

The distinctive features of kinship are grounded in biology; whatever it is that scientists say genetics is, is what constitutes descent. Similarly with farming or doctoring. One is not a legitimate farmer or physician if one does not follow the edicts of science and technology, objective disciplines that tell us "how it really is." Therefore, it is possible and legitimate to talk of such ad hoc

groups as the farmers, or the townspeople, or the Howard family. They are all the people who are related to an outside, objective, substantial quality, whether they relate to each other or not. One may use a generic term in such contexts either when one has to explain to an outsider what one does ("I am a farmer," "I am Irish") or when one is dealing with a group of persons not as persons but as people related to the objective in which one is interested. Thus the farmers are a group for the machinery dealers in town because their livelihood is dependent on what the farmers do—how successful they are at it. Who individual farmers are is irrelevant in this context.

The distinction made is that between dealing with man in his relations to nonhuman, objective reality—such as biological facts or technological areas—and interacting with another individual in a manner negotiated by the two for the duration of the interaction. American moralists have often argued that the latter mode of interaction is better than the former, precisely because it is individualistic and takes the personality of the other into account. In fact, America is also the culture that accepted most rapidly the rationalization of labor in industry, with its antipersonal implications. It is also agreed that any process that involves evaluation of an individual must be grounded in objective criteria that are not dependent upon the relationship between the evaluator and the evaluated.[2]

There is one apparent exception to the vagueness of the definition of the code of conduct: the fact that, as I noted, parents are not free not to take care of their children. It is recognized that small children cannot be physically independent, though they are considered to be emotionally independent at the earliest possible age. Thus it is somebody's job to take care of them, just as it is somebody's job to produce food for the rest of the population. This person is the parent, who must raise the child. However, parents and children are also individuals who have to interact, and thus as soon as the child is old enough to respond on an equal basis, a decision must be made as to the type of interaction—positive, negative, just polite, and so on—that will prevail between the two. This is why there is a formal end to the job of being a parent, both by law (the parent is responsible for a child for eighteen years) and by custom (the parent is responsible for a child until the latter's graduation from high school).

CHAPTER 3
Individualism in Religious Ideology

Only a very few of my informants oriented their lives specifically in terms of an explicit religious ideology. Many more rejected the idea that religion was the main driving force in their lives. Most of my informants, even among the churchgoers, when asked about the fundamental grounding of their morality would mention "democracy" rather than "Protestantism," political ideology rather than religion. They were in implicit agreement with Paul Tillich, who argues that in Protestantism, "just as there is no priest having a special religious function, for everybody is a layman and every layman is potentially a priest, so there is no religion *as a special spiritual sphere*. Everything is secular and every secular thing is potentially religious [author's italics]."[1] Conversely, it is a commonplace in American culture that religion holds an overwhelming place in political rhetoric, that the eventual validation for the existence of America as a political system is seen in its establishing a truly Christian society and offering it as a model to the rest of the world.

However, I do not want to get caught in a sterile discussion about the primacy of religion or politics as the explanation for American culture. There is no "core symbol" to the culture, and I am not searching for it. Thus, this preliminary discussion of religious ideas is offered simply to present certain variations on the theme of individualism when used in the context of religion.

In the second part of this book, I will deal at length with religious organization where the other basic category of American culture, community, and its place in the conceptual structure is best revealed. A full treatise on the religion of the people of Appleton would demand much more space than I can give to it. What I will do here and subsequently is to present a few aspects of religious life that best reveal the principles I have already outlined, although in different contexts. I realize that this approach cannot end with a definitive view of the nature of American religion, even restricted to an ethnologic view. Nor should my remarks be construed as intended to prove the validity of the preceding analysis. What I want to establish is that what I have already said about American culture through a study of personal life histories, trade associations, education, or family structure remains valid in other contexts of human action or interaction in Appleton.

A Religious Text

At the most concrete level of reality, religion is so pervasive in Appleton that it is somewhat difficult to know where to start. Thinking that the most arbitrary choice might be less biased than a pseudo-classification, I begin this discussion with a quotation from a monthly devotional magazine that enjoys some popularity in Appleton. Its general declaration of intent is printed above the table of contents:

> "GUIDEPOSTS is written for and by people of all faiths. Its purpose: to show, by inspirational personal experiences, how men and women from all walks of life have found strength, courage and hope through their belief in God. Its goal: to point the way to deeper faith, more creative living."[2]

This declaration obviously possesses a faint resemblance to the Farm Bureau Creed, which I analyzed earlier. It too is divided into three parts: (1) a definition of the audience, (2) a description of the means used by the organization or magazine, (3) a statement of the proposed ends. In this case an analysis of the differences will be more revealing than one of the formal similarities.

While in the Farm Bureau Creed action in society at large is intended to provide very practical results for the members of the organization, *Guideposts'* goals are much more abstract, spiritual, and moral. The former speaks of "comfortable living," the latter of "creative living." The dichotomy between the stated means is also very striking. The Farm Bureau goals will be reached through an "organized effort," which implies a union of the individuals involved and some activity on their part. On the other hand, *Guideposts* will use "inspirational personal experiences"—one individual talks to another individual—and it implies a certain passivity on the part of the audience. The editors of *Guideposts* certainly hope that their sermons will *result* in activity, but the process of listening to a sermon is totally passive compared to the process of organizing a marketing system (which will, however, eventually lead to a certain passivity toward the union when the economic goals have been reached). The most striking difference is certainly to be found in the definition of the audience. In the Farm Bureau it was defined in a very exclusive manner: "*these* friends and neighbors," not others. On the contrary, *Guideposts* is all-inclusive: "for . . . people of *all* faiths, . . . men and women from *all* walks of life."

The consistency of these differences is all the more striking since I chose the *Guideposts* declaration of intent by chance and not because it offered a good counterpoint to the Farm Bureau Creed. I believe that I could have made the same analysis using other religious texts, though maybe not so concisely. I will show presently that these reversals inside similar structures can be recognized in a much wider perspective. The systematic character of the reversals can be summarized in the following way: (1) the Farm Bureau is a *small* group of people *united* together for *practical* goals, and (2) *Guideposts* is for and about *all* men as *individuals* for *moral* goals.

Lévi-Strauss has often said that the diagrams he uses to illustrate his analyses are no more than illustrative and that too much importance should not be given to them. With the same qualifications in mind, I offer the accompanying Table 1 as a visual summary.

The regularity of the structure may surprise some and make them doubt the ethnographic value of the exercise. That is why I must emphasize at once that there is nothing strikingly new in the

TABLE 1. *Comparison of Farm Bureau Creed and Guideposts' Declaration of Intent*

		Farm Bureau	Guideposts
Audience	inclusive	−	+
	exclusive	+	−
Means	individual experience	−	+
	union	+	−
Goals	moral	−	+
	practical	+	−

substance of what I just said. It has always been known that religion in America is universalistic, individualistic, and moralistic, as distinct, for example, from religions with sociological and ritual overtones that are restricted to one race or that insist on the performance of certain specific acts to establish membership. The value of the preceding analysis lies mainly in its exemplary role: one self-contained text analyzed in detail can convey a more concise description of a structure than several pages of discussion of longer and more complex texts, interviews, sermons, and books that cannot be quoted at length. (I shall deal briefly with some of these data in chapter 10.)

As a last qualification, when I talk of American religion, I speak mainly of American Protestantism, either high-church, establishment, or moderate denominations, such as the Episcopalian, Presbyterian, and Methodist churches, or fundamentalist and Bible-oriented churches, of which many could be found in Appleton. The Catholic church in Appleton presents a more delicate problem because its authoritarian, Europe-centered nature has prevented it from evolving as fast as the Protestant denominations, although the shift away from European definitions was noticeable, particularly in the spontaneous reactions of the faithful.

However diverse Protestant denominations can be on points of doctrine, ritual, or in their approach to the moral life, there is an essential similarity among them that stands out when they are compared to other religions. For a nonspecialist and an outsider such as I, it is often very difficult to differentiate a Methodist sermon from a book by Billy Graham or from what is said about Seventh-day Adventists. For all of them, man is not saved by, or because of, his works, but because of his faith. In other words, man behaves according to the will of God not when he enters into certain relations with other persons in a prescribed way but when he as an individual, alone and free, decides to enter into a direct relationship with God.

This is expressed in different ritual ways by the various denominations. The fundamentalist churches interpret the moment of decision in a literal manner as the most important instant in the life of a man or woman, and they surround that time with a solemnity that stresses in action the individual character of the process of salvation. In certain churches the emotional aspect is stressed, and one is expected to present the same outward signs of "having received the spirit" as the apostles on Pentecost—"People thought they had become crazy," as one minister of a Pentecostal church told me—and those who are saved must show it in the same way.

In other churches it is necessary simply to come forward at the end of a service during the invitation and to declare publicly one's intention to join the church. In still other churches, it is not considered necessary to make a public profession of faith to be accepted as a Christian. It is enough to be baptized or confirmed, a more formal occasion when it is still assumed that the person has entered into a new relationship with God.

Let us examine a specific example of the way in which this theological interpretation is translated into ritual action. At the end of every service of the Protestant churches in Appleton, before the last hymns, the preacher says something like: "If there is anyone here this morning who has been moved by the spirit and desires to enter this community of Christians, let him come forward and confess his faith." To come forward means to get up from one's seat in the congregation, go down the aisle, and stand by the pulpit in front of the altar. There, a few questions may be asked by the minister, and then the last hymn is sung. Then one can mix again with the crowd going out of church and probably be greeted by many people introducing themselves and thus extending a welcome to the new church member. Any person who wants to join the church, even to transfer his membership from a church of the same denomination in another town, must go through this ritual.

This ceremony clearly demonstrates its quality as an initiation ritual, since it possesses the three phases of separation, liminality, and reincorporation that all such rituals possess, as Arnold Van Gennep and then Victor Turner have shown.[3] But it would be a mistake to interepret it in a purely formal way, as a transformation of a universal structure. It is also structured by specifically American principles. It is the passage of an individual into a community, the stress being put on the act of volition that an individual, alone in relation to God and indeed to any community, performs to join the group and give his life to God. As I will emphasize later, one of the most striking features of a Protestant congregation during a Sunday service is the essentially successful attempt at full unanimity of movement and appearance in a quasi-military manner. And yet all the members have once stood by themselves in front of the congregation. God addresses himself to the individual rather than to society as a whole through a consecrated channel. Any congregation or even the total community of Christians is an amorphous crowd during the service, and it is necessary to extricate oneself from this crowd to demonstrate salvation.

By way of contrast, the Catholic church, even after Vatican II, insists that it is in direct relationship with God *as a whole,* that although each individual Catholic may be estranged from God at any moment in his life, the whole cannot err, is directly inspired by Christ, in fact is "married" to him, as the "body" of which He is the "head," depending on the metaphor.

The inherent contradiction of the Protestant definition may have become perceptible by now. If religion is simply a matter of faith, something that concerns only God and the person as an individual, why should there be any organized churches at all? The case is similar to Mr. Howard's and his apparent refusal to recognize in certain contexts the help that he received from his family and friends. In other contexts he did recognize it. But he did not contradict himself, for individualism is not an absolute more or less actualized in concrete situations but rather a moment in a greater dialogue.

This dialogue remained fully implicit in everyday life. In religious thought, a necessarily more reflective medium, consideration was given to reconciling individual agency in relation to God with organized religion. Ministers railed against "those who call themselves Christian and would rather play golf on a Sunday morning than attend church." The arguments in favor of regular church membership and attendance are many, the two main ones being that (1) it is necessary to join others to worship God in a manner that will please Him, and (2) one has the duty, when one has been saved, to help others be saved. Depending on the church or minister, this latter reason for church membership means public witnessing and example for the most evangelical churches, or financial contributions. In the second argument can be recognized the purpose of *Guideposts.* Though this argument is somewhat stronger than the first one, it is not completely convincing for someone who advocates a totally individualistic religion. Nor does it explain what is indeed a structural necessity for organized churches.

The religious principles I outlined earlier demand only a personal declaration of salvation, and salvation, it is agreed, may occur in a private setting. Indeed, most stories of miraculous salvations stress the unlikely character of both timing and place—the more unlikely the better—and the duties of a Christian are simply personally to witness, but not necessarily in a public, structured manner. It is often argued that the best witnessing is that made to a friend or neighbor in a private setting not necessarily stamped as a religious occasion. It will be said, even by ministers, that attending church is at best merely a symbol of Christianity. From the point of view of the ministers, this is a counterproductive argument, since all the people I met in Appleton agreed that they did not like to do something that was not an actual means to an end—which does not necessarily mean that they never acted symbolically, but that they stopped performing an action once it had been labeled "symbolic."

Another argument and a more valid one in this context of efficacy is that it is good for one's own faith to meet regularly with people who share it; it is necessary to defend oneself against the evil influence of the pagan world "outside"—that part of the world that does not refer its actions to Christianity. One of my most sociologically conscious informants, a minister, argued once in my presence against a group of young people who were criticizing the need for organized religion. The minister maintained that it was a "normal" and "natural" process for a church to be founded. "Let us say that you have finally decided that Christianity is the only real answer to your personal and the world's problems and that you have discovered in yourself a strong faith in God. You cannot just sit there and keep it to yourself. You will go out and look for people who share your faith, you will meet regularly to speak of your faith, to pray or to plan, you will soon find out that one of you has more aptitude to lead the praying than the others, and you will essentially have started a new church. Later on, you will find out that it is convenient for practical purposes to be affiliated to a national organization, and you will have completed the whole circle. This is just how the so-called established churches in this town were started."

This statement is central to the development of my argument. It is clearly generated by the same mythical structure as generated what I was told about the organization of the Farm Bureau, its creation, and development. Conversely, it should be evident that however representative this statement is of the actual organization of churches and other voluntary associations in Appleton, it does not fit the definition of the relationship between man and God with which I started. Or, rather, because there is no insurmountable contradiction between these two aspects of American religion, it can be said that the creation of churches does not depend in a direct manner on a theological definition but that it depends on a different type of principle, which I sketched earlier: the overpowering need that is felt both consciously and unconsciously by people for the creation of smaller or larger groups in which they can relate on a personal basis, what I will refer to as "community." Thus, even though there is nothing in the basic tenets of the accepted theology that demands the creation of a church, most believers, particularly the more sincere, belong to a church and are active participants in its activities, with the paradoxical result that a religion that emphasizes faith over works produces much more actual work than a religion that is supposed to reverse the emphasis, such as European Catholicism.

This may seem to be a paradox. But one must remember that cultural logic is not syllogistic—"rational" in the narrow sense. It is poetic—*sauvage*, as Lévi-Strauss would say.

The Morality of Protestantism

The Farm Bureau Creed defines the goals of the association in very practical and limited ways: "a comfortable living . . . , education . . . , independence for old age." I emphasized how all these things were framed in an individualistic framework. This individualism is to be preserved through practical means: a precise set of actions specifically designed to deal with an external contingency in a rational way; that is, in a way that follows the natural logic of the situation rather than one created by the actor. The rationality referred to here is that of machines, rational answers to natural problems. In fact, the machines themselves, notwithstanding their obvious reality as cultural objects created by man, are prototypically natural in relation to the people who operate them, since relating to them is always fully determined by their structure. They are closed systems, just as the world is thought to be—only more obviously so. If one cannot loosen a screw by turning it counterclockwise, and if this is different from the usual structure of screws, it is probably because of certain aspects of the whole machine that make it necessary that it should be unscrewed clockwise. There are no other solutions.

I became well grounded in this type of logic during the period I spent working on Mr. Howard's farm, when repairs to the machinery were a constant necessity. On every occasion, I was struck by the fact that machines are utterly determined, that their code of conduct, or at least the code of conduct that one has to adopt in relation to them, leaves nothing to vagueness or personal whim. In the social world, associations such as the Farm Bureau, and indeed, even society itself, are considered such rational answers to natural problems—machines for the preservation of individuals. The main consequence of this is that no inherent value is attached to the *specific* rules, solutions, or whatever that are found necessary for the association to function. They may be necessary, they may be the symbols of human values, but they are not values in themselves.

This leaves religion with little, if any, relevance to the natural world. God laid down the rules of the game, man is learning them; God does not act directly on nature, man does. This is not so total a rejection of the presence of God in the world as it might seem, for God is given a place—and not only as creator of the rules of nature. He is also relevant to the behavior of the individual being, for it is through Him that one will reach a better life—"more creative living," as *Guideposts* put it; "authenticity," as others would put it. God thus changes the *quality* of an individual's life. He does not change its *quantity*, its specific character. In other words, since a person's specific acts are supposed to be directed by mechanical rationality, to believe in God, or have faith, does not necessitate a shift in these acts. Nature and its rationality remain the same whether one believes or not. What is demanded of the Christian is a shift in the meaning of these acts.

It might appear surprising to see Protestantism characterized here as being totally divorced from practical action in the world. There is a popular idea that religion is concerned with precise directives as to action in the world. It may have been more so in the past, and specific demands are still made on the congregations of certain denominations. The Seventh-day Adventist church still actively forbids alcohol, tobacco, and military service to its members. To these traditional taboos it has added keeping the Sabbath—Saturday—and a branch of the denomination holds to vegetarianism. This represents the most extreme development of taboos I could observe in Appleton. Most other churches, and all the larger ones, had done away with any sort of interdiction.

Yet even the specific taboos of the Seventh-day Adventists do not imply an action of God on the natural world: religion, here as elsewhere, is only relevant to moral action. Drinking alcohol displeases God; He has forbidden it. But this is not because of a culturally determined property of alcohol. Alcohol is forbidden not because it is somewhat polluting or sacred but because it is considered to be a threat to the quality of the person who takes some. It is a natural, rational threat. Even the vegetarianism of certain branches of the Seventh-day Adventists is justified by the "fact" that meat is neither necessary nor particularly "good" for one's body, that it might even be positively harmful and thus nonrational. Many denominations do phrase their rules in terms of the Bible. ("It is written in the Bible! How can you doubt that this is so?") It would be a great oversimplification, though, to suppose that the believers in the literal interpretation of the Bible use this "reason" blindly as the basic justification for their faith. Most of them are convinced that the Bible is history, *fact,* and that God is simply the guarantor of its truth. They support archaeological excavations in the Holy land, the search for the remnant of Noah's Ark, and are avid readers of popularized descriptions of the sociohistorical environment of Palestine. They consider learned a preacher who can paint realistic pictures of Christ's life, and their taste in religious iconography goes to posters purporting to describe incidents from the Gospel in authentic detail. They particularly resent the argument that the Bible is symbolic, for if it is merely symbolic, how can it also be true? The insistence on a literal interpretation of the Bible is thus more an attempt to escape from the idea that the world may possibly *not* be rational than the escape into irrationality that it is often made to be by outsiders to the faith.

The fundamentalist churches cater to a small part of the population of Appleton (see Chapter 5 for a table of church membership in the town). Most of the churchgoing population belongs to what I will call "moderate Protestant" churches, and most non churchgoers are close to the position of these churches in terms of moral ideology. In these churches most specific taboos have disappeared, and the divorce between religious and practical action is complete. It is a very rare sermon that demands a definite action on the part of the listeners, and this would normally consist of an appeal for money or for participation in a charitable or church-related project. There is even a tendency not to make demands for practical help during the actual sermon, but rather at the end of the service during the announcements. Sermons should be reserved, it is thought, for calls to lead a "better life."

In contradistinction to all this stands the Catholic Church. Even in the post–Vatican II version of it that I observed in Appleton, it was still insisted that the faithful perform acts *not* directly related to a practical means. The sign of the cross, confession, all the other sacraments, the formal structure and meaning of the Mass—all are interpreted as sacred acts that a Christian must perform to please God, even though they are not "practical" in relation to anything but salvation. These acts are, furthermore, the very core of religion. As I was told by a priest: "If one performs these acts, however much he may doubt their value or however much he may be sinful in his private behavior, there must be a spark of faith in him or he would not be performing them, and thus God will receive him." Of course, the reverse of this also holds true: "However good one's private life may be, if one does not perform any ritual act, one probably will not be saved because one does not have faith." Faith is not considered possible outside of some sort of ritual activity. The ritualism is thus rational in relation to God and salvation, while it is irrational in relation to the natural world.

My reference to the Catholic Church is not arbitrary. Historically, Protestantism started as a reaction against Catholicism, and today many of its choices are still explained and defined in relation to the theological choices of the Catholic Church. Furthermore, definitions of the "world" and "rationality" are very similar in the cultural backgrounds of both versions of Christianity.

The significant difference, in a quasi-phonemic way, exists at the level of the definition of the relationship of God to the world. The Catholic Church still expects God to act directly in the world He has created and to override when necessary the rules of a game He still controls. At a trivial level, the belief in the possibility of miracles expresses this idea; at a loftier one, the theory of transubstantiation, the doctrine of the actual presence of Christ in the consecrated Host, implies the same escape of God from the contraints of the rules of the natural order. How does He do it? It is a mystery, as one is taught in the catechism and in Catholic sermons.

The Protestant God does not have this power, or at least He does not use it. The bread and grape juice distributed during communion services are considered to be a symbol of the fact that the congregation is, or should be, a community; that is, a union of individuals coming together to help each other express salvation, wait for it, or nurture it. The bread and the juice are food for the body; this is why real wine cannot be served in churches that are still very close to their Puritan background. To serve wine would be a breach of the prohibition against alcohol. The food taken during a communion service is symbolic in the native sense insofar as too little is taken to actually feed one, but the difference between it and a full meal is quantitative rather than qualitative. Nobody sees these bread crumbs and grape juice as sacred.

The role of religion—what distinguishes religious acts from

nonreligious acts in the native mind—is thus very different from that of the trade associations, however much both domains may be organized in the same fashion from the point of view of social structure and however they may be used by particular people. While the Farm Bureau was a rational answer to a natural problem, religion is a moral answer to a cultural problem. Religion is not rational, because it is not given in the logic of the world—the existence of God cannot be proved. The problem is cultural because it has to do with the humanity of a person, with the transformation of an individual unit with its postulated rationality into a higher being who will transcend the natural self he or she was born into.

Religion remains *about* individuals rather than about their union. It is *churches* that are about the union of individuals in religion. Religion and churches are two different things, just as the belief in individualism that Mr. Howard demonstrated was a different thing from his involvement in the Farm Bureau. Individualism is natural; institutions like the Farm Bureau and society itself, as perceived by the sociology teacher and students, are the *result* of individual actions. As many of my informants implied, a newborn baby is already an individual, though not yet a member of society. Society is problematic. Churches are not fundamentally necessary to religious life. They may necessarily develop because of their pragmatic usefulness, but they remain artificial and open to question. And so does a trade union like the Farm Bureau.

But the fact that informants saw the Farm Bureau, the family, and indeed society itself as derivatives dependent on individual action does not mean that they did not live in a society in constant interaction with other individuals. The existence of churches may be fortuitous. They may not be necessary, theologically speaking, but when I was there, there were still more than a dozen of them in Appleton, and they were very much alive. Indeed, two new ones were created during my stay. Individualism, in the context of American culture, is not an overarching solution to a problem. It is, on the contrary, the setting up of a question, a dilemma that can often take tragic overtones. The question is: How do we go from individualism to community?

PART

From Individualism to Community

There were opinions at Woollett, but only three or four. The differences were there to match; if they were doubtless deep, though few, they were quiet—they were, as might be said, almost as shy as if people had been ashamed of them. People showed little diffidence about such things, on the other hand, in the Boulevard Malesherbes, and were so far from being ashamed of them—or indeed of anything else—that they often seemed to have invented them to avert those agreements that destroy the taste of talk.
—Henry James, The Ambassadors

Introduction

When talking about his life, Mr. Howard did not feel the need to refer to the help he may have received from his parents, siblings, or friends. Even after his wedding, "his" story did not become "our" story. In the same way, his wife's story was the story of an individual encountering the world and transforming herself in reaction to perceived changed in this world. Mr. and Mrs. Howard did not seek to transform the world so much as to use it most effectively for their own ends.

That they did not talk about their social environment in these contexts did not mean that they did not have friends or that they were not aware that they did. But this awareness came only in certain contexts, different from the one constituted by the telling of "his/her" story. The basic thesis of this book is that the distinction between these contexts constitutes one of the fundamental oppositions around which American culture is structured.

However, as I will try to demonstrate, this opposition, which can be perceived by sensitive natives as involving a moral dilemma, is a logical opposition in which each term implies the other. In other words, the internal organization of American individualism shapes, and is shaped by, the internal organization of the American notion of community. The opposition is dialectical and generative. Each term may appear to deny the other, but, in fact, implies it.

All this means that the structure is not linear. Mr. Howard is neither a rugged individualist nor a conformist in his chosen community. He is both at the same time, although his statements were framed in either one mode or the other. To understand these statements in their totality, it was necessary to know something of other statements that he made. This explains, I hope, a certain awkwardness in the presentation of my data, which must necessarily be linear. I had to present "individualism" and "community" separately, referring to each pole of the structure while talking about the other. I also had to make a choice as to which I would analyze first.

Structurally, neither individualism nor community is primary. They are contemporaneous, though distinct. However, this is so only for an outside analyst. My informants perceived that individualism generates community. For them, individualism is natural, community problematical. *Society has to be built.* This is a statement that must be understood both as a model *for* behavior ("Let's join together to make this a better world") and as a model *of* behavior ("This is the way the United States began"). Society was created by a joining of individuals for the greater good of each of them. And the institutions of society down to the Farm Bureau were created in the same manner for the same purpose.

It is because my informants put individualism first that I also decided to deal with it first. And it will help the reader, I hope, not to read the forthcoming discussion of *ideas* about social organization as if it were a study of the dynamics of social structure as a separate domain. In the next four chapters, I will continue to deal with the *cultural* subsystem of action, with the natives' perception of their society, what one might call "ethnosociology." In these chapters when I talk about a "group," a "community," or "they," this must always be understood as in reference to a whole that is *not* necessarily greater than the sum of its parts. This is so radically opposed to what I as a social scientist consider to be the true reality of the human condition and what I take to be the central message of the social sciences in general that it must be stressed at the onset, and the organization of the presentation itself must reinforce the point.

CHAPTER 4
Everybody and the Foundation of the Social Structure

Two or three weeks after my arrival in Appleton, I met in the shopping center the nineteen-year-old daughter of one of my first informants. I had seen her briefly at her parents' home, and I knew that she had a somewhat controversial boyfriend and went out in the evening very often. I took the occasion to tell her that I would be glad to go to a party with her and her boyfriend. She answered, "Great! We had just been talking, John and I, about inviting you. He would like to meet you. But we weren't sure you would like to go. We'll pick you up Saturday evening at eight."

John and His Friends

Around eight the following Saturday, John and Sue came to my place. I offered them a beer, and we talked for a little while. We left then, and all three of us piled into the front seat of John's Chevy. We stopped at his place briefly, a rundown one-bedroom apartment with half-destroyed furniture, dirty walls, psychedelic posters, and a black light, the type of place associated with radical students or archetypal hippies. It contrasted somewhat with the rather neat personal appearance of John and the even more conservative dress of Sue. We moved on again to pick up two friends who lived fifteen miles away in another town, had another beer, took off again back to Appleton, all of us still in John's car. There was "necking" in the back seat and beer drinking everywhere.

The party was held in a house in Appleton. There were about thirty people present—twenty in the darkened living room where a stereo was blaring in one corner while someone was trying to play the guitar in another, and ten seated around the dining-room table, apparently in earnest discussion. There was no dancing, and there would not be any; John told me that dancing was very rare. There was only drinking and joking, with more and more sexual emphasis as time went by. An attempt was made to have a sing-along, but apparently everybody was too drunk to go at it seriously and the songs never went beyond the first bars. This is the way the party went from ten o'clock to twelve.

Shortly before midnight, when things were getting louder, about half the people left without any apparent effect on the other half, who continued as before until someone proposed that the party move to a restaurant, a suggestion that was accepted matter-of-factly, without any visible decision-making ritual. So we all (now only eleven) climbed into cars and drove five miles to a restaurant on the interstate highway. We had hamburgers or sandwiches and coffee. Everybody was really "gone" (as it was termed) by then, the joking reaching extremes, even though we were in a public place. Things went on like this for about an hour, and then everybody went home.

John told me the next day that this had been a particularly "wild" party, but, with a little laugh: "They are all like that." Indeed, they were all like that—with variations, of course. There were not often so many people present (normally not more than a dozen); going to a restaurant at the end was frequent but not necessary; and jokes with a sexual emphasis were almost as rare as dancing, which did take place two or three times. People were more or less dressed up, the singing was sometimes better (most of the time about as bad, though the quality of the guitarist improved), beer was sometimes replaced by marijuana or hashish, and so on. The basic form—three to four hours of heavy drinking or smoking to reach a certain degree of intoxication—persisted, though, and of the fifty-two Saturday evenings of the year I spent in Appleton, at least forty-five were occupied in this fashion by this little group of people. And even more important from the point of view of social organization, the same core of twelve people was present at most of these parties, and their "friendship"—to use a native term—extended far beyond going to parties together, as I soon discovered.

At the end of the party I have just described, John said to me the usual thing to say after a first meeting: "Drop in anytime." I say "usual" because many people said the same thing to me many times, people of all ages, from all backgrounds. So I "dropped by" John's apartment the following day. I found him and three other men whom I recognized as having been present the night before at the party and at the restaurant watching a football game on TV. John was very sloppily dressed, unshaven, and he told me he had a headache and a hangover from the night before. He was sprawled on the dirty couch, and the other men were in similar postures on the floor or the chairs. One of them was rather well-dressed, but there was no feeling of stress. Nor did my entrance appear to make much difference. The polite formulas exchanged were kept to the bare minimum of "Hello, how are you?"

The talking rambled slowly along, about the plays in the game and what I was doing in Appleton, but even this was asked less from curiosity than from a desire to be polite. In fact, it took a long time for people in the group to realize what I was doing, and some never did. I just continued to be accepted matter-of-factly, more and more so as the year passed. This first afternoon went slowly by. Sue arrived, then another girl, a man left, another came, we continued to talk aimlessly, to watch TV—the set remained on all the time, even though it was watched only when there was a lag in the conversation, more as one would stare at the flames of a fireplace than from any interest in what was going on, especially after the football game ended. Around six it was decided—again "naturally," so to speak—to go to a restaurant and have a snack. We came back, and the evening was spent like the afternoon, until about ten-thirty when everybody started to go home.

There were many variations of detail in these Sunday afternoon or weekday minigatherings. What was striking was the regularity and frequency of the meetings between the members of the group—often four to five times a week, every day and several times a day if it was at all possible—for coffee in the morning, at the bar at night, at the bowling alley, or just at home. It was rare for the whole group to meet together more than once a week. During the week the meetings happened almost by chance and rarely involved more than two or three persons in the group. In these averages I have not included the meetings of the couples, husband/wife, boyfriend/girl friend, or those of the three persons who worked in the same office. I am talking only about activities not directly influenced by professional duties. As for the case of the man/woman couples, that is more complex and will be dealt with separately. Let us say simply that counting the meetings between those units, as I probably should, would simply raise the average rate of meetings in the group as a whole and thus reinforce my point.

Beyond "having fun together," this group of friends had

another function more typical of social groups. It was also, though in a much more implicit way, a closed cycle of exchanges of certain services: if a friend asked you to do something for him, it wasn't possible to refuse. Of course there were limits to what one would ask, and the service requested could not surpass the capacities of the person involved. Nor could one demand a long-term engagement on a specific project; only the association itself was such a "project," which, I could say, was made up of short-range actions. The most current services exchanged were moving furniture, carpeting a room, lending a car or giving a ride, providing a room for the night, or cutting hair. The list cannot be exhaustive because the point was precisely to leave it open. To my inquiries about what could be asked, I was answered: "Anything."

The most important of the services exchanged—psychological help in periods of depression—does not appear on the list because it is of a different nature and was not consciously recognized as a service by the people in the group. They treated it differently. While the first set of services consisted of a definite series of acts bounded in time and place and thus could be considered eminently suitable for exchanges, psychological help rarely entailed anything beyond listening patiently and regularly, for it was rare for a period of depression to be clearly bounded. What is more, the depression rarely ended through an action of the listener, who remained, at most, a sympathetic spectator to a drama taking place outside his sphere of influence. I personally was considered to be good in the role of listener and was often used as such by members of this group and by members of other groups, but the service was often exchanged between participants. (I will give a long example of this process at the beginning of Part III.)

The two main social qualities of these services were universality and equality. There were no explicit rules as to what should *not* be asked of one's friends. There were some implicit ones, which were part of the similarly implicit covenant on which the association of these twelve people rested. But the exceptions—and they were few—were left unsaid, while universality was affirmed. The real limits were those set by the necessity of equality: a service given necessarily implied a service given back of the same value or quality. To return more than one had received might be considered an attempt at shaming the receiver and would eventually lead to the expulsion of the deviating member from the group. To start off with a gift that one knew to be impossible to match would have the same result. Conversely, a systematic inability to manage the average level of gifts exchanged inside the group would also lead to expulsion. For example, this particular group spent from two to five dollars per person per party or night on alcohol or entertainment. One could not have been a full-fledged member of the group if one had not been able to follow this level of spending or if one had wanted to spend much more.

But just as the basic services exchanged were nonmonetary, the expression of the necessary equality should not be interpreted only in economic terms, however important these might also be. A certain equality of behavior or conformity to the specific rules accepted by this group was necessary and expected. In terms of dress and external appearance, it was understood that one could not wear dirty clothes to a Saturday night party. There was no need for anything beyond clean jeans (for boys and girls alike), although more elaborate pants and shirts were permitted and often worn. At the other extreme, I never saw anybody wear a suit and tie to a party, and the one or two times I arrived dressed this way I was asked jokingly, but with insistence, to take my jacket and tie off so that I would be "more comfortable." Politically, one could briefly defend liberal positions but only as long as a nationalistic, conservative position remained as the accepted framework. National origin or religion was not considered relevant, but one should not stress a strong sense of identification with either as long as one was behaving as a member of the group: the group had to be the primary referent of social loyalty. The same thing could be said about jobs: jobs were not relevant, but one should not stress his belonging to a certain socioeconomic category.

I could go on for a while listing traits by which the group could be recognized and differentiated from other groups. It would not serve any real purpose, because this group might have been the only one in Appleton to have these particular characteristics. If there was another one, the people in the group did not know about it. As far as they knew (and as far as I know), they were unique. They did know several other groups to which they felt close and from which they wished to differentiate themselves strongly. On one side there were the "greasers," with a slightly more conservative outlook, at least from the point of view of the reference group. (I could not really have told the difference.) On the other side there were the "freaks"—long-haired, aggressively dirty, more radical in their ideological outlook, more deeply immersed in the drug culture, and so on. John's friends felt themselves to be "in the middle," at a sort of rational place between two extremes.

The Social Organization of an Elementary Group

The stable core of the group during the period that extended from November 1970 to August 1971 was made up of:

John Lawrence—blue-collar worker; first unemployed, then a salesman; "Italian"; raised Catholic; twenty-seven.

Sue Elliott—secretary; "WASP"; raised a Methodist; nineteen; girl friend, then wife, of John Lawrence.

Robert Penn—in management; no definite ethnicity; raised a Catholic; twenty-three.

Mary Segala—no profession; "Italian"; raised a Catholic; twenty-three; wife of Robert Penn; sister of Alexander and Harvey.

Ralph Steffof—in management; "Slavic"; raised a Catholic; twenty-three.

Sylvia Suboski—no profession; "Polish"; raised a Catholic; twenty.

Alexander Segala—engineer; "Italian"; raised a Catholic; twenty-five; brother of Mary and Harvey.

Ruth Johnson—schoolteacher; "WASP"; no religion; twenty-one; Alexander's girl friend.

Harvey Segala—engineer; "Italian"; raised a Catholic; twenty-seven; divorced; brother of Mary and Alexander.

John O'Connell—barber; "Irish"; raised a Catholic; twenty-seven.

It is important to note that religion and ethnic identity are indicative of a background rather than of any activity on the part of these persons. The quotation marks express the fact that when the subject was raised, the different persons would claim membership in one or another ethnic category. "WASP" was not a fully developed category. Sue would first say that she was "nothing"; if pushed, she might say "a mixture," and she would understand "WASP."

One of the stratification subsystems with which I will not deal at length is that based on sex. Except for one case, the women were accepted into the group through their husbands and boyfriends. But this is only one of the idiosyncrasies of this group and does not reveal any cultural necessity. Indeed, I have experienced groups in America, though not in Appleton, in which a woman was the focusing person, even though there were many men in it.

A rapid glance at the list reveals that most of the group have a Catholic and "ethnic" background, and almost half are Italians. Furthermore, the three Segalas are brothers and sister. Finally, the management and white-collar jobs of most of the members imply a somewhat high income. Indeed, in terms of consumer goods, the group could be considered very well endowed: ten cars (one per person), three motorcycles, one boat, five television sets, four full stereophonic ensembles, well-equipped and -furnished homes (except for three of them), and so on. Finally, the three older members of the group had gone through school together, and their friendship could be considered a carryover from that time.

These data might lead one to expect a social structure based solely on economic criteria compounded by ethnic and religious factors. From what I said earlier and from the data I am now going to present, it will become clear that this is not what happens empirically. An analysis that would insist on the sole relevance of these factors would be inaccurate from a cultural point of view.

Let us first consider some of the facts that go against a simple sociological interpretation. There were two men in the group whose level of income remained very low through nine of the eleven months of the study, and who lived in substandard apartments. But they were not outcasts. In fact, John Lawrence was the center or the heart of the group, the link between certain people who did not have such close relationships with each other as he had with everybody. For example, he was much closer to Robert Penn than Penn was to Harvey Segala, who slightly disapproved of him as a suitor for his sister.

Furthermore, if the process of inclusion in the group ignores to a large extent the sociological background of the person invited, the process of exclusion reveals the same attitude. These ten people formed a very tight group, but they were not totally closed. From time to time other people were invited to parties or just "dropped in." These people formed a sort of amorphous fringe of the reference group; they gave their loyalty to other small groups of the same general character as the one I am describing, but they participated in some of its activities. Thirty to forty people formed this fringe, some closer to, some farther away from, the core, the distance being calculated in terms of frequency and type of interaction. Some of them would have been totally acceptable to the group if they had decided to participate regularly. Others would not have been.

Further removed were the "freaks" and the "greasers," people who could clearly be identified as being a "different" group (from the point of view of our group—they may or may not have had any social reality), some members of which belonged to the outer fringe, some of which did not. I knew some of them, and many corresponded very closely in general background or even present behavior to the characteristics of our group—there were young white-collar, upper-middle-class types who were indistinguishable from Ralph Steffof or the Segala brothers. There was, for example, John Lawrence's brother, who was completely immersed in the "freaks" group. Ralph Steffof's brother, on the other hand, led a normal style of life completely outside any of these groups, was never heard of, and yet was Ralph's business partner! Among the women, the same types of behavior could be observed. Sue Elliott's sister had had nothing to do with John when they were in high school together (and vice versa!), and she still "could not understand what her sister found in John." Ruth Johnson's sister was married to a totally middle-class husband, had three children, and they related only during rare family reunions.

In just the same manner as the Farm Bureau and its Creed emphasized "*these* friends and neighbors", John Lawrence and his friends did not get drunk together because they were Italian or ethnic or Catholic or middle class, not even because they belonged to a certain age group or had gone to school together or shared a certain ideology, but because they "liked" each other. John told me of the beginning of his friendship with Robert Penn: "At that time Harvey was married. They invited me over one night. You know Roger, don't you? Yes. He was married, too, then, but to another woman. Cathy is his second wife. His first wife knew Robert, and he came with them that evening at Harvey's. Well, we just hit it off right away, Robert and me. I don't know why, we just liked each other, and we have continued ever since." Conversely, I was often told about people whom I knew to be unacceptable: "I don't know why I don't like him. He is really a strange guy. Don't you think so?"

From the point of view of a sociologist, these answers are often exasperating, and one can easily fall prey to a temptation to find "reasons" where the natives do not see any, and call these reasons "unconscious." But such unconscious reasons cannot really account for the process of formation of these small groups. The natives are expressing an ideological truth when they say that they "don't know," that they just "like" or "don't like" a certain person. What they are implying is that they like somebody—that is, enjoy being with him—if this person is in some ways *like* them, if they can communicate with him from a point of view of equality, if they can exchange equally. Being based on communication and exchange, the groups are eminently social phenomena, yet their basis for existence is personal if not psychological—in other words, individualistic, which takes us back full circle to our starting point.

John's Friends: A Historical and Processual Analysis

The two members of the group who had known each other for the longest time were John Lawrence and Harvey Segala. They were childhood friends, went through high school together, and graduated in 1961. Shortly after that, John and some of his friends organized a rock band in which Ralph Steffof played. The band remained together for a few years performing at local schools and bars. They even recorded a song that succeeded honorably on Midwest hit parade charts but didn't make it all the way to the top. Eventually they disbanded. In the meantime, Harvey had married, and he ceased for a while to participate directly in John's social life. It was at the end of this period that John met Robert Penn. Then Robert and Ralph were drafted. John married, got a good job, and moved to another town. Two years later he got a divorce, came back to Appleton, remained unemployed, or underemployed, for two more years until he met Sue. He married her and returned to the outwardly more middle-class life that he had abandoned after his divorce. (See chapter 8 for a fuller account of his "journey.") During this period he remained in contact with the people who were to form the group, and met regularly with some of them, but it was only when Ralph and Robert returned from the service, sometime in 1969, that the present group came into existence as a social unit. They aggregated into it their girl friends or wives, rejected some people, saw with regret others leave.

Thus when I arrived and began the process of my own integration into the group, it was relatively new as a social unit, and at the end of my stay there were signs of disintegration as the two unattached males moved to another town, something that made frequent interaction difficult. (During the following three years, John O'Connell married and then was divorced, and Robert Penn and Mary Segala were divorced.) And yet while it lasted, the strength of the bond, the unity of the group and of its self-definition were very strong. During their frequent meetings any mention of other loyalties, even to one's family, had to be made with apologies, disparaging remarks, and comments to the effect that one's real duties were to the group. Nowhere was this feeling of unity more strongly felt than in the process of integration and segregation, which will be illustrated by the following examples.

In the fall of 1970, when I arrived in Appleton, Elaine Schneider was a member in good standing of the group. She was getting a divorce from her first husband, was going out with Arthur, an "associate member" of the group, and was respected enough to become a core member of it. The relationship "did not work" between Arthur and Elaine, and around Christmas she was officially recognized as "unattached," which meant that she had to be "fixed up" with somebody. Harvey thought Elaine should go out with Robert because "they are both very business-minded." John encouraged me to ask her out on dates: "You know, she is really intelligent, just like you." For a brief time later on, it appeared that Harvey himself was falling for her. About this latter development, Sue said: "I hope it works out, it would be very good for both of them." All of these efforts were totally endogamous, and the success of any of them would have created no problem for the group. But they all failed, maybe precisely *because* they were too strictly endogamous. It is also interesting to note that all the rationalizations about why it would be good for Elaine and one of the men to go together were based on psychological grounds. There were differences as to what would make the match possible; still, what was looked for was an assumed shared psychological trait (a business head, intelligence).

Then, suddenly, the word spread that Elaine had fallen in love with a man from La Crosse whom she had met at work and whom nobody knew and about whom she said marvelous things. "I am sure you will like him," she told Sue. "He is just like John." But Sue's opinion after she had seen him was: "My God, where did she find him? He's a complete nothing. How can she think that John is anything like him?" John's impressions were: "They came to see us, and they spent two hours telling us how beautifully they got along together! Truly!!" Harvey said: "Did you see the guy Elaine has found? Who is he? He looks completely stupid to me. She is going to *marry* him?!!" And so on.

Suddenly Elaine disappeared from the parties, she was not invited anymore, her invitations were not accepted, and John said one day: "I used to think she was pretty intelligent. But I don't know anymore, maybe she just fooled us." That was it. It is very possible that the dislike was mutual and that Elaine's friend did not want to join the parties. Unhappily, I have very scant evidence on this point. Yet the rejection is evident. This was the clearest example of rejection I came across. Other examples include parties to which members of the group had been invited that were rejected out of hand. John said about one such invitation: "I am not going to go there." Why? "They are just a bunch of teenyboppers, and the talk will be completely stupid." From my point of view, I would say that after the third beer or the second joint, the discussion in any group did not make much sense, but this, of course, was not John's point!

Cases of integration involve the same processes. One of them involved me personally, but since at the time, I feel, I was very well integrated into the group, they have ethnographic relevance. Through a friend of mine, totally outside not only the group but also their general life-style, I met a student at the state university, Cathy Ford, twenty, Dutch Reformed, a senior majoring in Spanish. She came from a nearby town where her father was a well-to-do insurance agent.

Upon hearing all this, John and Sue picked up on the fact that she was a college student and they were clearly afraid of her being "highbrow," since she would be better educated than anybody else in the group. (It is interesting to note here that Cathy's ethnic background and her religion were *not* considered relevant by members of this group, while education was. Once again, this does not mean that ethnicity is not relevant for small-town conservative liberals in their twenties but that one should not systematically explain stratification in America through ethnicity or any automatic criteria such as class, job, or educational level.) What they expressed was hospitality: "Why don't you bring her over one night? I am sure it will be all right." The implication was: "You are a member in good standing of the group. If you like her, then we'll like her." This is the same discussion that had preceded my own presentation to the group, as I was told once, and also the same as that which had taken place the first time Elaine had spoken of her new friend.

I felt Cathy would not stress her education too much, and, partly as an experiment, partly for personal reasons, I took her once to John and Sue's. We watched TV, drank a couple of beers, John and Sue satisfied themselves that there would not be any problem on the drug question, and the following day I was greeted by highly positive statements: "Wow, she is really a nice girl [with both physical and spiritual implications], you'll have to bring her to a party." I did, and she fitted right into the group without any problem. I started receiving invitations to other parties specifically including her. ("Why don't you bring Cathy Saturday?") After the second or third party, it became accepted that she was my girl friend, and, in fact, this gave me a higher standing in the group.

It must be stressed that all these decisions as to group acceptance or rejection of a new member were made by the whole group. There was no formal decision-making process—a grunt or a slight movement of the body was enough for everybody to know the opinion of a particular person on any subject—and it was only after assurances had been given that a position was widely shared that verbal, public statements could be made in a definite fashion. This does not mean that unanimity was constant. For example, there were Harvey's objections to Robert; but I never heard him comment on Robert, except privately to one or two persons at a time and as if in passing. The group was close enough, its unity so naturally accepted, that opinions could be transmitted through nonverbal communication—moods were more important than words. As I will say later, it is only in groups that do not possess such a strong sense of unity that formal methods of decision making have to be used. Another consequence of this closeness of the members to each other was the fact that they disagreed very rarely on important decisions. Of course this was also a cause for the establishment of this closeness in the first place. But just as in the life of a husband/wife couple, the process of adaptation goes both ways.

Other Groups

I may have given a stronger impression of this group's independence from other such groups than is warranted. I did mention the existence of a fringe group and also of two others, the "freaks" and the "greasers," who were felt to be somewhat in competition with John's group. But competition does not only mean differentiation, it also means communication.

One evening late in my stay in Appleton, I met for the first time a young man in a situation totally foreign to John and his friends' group: a townwide activity catering mainly to established middle-aged Presbyterians and Episcopalians. In outward appearance I would have classified Jim as a "normal college type"; that is, with well-to-do parents and liberal tendencies. I recognized that he was more radical than his appearance suggested when he answered my question about what he was doing by saying: "I do nothing, I am just a bum. . . . Well, in fact, I have been working in a garage for the last few weeks." As I realized later, Jim was very much out of place in the conservative association in which I had met him, particularly since he was not related to anybody in it. He had been invited by a former high school teacher. It was the first time he had gone to a meeting of this association, and he never reappeared.

Later that night I drove him home and he invited me to come in. He first showed me his bike, a huge machine in perfect shape, and then we entered the house. About half a dozen men and women, apparently in their early twenties, were sitting around. Everybody was drinking wine, but the atmosphere was subdued. The TV set was on, but nobody was really watching it. The whole thing felt more like an evening in one's home in a family situation than a party. I was interrogated in the usual way about my background and apparently passed the exam. It is never difficult to do so if you show that you generally agree with the two or three main idiosyncrasies of the group. So I did not show any disapproval when they told me such things as: "There really is nothing in this town," "If we had a campus, we would burn it down," "We do not have police here, we have *PIGS*. I mean it." I accepted some wine and did not show any surprise when talk of drugs arose. I was "all right."

During the hours I spent there, people moved in and out of the house without formality, and I got an inkling of the social organization of this group. Apparently Jim was supported by his grandmother, who owned the house and let him use it. The house appeared to be a sort of meeting place for his friends, a place where one could eat, drink, and probably sleep in an almost communal fashion, with most resources held in common. I heard talk of food being used by the first person who needed it, even though it had been bought by somebody else, of a pair of blue jeans that had "disappeared"—all in good humor and without apparent resentment. The whole thing reminded me of descriptions of the true hippie life. In this respect this group was clearly much further "out" than John and his friends, whose reactions were much more traditional, particularly as far as private property was concerned. Their evident goodwill and hospitality had a different quality to it from that of Jim's group, even though they obviously used the same structural parameters. When I left, I was once more given the usual—and, I am sure, sincere—advice to "Drop in anytime. My door is always open, and there is always somebody here."

Although I thought I had never met Jim before, one of his friends reminded me that we had met several months before when John, Harvey, and Roger had played hockey with him, his brother, and two or three other men, whose social position I didn't know. I know for sure that none of these men was a member of John's group, not even of its fringe. Yet they knew enough about each other to organize a few afternoons of hockey.

I observed a second example of communication. The day after my first meeting with Jim, I went to have my hair cut by John O'Connell, and he greeted me with: "I know what you did last night!" He had had coffee with Jim that very morning. Now, as I said earlier, Jim was not a member of John's group (in 1970–71), while John O'Connell belonged to its very core. Of course, the relationship might have been diachronic; that is, a survival of the time when the two Johns were much farther "out" than they were then. It could also have been partly for kinship reasons—I was told afterward that John O'Connell's brother "ran" with Jim's crowd. And of course they all behaved according to variations on the same ideological theme: the "hip" theme.

This is evidence that there was some communication between the groups. And yet they maintained their separate identities. Later the same day, I conducted a kind of experiment. I hypothesized that if John O'Connell knew Jim, John Lawrence would know him, too, and probably Sue, also. I met her for lunch and was told: "I think he thinks a lot of himself, but he is not very bright. He runs with a much younger crowd than we do." John talked about "teenyboppers".

Segregation, in fact, implies a certain form of communication—segregation is not ignorance, properly speaking. It involves the perception—a form of knowledge—that an alternative exists, and its rejection. Racial segregation is not an exception. Civil rights leaders are correct in stressing the importance of "ignorance of the fact that differences in the behavior or appearance of human beings do not mean differences in their moral worth." But this ignorance is a form of knowledge of the behavior of the other that derives from a certain amount of (mis)communication. Prejudiced whites "know" what blacks are and what they do, and it is because they know that they reject behaving in a similar manner, even though they may in fact end up doing very similar things. The belief that one is different and the presence of a few symbolic differences are often enough to express the distinctiveness of a group. If segregation demands communcation, then people from different groups must meet in one way or another.

The young adults who belong to the various smaller groups I have been describing do meet each other, but outside the party or evening-at-home situations that are restricted to members of the group. They meet most often for breakfast or coffee in the morning or in the afternoon. I had noticed several times that John, Ralph, and Harvey, when they happened to be in town, more or less regularly had coffee at one of the two coffeehouses downtown. I had also noticed that when I joined them I was often introduced to people of the same general appearance as themselves but whom I would never see on any of the occasions when the whole of John's group met. I thought it odd until the incident I just reported made clear to me the meaning of these all-important coffee breaks in the life of Appleton (not only for the hippie fringe but also for the businessmen) and their structural role. Coffee breaks are the time when news of each other's doings is exchanged, when the groups communicate, when one decides whether to maintain the segregation that one enforces against a certain person. From time to time, one may try to invite somebody again to see whether he can be made to join one's own group. This may lead to "mistakes"; I heard of some. And of course groups shift, often quite quickly. Thus it can be understood why somebody who never goes to have coffee "doesn't know what's happening in town," a comment I heard many times, even though, as I observed, it was rare that highly interesting political news would be passed. More often the news concerned the weather or a football game. The real news that made the coffee breaks interesting was of a different nature.

On the other hand, there were also definite limits to the amount of communication taking place among the groups in town. For if the grapevine functioned well between hippie or almost-hippie groups in Appleton, it did not work in quite the same way between these groups and the many groups formed by people who attended the regular Protestant churches, or between these and the fundamentalist churches, between the Protestants and the Catholics, between the townspeople and the farmers, between the merchants and the workers in the factories, and so on.

These groups generally knew about each other's existence, and to this limited extent there was "communication," but they had only the faintest idea of the life-style of the people in them. Whatever idea they had, they gained indirectly, often from the mass media. They had even less idea of the details of each other's histories. During my stay, there was no issue of great enough import to involve all the groups in the town—not even the firing of the school superintendent and what the people involved considered a hot race for school-board seats. I myself was certainly not such an issue. Most people had no idea at all about what I spent my time doing when I was not with them.

This allows for an interesting phenomenon that I will call "double allegiance." Double allegiance among adults was relatively rare. It was very frequent in parent/child relationships when grown-up children had decided to shift their primary allegiance from their parents' larger groups and from their families to a group of their own. But for a while they continued to participate as full members, if not of the parents' full group, at least of the family.

During that period young adults often had two different sets of behavior according to whether their parents were present or absent, but they very rarely informed them of the details of their behavior when they were with their friends or of the ideas that were current and accepted in their group. Conversely, parents were a subject that was rarely discussed in the public meetings of a group, for reasons very similar to those that emerged in the opposite situation: to speak of one's allegiance to a group ideologically very different from the one in which one happens to be at the time is unpleasant and disquieting. It implies that one is not so totally a member of the group as one is supposed to be. A feeling of guilt is also often raised because one has to confess to doing things and making statements that go against the accepted mores of the group that one believes he should be accepting without restriction while he knows that, in fact, he doesn't. These matters may be raised privately but always in a context of anguish and guilt and often hostility for being forced into a position of guilt. Shifting allegiance may be possible and frequent, but it is rarely easy emotionally. It may not be going too far to say that the creation of this feeling of guilt, which may take the form of hostility or dread vis-à-vis other groups, reinforces the segregative tendencies of American groups.

Farmers and Townspeople

A sharp split between wider groups is not a privilege solely of the parent/child relationship. The necessary split between them—the generation gap as it is called in Appleton—possesses many characteristics of a *rite de passage,* with the identifying of the child with one social group, the family, at the beginning, a rite or a series of ritual situations emphasizing illegality (booze parties, pot, "parking") and thus separation, and an ultimate integration of the now "adult" child into a different social situation that often involves different social groups, though not necessarily.[1] It remains that being an active member of a strong group is not simply an aspect of the ritual passage into society, it is also the place to which the passage leads. I will not spend time exploring all the adult smaller or wider groups into which the people of Appleton were organized, because the literature is copious enough already.[2] What I want to do is give an example of what happens when representatives of two different groups are forced to meet face-to-face because of events outside their control.

The occasion was an encounter between representatives of the merchant/professional men of Appleton—the "town," as they liked to call themselves—and the representatives of some of the farmers who depended on the town for services—the "rural community," as it was sometimes called. The democratic representativeness of these people could be discussed, but it will suffice to say here that the people involved felt themselves to be somewhat representative and they behaved as one is supposed to behave when one *is* representative.

In a more specific way, it was a meeting between the Appleton School Board and the last members of the Johnson Community

School Board. Johnson Community is the name by which the northwest corner of Appleton township used to be known (Johnson was the name of one of the oldest settlers of the area). This area used to sponsor (until the middle 1960s) a one-room elementary school. It formed a politically autonomous school district that had been integrated into the larger Appleton School District shortly before. The changing demographic character of the neighborhood, economic conditions, and the belief that it would be possible to give the children a better education in a larger school system— all these factors led to the consolidation of this district into the Appleton School District. The old building stood unused, and one night it burned. The question was: Who was to pay for the removal of the ruins? Legally the matter was not clear: the building had been donated to Appleton, but apparently only verbally and matter-of-factly, with several riders. The records could be read to say that the building was the responsibility of either Appleton or the Johnson Community.

The last president of the Johnson Community School Board felt somewhat responsible for what would happen. He rounded up two or three of the members of the old board, and they decided to talk about the situation with the Appleton School Board. I happened to be present at the study session when the matter was discussed. The situation was defined by the members of the Appleton School Board as a "study session," implying serious discussion, sharp questioning, and an absence of formality, particularly in dress and outward bearing. Open-necked, short-sleeved shirts, corduroy pants, and almost horizontal relaxation in an armchair was the accepted appearance for the university professor, lawyer, high-level public servant, two well-to-do merchants, the minister, and captain of the local state police post representing the Appleton School Board. However, the two representatives of the Johnson Community, both farmers, entered the room nervous, in their best Sunday clothes, and they remained uneasy and on the defensive all through the meeting.

The opposition between farmers and townspeople was strongly visible, and there was no doubt about social ranking. The townspeople felt themselves superior to the farmers, and the latter felt inferior. Eventually the farmers won their point, but not specifically on the strength of their case, as the exchange of comments that followed their departure reveals:

"Who are those people?"

"They are among the richest farmers in the area."

"We don't really *have* to do anything about it, do we, legally?"

"We don't, but they have some political power. If we don't placate them, we might lose some votes on the next bond issue."

The question of political power, real or imaginary, does not interest me so much here as what the confrontation reveals in terms of the social structure. Note the symbolic differences in dress and behavior. They are all the more striking since the farmers knew beforehand they were going to present their case in a study session, and also since at their own business meetings—at the Farm Bureau, for example—they would behave in much the same relaxed and casual way the school board usually adopts. I should then emphasize the ignorance displayed by most school-board members as to the identities of these farmers, an ignorance partially understandable since many of the former were relatively new to Appleton, but not totally so, since one of the farmers was president of the county-level organization of the Farm Bureau and his name, picture, and activities had been publicized several times in the local paper. But townspeople did not generally read news relating to farmers, and most farmers did not know who the president of the town council was.

The situation was finally saved for the two farmers because of a case of double allegiance: both of them belonged to the church whose minister was a member of the school board and thus belonged also to the "town." As minister of his congregation, he was a member of a subgroup that included both townspeople (not all of whom were the "town"!) and farmers. *He* had experienced in his congregation the power of these farmers. However, during the meeting he remained neutral and silent, even when the tone of his follow board members was particularly sharp in their attacks against "Johnson Community pretensions." He just explained who the farmers were and what positions they held in the informal social structure of the township. In other words, he personalized the situation and thus laid the ground-work for a subjective resolution of the conflict.

All the people involved in this affair considered themselves to represent rather large groups of people. It will come as no surprise that the true representativeness of the two sets of people who participated in the discussion was very limited. The school board presented itself as representing the whole of the school district, which it did, of course, by law. As a social unit, the Johnson Community had died many years before. It never had any administrative reality apart from its school district, and this had also dissolved.

No elections to its school board had been held in years, and legally speaking, the farmers involved had no right to speak in the name of anybody but themselves, a matter that would have been raised if the affair had taken on some importance. Conversely, the Appleton School Board, though the legal representative of the school district, was given its mandate by a very small number of voters, and, strictly speaking, it could be said to represent only the relatively small group of people in Appleton actively interested in the administration of the town in general or, specifically, its school system—a few hundred at most of the several thousand people inhabiting the geographical area of the district. Furthermore, all members of the school board resided in the town, none came from the outlying areas.

The participants were rather well aware of the complexity of the situation and operated easily on the several levels of the social structure that were involved. At the most formal level there were two school districts considered to be of equal administrative standing who had got caught in a routine conflict to be resolved in a court of law that would balance the legal merits of the case and make an objective decision blind to the personalities involved. At a less formal, though still rather abstract level, there were the two communities represented by the respective boards. They were the realities behind the boards, what the boards "represented." Then there was the opposition of townspeople versus farmers. And finally there was the most immediate structure, that of two informal cliques, powerful men in the town and powerful men among the farmers settling their disputes directly in a face-to-face encounter where the subjective factors of power, ideology, and life-style were the primary motors.

Each of the informal cliques existed directly as a small group structured according to the same principles that structured John's group: conformity to a certain life-style (public service) and shared interests (political power, a better education, the "welfare and prosperity of agriculture," and so on) dependent on an individual choice (many farmers and townspeople who could have claimed to powerful status just weren't interested). Furthermore, both the farmers and townspeople involved in the incident were powerful in what was in other situations *one* community. They were all generally small-town conservative Republicans in their disputes with the large urban centers of the state. At this very abstract level they were one, and they would easily recognize it.

They *would* recognize this unity as they would recognize that they were part of the state (and root for the state university's football team), the nation (and feel personally honored by the feat of landing men on the moon), the human race (and point out that the landing on the moon was "really" a step for "mankind"), the middle class, the Italians, and so on. But they would recognize this unity most comfortably *away* from face-to-face interaction with people whom they might also accept abstractly as "one of us." This is true not only of references to mankind. It is also true at the most local level.

The townspeople rarely interacted with farmers, except in shops. Even in town churches where the congregation was mixed, there was segregation. In the same way that the members of John's group were more offended if I implied that they were somehow like the "greasers" than if I implied that there was not so much difference between them and their parents, the townspeople, particularly the newcomers who had moved into the town for its "country" atmosphere, would have nothing to do with what actually may have made it "country." They had their church or church organizations, and the farmers had theirs.

Similarly, there were many subgroups within the townspeople. They belonged to many different churches, and within each church there were various cliques vying for the possibility of defining the character of these churches. This is why it would be a mistake to give too much importance to incidents such as the one I just reported. For the dispute over the burned school was not a small episode in a larger fight between the town and the farmers. For such a fight to take place, there must be definite protagonists. But beyond the few people actually involved in the particular dispute—two small cliques at most—there was nothing, and certainly not a mass united by its antagonism toward the other.

References to the farmers might be made by people who believed that there is such a mass. And yet if one examines closely the context in which these references were made, it appears that they were always abstract and irrelevant to everyday life. For in every day life what my informants lived was the constant shifting of communities, the essential quality of which is fluidity. For example, only some of the old Johnson Community School Board got involved in the case. The others pleaded that they had no right or responsibility to get involved since there had been no elections, and they remained on the sidelines.

Everybody

This fluidity is tragic for many, and a lot of time is spent trying to make believe that it is not there as an integral part of the daily experience. Not everybody is involved in this dizzying movement, but every community, however small, closed, conservative, has experienced the loss of longtime members due not only to death or the geographical nomadism of middle-class Americans but also to ideological and life-style shifts that strike at the heart of the original community. This fluidity is a direct concomitant of the responsibility that is laid upon the individual to create society and then to maintain it by his constant activity. For a European, this constant worry is probably the most exotic aspect of American life, since a European would probably see society as an essentially indestructible, blind, and overpowering force from which individuals must withdraw even if this means building walls around one's house and not talking to one's neighbors. Even American society, to an outsider like me, is so obviously an infinitely strong, solid environment and so redundantly structured that I believe only the strongest input could really rip it apart. This did not seem obvious to most of my informants, who did not see their society or community that way. For them, it was forever "falling apart" and in constant need of conscious, revivalistic efforts to "bring it back together." One way to do this rhetorically was through the concept of "everybody."

When I was invited to a party of John's group, I was often told that "everybody" had been invited. This could mean all the members of the core group or all the members of the larger group. The word was used by many people on many different occasions to refer to the same sort of very small unit. Its use was particularly striking in the context of discussions of ideological questions. It seemed very difficult for most people to accept the idea that they might be unique or even in a minority on a particular subject. Any position had to be legitimized by reference to the fact that "everybody" held it to be valid, not only the actual group in which the position was uttered but any intelligent, sincere person. Some of my informants could literally be brought to tears if someone they considered close to them appeared to seriously disagree with them. And in cases where it was well known that only a minority accepted the idea or the form of behavior—drug taking, for example—the argument easily became that "everybody" would accept it "if they knew what it is really about."

"Everybody," then, is both an integrative and a segregative concept. When members of John's group referred to themselves as "everybody," they were expressing their unity (integration) as against those who were not members of the group (segregation). The latter function is inextricably tied with the first. Small-group integration demands segregative processes against those who just could not be invited. But there was little expressed recognition of this, and, to a large extent, references to the small group as "everybody" is a way to avoid the facts of segregation, both the segregation that is generated by the group against other groups and the segregation that is generated by other groups against the group. This is particularly striking in the rhetoric of elected governing boards.

All members of local "community" boards were elected to their position by a very small percentage of the eligible voters. The more local the board was, the less interest there seemed to be in participating in it, through voting, at least. Some people did participate. They were often informally organized into two small cliques, one composed of most of the members elected to the board and the other of the people who opposed them. The latter clique remained latent most of the time and became activated only when the board took a controversial position. Membership in the opposition clique was transient and constantly shifting, and the people who participated had, of course, not been elected to their positions. They were self-proclaimed. Both cliques pretended in certain contexts to represent "everybody," "the people," the "district," the "community." Of course, the people who had been legally elected to the boards possessed the legitimate claim. They had submitted to a rite, they had been anointed, and they were by definition representative of their constituencies.

The claim of the elected members may be legitimate, literally speaking. It is no more justified than the claim of the opposition or the claim of John's group that they were, or represented, everybody. That elected officials are rarely truly representative of those they are supposed to represent is an interesting thing in itself, and it has been noted by many critics, political scientists, sociologists, or politicians in the opposition. It is, in fact, part of the general popular wisdom. But this does not deter these same people from continuing to press the claim—defensively as justification for the value of their intervation, and offensively as an attack against the value of the intervention of the other cliques. The legitimacy of elected officials is grounded in the fact that everybody can vote (universal suffrage). The (popular) legitimacy of community groups who revolt against decisions made by elected boards lies in the argument that the election was rigged both at the nominating and at the voting stages, so that only a few, and not everybody, or even a majority (which is an equivalent of everybody, since in democratic theory majority decisions hold for all), participated.

In fact, neither the board nor the rebels are everybody. "Everybody" is probably a notion that cannot be actualized in such a diverse and complex society as the United States, or even Appleton. The persistence and pervasiveness of its use must thus derive from something other than its experiential reality. Etymologically (every body) and in its polemical use, it is a statistical notion. The evaluation of "everybody" is numerical and is supposed to be literal within the predefined population. The question: Has everybody been invited? must be answered by an assurance that each, every, and all members *have* been contacted and invited. The absence of even one person raises the questions: Is he sick? Are they snubbing me? And yet it would seem that the notion is used precisely to escape the pressure of numbers since the population that is everybody is constantly being redefined so as to preserve the appearance of universality.

In everyday usage, "everybody" refers to all the people who actually participate in a community's life. The fact that the group to which this refers is either extremely small or totally abstract does not make the need to use the word less pressing. What makes it necessary is the risk of disintegration of the community, a risk that is perfectly real at the microlevel of small groups of friends, as I emphasized earlier. At the level of local governing boards, the risk that other competing groups will challenge the legitimacy of their claim to representativeness is also ever-present. There is always a dissatisfied clique ready to mount a campaign if the members of the board have not been able to manipulate the symbol of universality successfully. This is a very difficult thing to do, particularly when there is wide interest in the tasks of the board. The members are always individuals isolated in the middle of small cliques, cut off from most of the people whose confidence they need, so that their claim to universal appeal is very weak. Most of the board members I talked to knew this.

At broader levels, like that of the town or the school district, the risk of disintegration takes a different character, though it remains a distinct possibility in the minds of most people. The town as a physical entity is very resilient. Towns do die if their population dwindles to nothing, the post office is closed, and maps cease to carry their names. They also die as discrete units if they are incorporated into larger units. But it is not this physical risk that "everybody" is intended to mediate. At the most microlevels, to refer to half a dozen people as "everybody" or as representing everybody, mediates the group in its aloneness with the rest of society by denying the relevance, if not the existence, of alternatives: outside of everybody there is nobody.

It is the same sort of risk that the concept mediates at the larger levels, like that of the town—or the "community," as it is commonly referred to in such contexts. Communities can be broken by dissension. They are broken if disputes come out into the open, when it is affirmed symbolically that a population that ought to be one is, in fact, many. It is important that any disputes be handled within the rhetoric of universality and transcendent unity and that the appropriate rites—elections, the use of parliamentary procedure by elected boards—be performed.

CHAPTER 5
Religious Organization

There were thirteen established churches in Appleton when I arrived. They were, as listed in a local publication written for tourists: "Trinity Lutheran, First Methodist, First Presbyterian, Full Gospel Pentecostal, Church of Christ, Church of God, St. Mark's Episcopal, Seventh-day Adventist, Assembly of God, St. Mary's Catholic, Jehovah's Witnesses, First Baptist, Church of the Nazarene (rural)." These churches offered widely divergent forms of worship and theological tenets, and also several versions of a basically similar brand of Protestantism. I will attempt to analyze to what degree these churches were the same, and to what degree they were different, and how these similarities and differences ought to be understood.

To begin with, I want to point out the absence of any sort of classification—be it religious, social, historical, or even alphabetical—in the listing that I have just quoted. Similarly, the order in which church notices were printed in the local newspaper was totally haphazard, though different from the order I just referred to. This is a reflection of the main ideological attitudes toward the multitude of churches that could be found in Appleton: the idea that because all of them accepted the divinity of a supernatural being in the same Western tradition of Christianity, they were all "much the same" and "just as valid." This attitude was widespread, but it was only expressed in the same type of *public* situation, when unity had to be stressed. A tourist brochure intended to show how friendly a *town* Appleton was, was one of these situations, and so was the newspaper whose editor felt his role to be one of "bringing together" what he himself perceived to be the essentially disparate parts of the town.

The importance of religion in Appleton was quite great, although perhaps not quite so great as it was said to have been in earlier times. All civic occasions—Memorial Day, high-school graduation ceremonies, dedications of public buildings—required the presence of a minister or two and the saying of prayers and blessings. Churchgoing was considered by many to be a sign of respectability, and most holders of public offices were churchgoers. Yet disinterest in any form of religious activity within the confines of an established church was great also, particularly among the younger generation, which did not feel any strong pressure to join or attend any church. In 1964, Surajit Sinha gathered the figures on church membership in Appleton shown in the accompanying Table 2. Because of a great number of variables, the table can be indicative only of the relative importance of churches. Since it was clear to me that relative size had not varied much since 1964, I did not attempt to take a census of my own. Furthermore, Sinha lists only eleven churches, the brochure lists thirteen, and while I was in Appleton at least one more church was established. It is evident

TABLE 2. *Church Membership in Appleton Township*

Church	Number of Families	Percent of Total
Standard Protestant		
1. Presbyterian	160	13.0
2. Methodist	150	12.0
3. Lutheran	90	7.1
4. Episcopal	25	2.0
5. Church of Chist	25	2.0
	450	36.1
Fundamentalist Protestant		
1. Baptist	15	1.2
2. Assembly of God	10	0.8
3. Seventh-day Adventists	29	2.3
4. Pentecostal	2	0.2
	56	4.5
Roman Catholic	400	32.1
Jehovah's Witnesses	2	0.1
Miscellaneous Churches Outside Appleton	25	2.0
Jews	3	0.2
Unchurched	309	25.0
Total	1,245	100.0

S. Sinha, "Religion in an Affluent Society," p. 191.

that the number of churches and their relative size is not a matter of structure. Only the very multitude is.

The figures in the table inflate somewhat the real dimensions of religious life in Appleton insofar as they deal with *membership*; such figures are always disproportionate to attendance and involvement. For example, in 1969, the Methodist church had a total membership of 392 and an average attendance of 153, or 39 percent. (The figure 392 refers to the total number of baptized and confirmed Methodists, while Sinha's figure for the Methodist church, 150, refers to families. It is also possible that the church grew under the impulse of a very active minister. In any event, it is necessary to shift the figures to compare membership with attendance.) This phenomenon is general in all the churches I went to, except the Catholic church and certain of the smaller fundamentalist churches, whose average attendance, compared with their membership, was better. Another fact to be noted is that none of the churches was limited to people from Appleton per se; an important part of the membership of all congregations lived outside the town limits—no two churches included members from exactly the same area of the county.

Differentiation and Ranking: The Social Organization of Protestantism

At the most general level, the three main currents of American religious thought are represented in Appleton. There are the moderate Protestant churches, such as the Presbyterian and Methodist, characterized by a minimal insistence on any specific theological background. There are the fundamentalist Protestants, such as the Baptists or the Assembly of God, with a theoretical insistence on a literal interpretation of the Bible.

Finally, there is the Catholic Church, which includes, principally, recent immigrants from Catholic parts of Europe, their children, and a few converts interested in the more complex and systematic theological justification of the beliefs and liturgy of this church. The historical establishment of Catholicism in the United States is not really recent, but its ranks have constantly been renewed as immigrants came into the country, and its superficial organization is still more European than American. Yet the process of Americanizing the Catholic Church in Appleton is certainly well on its way, as the influx of new immigrants has almost stopped.

I will focus first and foremost on Protestant churches because they reveal organizational realities at the most visible levels.

The distinction between the two brands of Protestantism or between Protestantism and Catholicism can be made to seem much sharper at a theoretical level than it is in reality. It is well known that the Episcopal and Lutheran churches incorporate many traits typical of the Catholic Church, such as complex ritualism and a religious hierarchy that limits the autonomy of the local congregation. Similarly, the Church of Christ, with a theological orientation that equates it with the moderate Protestants, incorporates the "coming-forward" ritual and baptism by immersion typical of fundamentalist churches. On the other hand, the Baptist church of Appleton held services whose structure was very close to that of the moderate Protestant churches. From that point of view, the Protestant churches are positioned along a continuum with "high ritualism" at one extreme and "high emotionalism" at the other, the order being: Episcopal, Lutheran, Methodist, Presbyterian, Church of Christ, Baptist, Seventh-day Adventist, Assembly of God, Jehovah's Witnesses, Church of God, Full Gospel Pentecostal. (The ranking could be different elsewhere.)

This order loosely conforms to a sociopolitical order insofar as members of moderate Protestant churches held all the direct political power and most of the wealth that Protestants possessed in Appleton. Fundamentalists rarely participated in any political or social activities with members of other churches, even though they were often invited and most of them would have been perfectly acceptable almost anywhere. The Catholic church was a special case, since it included many of the richest and most powerful people in town (those who were not Protestant) and also a wide selection of people from all social levels. Therefore, it would be meaningless to rank it with the Protestant churches. These churches were much more homogeneous in their membership and could easily be characterized socially if one accepts that the people who dominated each congregation in some way represented the sociological reality of these churches.

As perceived by many people in Appleton, the Presbyterian church, for example, was supposed to be "intellectual" and "sophisticated"; the Methodist was the church both of older, established small farmers and younger, "up-and-coming" businessmen in the town. Indeed, the Presbyterian church appealed mainly to professionals and high-level civil servants, the Methodist to merchants. The school board was dominated by Presbyterians, the town council by Methodists. There was clearly a feeling of competition between these two churches, the most important ones in Appleton. For the time being, the advantage appeared to lie with the Presbyterian church for the top spot in the ranking system.

The Episcopalian church, being very small, did not play a very noticeable role in the social and political life of the town. The income of some of its members was very high, but the most active members, a handful of them, congregated mostly with Presbyterians outside of church activities.

The Church of Christ was quite close to the Methodist in many ways, but its atmosphere was very quaint and its congregation did not try to compete socially with the others, although one could feel a certain desire among some members to do so. Its members were often close to people in the Baptist church, with whom they felt more at ease on religious matters than with the more liberal Methodists. They were generally not fundamentalists, but they preferred this position to the liberal Protestantism preached by other churches.

The Lutheran church was quite outside this ranking system, probably because a large number of its members came from areas outside the town and because of a strong plurality of German immigrants in its ranks. In outward appearance, its membership consisted of many people whose socioeconomic background was very similar to that of the Methodists, and they could have competed with them, but they did not, and remained withdrawn.

An absolute ranking for the fundamentalist churches would be even more difficult. The Full Gospel church appealed mainly to very poor white migrants from the South, many of them unemployed, and all with large families. They contrasted strikingly with the congregations of the moderate churches, in which people of this type were exceedingly rare. I could say that the Full Gospel church fell at the bottom of the social scale.

The status of the other fundamentalist churches, though certainly lower than that of any of the moderate churches, is much more difficult to determine. On the one hand, none of the people who held political power or offices, whether in the school system or the town or county government, belonged to any of these churches. On the other hand, most fundamentalist church members held jobs and, more importantly, followed a life-style totally acceptable to, and often encountered in, the moderate churches. As long as religious subjects were not approached, it was often hard to distinguish between a churchgoing Methodist and a Seventh-day Adventist or

Baptist. They were, in fact, regularly invited to participate in the ecumenical activities planned by the moderate churches, and just as regularly refused.

It soon became evident to me that the absence of any Baptist or Seventh-day Adventist in most townwide activities was the result of an ideological choice: "worldly power" was evil and corrupting and should be avoided. This was not a rationalization in the face of segregation. Many individual Baptists would have been politically acceptable. But if they *had* joined the political cliques in town, they could not have remained Baptist. They would have been rejected and, conversely, accepted in, say, the Methodist church. Socioeconomic differences among the fundamentalist churches were minute. The only differences among most of these churches were religious and theological; they were essentially "equal" among themselves, and their organization was based on principles similar to the organization of the groups of young adults discussed in Chapter 4.

All fundamentalist churches were very small, each comprising only four dozen families. And the smaller they were, the tighter and more segregative they were. The Seventh-day Adventists were the best example of this process, with their insistence on keeping Saturday rather than Sunday as their holy day. Their reason for doing so was, of course, a typical fundamentalist statement: "This is what the Bible says." They believed themselves to be more fundamentalist than all other fundamentalist churches combined because *they* kept the Sabbath and the others did not. On the other hand, their interest in health, nonviolence, conscientious objection to military service, and social service did not derive from a wholly literal reading of the Bible. They seemed to insist relatively less on salvation than other churches.

All fundamentalist churches present such a mix of literalism and interpretation with regard to the Bible. They have to be literal to justify their existence, and they have to be interpretive not only because of the ambiguous character of many biblical passages but also to differentiate themselves from other fundamentalist churches. By keeping Saturday as their day of worship, the Seventh-day Adventists devised a particularly efficacious way of differentiating themselves from the rest of the population. It made communication with other churches a little more difficult, contributing thereby to the strength of the bond among church members.

To be unlike all other churches was the main raison d'être of

most of the smaller churches. The differences based on disagreements concerning the interpretation of biblical passages
played the same minor symbolic role as the presence or absence of
flags in the churches. The Baptist church had two flags around the
altar, an American and a church flag, plus a large cross painted on
the wall. The Seventh-day Adventist church displayed a large
American flag just by a lectern with neither altar nor cross. The
Full Gospel church had a lectern and a bench for people who came
to "receive the Spirit," but neither flag, altar, nor cross.

The differences among churches were also expressed by the
use of different prayers during Sunday services or by small shifts in
the organization of the service: some churches would use both the
Gloria Patri and the Doxology; others would use only one at a time;
some would use neither. There were variations in the frequency of
communion services or in the order of the different steps of a
service; communion generally came after the sermon, but it might
be placed before, and the consecrating prayers might be said by the
pastor or by one or several elders. These variations were quite
important symbolically because of the relatively large amount of
communication that existed among the congregations of these
churches. People frequently attended services at churches other
than their own and thus found out how other churches went about
doing things. Practical help was often exchanged, and friendship
networks existed across churches. Here also segregation demands
communication.

I characterized the Episcopalian congregation as rich and in
the orbit of the Presbyterian church. It was rich because it was clear
that it could count on more money per member than any other
church in Appleton. In spite of the small size of the membership, it
could afford a full-time minister and a church fellowship hall complex at least as large as the Presbyterians'. Proportionally, this made
the Episcopalians richer than the Presbyterians. On the other hand,
the Presbyterians were much more active in politics and other aspects of the life of the town, while the Episcopalians were under-
represented. What does all this mean?

There were 80 names on the mailing list of the Episcopal
church and 200 baptized Episcopalians in Appleton. About 150
people practiced, and the average church attendance was around
80 (none of these subdivisions offered to me by the pastor cover
exactly the same units; statistics cannot be very precise, just indicative). In general, people holding high-status jobs (professionals,
managers, civil administrators, small businessmen) made up about

40 percent of the congregation. People with lower-status jobs (clerks, secretaries, blue-collar workers) comprised 35 percent. Retired persons (25 percent of the congregation) were, in general, not very well-to-do, except for the two widows of Chrysler and General Motors executives, who were very well off and accounted for the relative wealth of the church; the large fellowship hall had been donated by one of them. Finally, no one in this church played the role of "old aristocrat." Even among the upper half of the congregation many were new, both to Appleton and to their social position. None of these people would have been unwelcome in the Presbyterian church. Nor were Episcopalians totally snobbish toward Presbyterians; there were many extra-church relationships between the two congregations.

The statistical composition of the Methodist congregation does not vary significantly from the Episcopalian: 35 percent of the people on the membership list (266 "units," 410 people) could be classified as "higher" (both in status and income), and 56 percent as "lower." There were also 9 percent who were retired and unaccounted for. (My criteria for determining higher or lower status are the same as those I used for the Episcopalians. My data are purely occupational; that was all I could get from my sources. Once again, these statistics are intended to be indicative of the type of people who were on the mailing lists of the respective churches.) The average and median incomes and jobs were thus most probably slightly lower for the Methodist than for the Episcopal church, a result well in keeping with the findings of sociological studies of American towns. The question is: To what extent is this difference in income averages relevant? To be more precise: Why is it that university professors, white-collar workers in a large chemical complex, and blue-collar workers in a Ford automobile factory could be found in all three churches—and, in fact, of course, in all the others? Why is it, furthermore, that the Episcopalian church gave an outward appearance of wealth and gentility, the Presbyterian one of intellectualism, the Methodist one of *nouveau riche* pride and self-consciousness, although the statistics reveal that the composition of the congregations did not vary significantly?

The answer to the first question is very simple: One belongs to one church or another primarily for *personal* reasons. A person does not join a group or a church *because* he is a university professor (or in spite of being one) but because he wants, for whatever reasons, to be a member of this or that church. A Methodist survey found that the three main answers given to this question were that one joins a church because it has a "good" minister, a "nice" church building, a "congenial" congregation.

A young couple I interviewed who had just moved to Appleton from Detroit, where they had not belonged to any church, decided that they should "because it would be a good example to the children," even though the husband said freely that he did not really believe in the utility of church membership. One Sunday morning, one of them went to a Methodist service, the other to the Presbyterian church. The Methodist minister made a sermon about "preparing a birthday cake for Jesus on Christmas . . . Good grief!" The wife decided that it would be difficult to find anybody giving a better sermon in Appleton than the one she heard the Presbyterian minister preach. Their social position at the time was rather beneath the image the congregation presented. The church was also more conservative than they considered themselves to be. However, they "adapted" and joined the Presbyterian church and are now very active in it.

Another couple had moved from Ohio to Louisiana to Appleton. They had been raised Unitarians, could not find the denomination after they left Ohio, and joined the Presbyterian church in Louisiana. Their experience there was very bad. ("People were so unfriendly there. They were polite on Sunday, but nobody ever called on us. I even proposed myself to teach Sunday school, but they said they didn't need anybody!") In Appleton they also joined the Presbyterian church and found it very congenial. A third couple was invited to the same church one Sunday by friends, who explained: "You'll probably like it very much there, and we would be so pleased to see you."

All three couples were relatively young. One husband was a high school teacher, the second was the head of one of the services in the county administration, and the third was a salesman for a large company (he was only in his twenties). They could all have joined any church in Appleton. The third couple could have become "almost hippie"; the first couple, though they could not have belonged to any such group—because of their age, mainly—knew John, Sue, and some of their friends relatively well. Nobody made theological comments. They answered questions about the differences they thought existed among the moderate churches by saying that they did not believe that there were any from the religious point of view. ("We all believe in the same things.") They were hard put to give an explanation for the existence of such a number of moderate churches beyond the statement that "some people are friendlier than others."

Building programs played a role, too. Ten years before, the Methodist church had been dominated by older people, had had a mediocre minister, and its church had been old, damp, and dark. (Architecturally, it had been one of the best buildings in town, but that did not count.) A new minister arrived, a younger and more energetic man. He organized membership drives and a very successful building campaign, the product of which was a brand-new church/friendship hall/office/classroom complex with lawns and a large parking lot, at the outskirts of the town.

The result was a greatly enlarged congregation that included many younger adults; they worked hard for the church and changed its outward appearance. What these new members liked was the feeling of activity, development, and improvement displayed by the congregation and "symbolized by the new building." I often heard scornful comments about "the church that is not going to start a building program for a long time," meaning the Presbyterians, whose facilities were well below the size and plushness of the other church's buildings. Presbyterians said among themselves that "outward expenditure of money is no proof of Christian worth," which, of course, must be taken with a grain of salt, since most of them were as much "conspicuous consumers" as any Methodist!

These examples of choice in church membership, however interesting in their explicit evocation of a structural reality, should not cause one to overlook the fact that many people belong to a church because at one point in their career it was the "only" church in town. Joining a church affiliated to a national denomination of which one was not previously a member might be a disagreeable process for certain adults, since it sometimes implies instruction in the basic tenets of the denomination or interviews with elders or even a new baptism, in some cases by immersion. It is always much simpler to transfer membership.

Even in the most extreme forms of congregational autonomy, to be found in Appleton in the Presbyterian church, transferring membership from a Presbyterian church in another town implied only a ritual acceptance of the person and his family by the congregation. In this case, the prospective member was presented by an elder to the congregation during a Sunday morning service, and the matter was put to a vote. At this stage there was, of course, no chance for a negative vote: segregation processes always have a subdued character. A public negative vote or even a nonunanimous one would have been scandalous and an impossible affirmation that the church was not a "community." If a "mistake" was made, the congregation's recourse was "unfriendliness," the refusal of social intercourse with the new couple.

Segregation was, of course, just as current a process as integration, although it was never so well publicized. Cases of people "dropping out" were usually repressed—by both sides. Surajit Sinha reported a few expressive comments from people who had refused to join any of the churches because of what his informants called their "hypocrisy" and the impression the congregants gave to the prospective members of feeling "superior" to "ordinary folks." (Mrs. Howard's reasons for dropping out of the Methodist church first, and then the Presbyterian, were similar.) Such comments would have raised shudders of horror if told to the people concerned; they might even have gone so far as to say that they were glad a person who said such things was not a member of their congregation. ("Such a great group of people in which everybody works together so well!")

In fact, it is possible that the informants were, or felt, rejected. One would certainly feel rejected by any Protestant church, particularly the upper churches, if he came to church in anything but his best clothes. And he would eventually *be* rejected if he did not get the message and persisted in attending. But such an occasion must arise only rarely. An initially cold reception from the congregation would be enough to drive anybody away. Any well-encultured American would interpret his exclusion from the outwardly warm and friendly salutations exchanged among integrated members as a clear rejection of himself as an acceptable candidate for membership.

I personally have not directly observed any examples of an individual's rejection by a church. I have often observed, on the other hand, rejection of a certain form of religious worship by an individual, particularly by the young, but also in two cases by adults, one being Mrs. Howard, the other being a member of the Full Gospel Pentecostal church, who testified that she had abandoned the Presbyterian church when she realized its teachings were heretical, its congregation hypocritical, and the whole "inspired by the Devil rather than by God." In many such cases the rejection is mutual. This is particularly true of young adults, whether they decide to abandon churchgoing altogether or to join a church different from the one in which they were raised. Such a shift is often associated with a move to a different town and is part of the last step in the long *rites de passage* an American youth has to endure.

There are also many examples, both in the sociological literature and in novels about American life, of people who would like to join a church, association, or clique they consider "higher" and are prevented from doing so by the resistance of the members of these groups to their application. Most of this literature (Dreiser, Lewis, Marquand, Warner) is critical of actual American life, and one can raise some doubts as to the validity of their analysis of motives, with their insistence on jealousy, envy, snobbery and other "evil" things as the primary motors of social stratification in America. But there is also little doubt that their descriptions correspond to a certain reality.

Most people in Appleton would insist on what they would consider to be the positive aspects of group formation; they would insist that anybody is welcome in their midst if he is an "interesting" or "good" or "respectable" person—which means, among established, successful, white middle-class persons, as well as among their young, "radical" children that the applicant for membership is willing to conform to the rules of the group as defined by its dominant clique at the time of the application.

If a blue-collar worker wanted to join the Episcopalian church or even simply to remain in it without feeling too uncomfortable, he certainly could do so in Appleton; there were several blue-collar workers in the church. His problem would be that he would not find many of his kind in the dominant clique, that he would have to play the game of sophistication in speech, dress, and outside interests, which he might be disinclined to do. On the other hand, the church might just happen to be dominated by blue-collar workers, and so he would not have to play a role too different from that of the majority of his fellow-workers. The Episcopalian minister had served in just such a parish before he came to Appleton. On the other hand, a blue-collar atmosphere might not appeal to the wife of a retired executive. But then again, it also might.

My argument here is that two things must be distinguished. First there is what might be called the sociological reality of the congregation, a reality dependent on the amount of money it controls and is willing to spend on church-related activities. Then there is the appearance it conveys by the use of certain symbols and by the activities of the group of people, always rather small even in the large churches, who hold most committee positions, meet informally regularly, and thus control the church. The interesting thing is that the two things are not necessarily related, something that has escaped many sociologists concerning American religion. There is a relationship between economic power and church membership only if one considers the churches in groups. But within each level there can be several competing churches, each a slight variation on the general theme. Thus the Presbyterian church in Appleton was not "intellectual" because there was a predominance of university professors and school teachers in it, but because several of the most active members of the congregation, those who planned and organized church activities, had enough influence on the minister to orient his sermons in a direction that they considered "intellectual," were interested in some sort of cultural life, and pushed the congregation to accept it.

Because the characterization of a church depends so heavily on an active clique, it is also something that can easily change as people leave or join the church. Sinha related that the conservative elements in the Presbyterian church were strong enough ten years ago to obtain the resignation of a young, rather liberal minister who had preached strongly in favor of renting a piece of church property in the best neighborhood in Appleton to a black family. (The congregation now accepts a youth service complete with rock music, protest songs, not-so-clean T-shirts, and bare feet.) Some members of the congregation wanted to set up a treatment center for people with serious psychological troubles, particularly drug addicts. The project had a hard time getting off the ground because of the lack of enthusiasm, if not the opposition, of other influential groups in town whose help would have been needed; it was too liberal, if not radical, for them. It may well have been too much for certain Presbyterians also; I heard that there were rumblings in the congregation, particularly among certain middle-aged members who thought it was going too far but who did not have the time and energy for a campaign against the trend-setting clique.

The Methodist church's transformation from an older, traditionally conservative church into a younger, modern, conservative church is another example of the same process. Many of the people who gave the church its character in earlier years are still around, but they were pushed out of their positions of power, probably gently but nevertheless firmly. The average age of people serving on committees is around forty-five, and it is the people in this relatively young age group who are the most visibly active. Yet their interests lie in very different quarters from those of the Presbyterians, whom they know quite well. They feel the need to maintain a perfect outward appearance more consciously than members of the other churches, and they are ready to sacrifice a lot, in time and money, to achieve it; their answer to the youth-service experiments of the Presbyterians (in which two or three nominally Methodist youths participated) was the creation of "sacred dancing," as it was called, which consisted of a troupe of young girls in their early teens who performed classical dance pieces during certain Sunday services. Solo pieces or special musical pieces sung by the choir were performed more regularly. From the point of view of traditional Protestantism, these experiments may have been much more radical than the youth service. After all, singing hymns has always been a respectable activity for a service, while artistic performances, particularly dancing, have never been favorably looked upon by most Protestants, especially Methodists!

Here again, the opposition of conservative versus modern or liberal does not have much meaning. Any group is always "modern" and "conservative" at the same time. For example, the Methodists accepted dancing in church but showed a certain lack of enthusiasm for the large and successful local amateur theatrical troupe that was open to anybody interested (even people known by the director to belong to the hippie fringe were invited in my presence—the invitation was rejected). A statistical breakdown showed that Presbyterians, Episcopalians, and unchurched persons made up 80 percent of the troupe, while only 12 percent were Methodists and 8 percent were Catholics.

What this choice of symbols to characterize a church reveals is that the true role of these symbols is not so much to express the inner reality of the particular group as to differentiate it from those groups closer to it and in interaction with it. Youth services and dancing, a new church, or a theatrical troupe play the same role in the social organization of moderate churches and belong to the same category of phenomena as the presence or absence of crosses in fundamentalist churches or the length of hair and quality and frequency of drug usage in hippie groups.

The manipulation of these symbols for purposes of differentiation and identification has a distinct totemic quality to it. Each group is differentiated from all others by the symbols it uses to express its existence. These symbols almost never spring from the infrastructural reality the groups may also possess. They are also very rarely invested with any emotional meaning for the members of the group: they are not sacred. They are essentially intellectual means by which the need for a multitude of groups and communities is solved.

The totems are not sacred, nor do they represent in any sense the "true" reality of the groups as seen by the members themselves. They are, as they would say, just "symbols" of the essential humanity of the members. I was told many a time: "What matters that we be Methodists, Baptists, Seventh-day Adventists (or even Jews)? We are all Christians (human beings) worshiping the same God." The totemic diversity of the social organization is a matter of surface appearance that hides an essential, and obviously very abstract and ideal, unity—the oneness that comes from the fact that all the members of these communities remain individuals whose attachment to their communities and its symbols is of the same nature.

All this must be stressed if we are to understand American culture. If America were simply "egalitarian" as de Tocqueville, for example, argued, it would have all the elements to evolve a clanlike social structure and—who knows?—it might still evolve into such a society: ethnic groups, religious minorities, "counterculture" followers could solidify into probably endogamous groups. Yet this would entail a radical shift in the definition of man: there would have to be an admission of mutual differences in the nature of human beings according to the group into which they were born. That the system would evolve in this direction seems at present almost unthinkable.

Protestant Ritualism

Max Weber saw in the question of the importance and relevance of ritual in worship the "decisive difference" that led to the schism in Christianity between Catholics and Protestants. Protestant theologians rejected the idea that there is an inherent value to ritual action or that it is only through such actions, "sacraments" as the Catholics call them, that men can get in contact with God or receive grace from him. This difference about the need of a mediation between God and the individual is still very much alive. The Catholic theologians Karl Rahner and Herbert Vorgrimler still say: "When the Church, engaging its whole being, makes absolute in God's name and Christ's this pledge of grace for the individual at the decisive moments of his personal saving history, we have the *opus operandum*—a sacrament."[1] Paul Tillich, on the contrary, says: "The Protestant principle overcomes the gap between the sacred and the secular spheres, between priesthood and laity, Protestantism demands a radical laicism. There are in Protestantism only laymen."[2]

Most of my informants would agree with Tillich. For them, the rites that were performed in their churches at most "expressed the unity of the congregation" or "contributed to the smoothness of the worship service" as a symbol—in the native sense—of a higher, nonritualistic reality and as a practical means of solving a natural problem. As Tillich says: "One can say in general that withdrawal from communal devotion is dangerous because it easily produces a vacuum in which the devotional life disappears altogether."[3] All this was translated, in the stereotype generally accepted by people in Appleton, as meaning that the Protestant churches are not ritualistic (though some are more so than others) while the Catholic Church is.

This rather stereotypical description of the ideas on liturgy held by the two main branches of Christianity found in Appleton and the United States in general is accepted matter-of-factly by most sociologists. Even in Warner's *The Living and the Dead,* one of the best attempts to date at an anthropological analysis of the symbolic life of Americans, there is no analysis of the Protestant service, although long pages are devoted to the Catholic Mass.

Although it is certainly interesting to note that the Protestants have the feeling that their choices are devoid of "meaningless" rituals, there is no reason to believe that large groups of people could meet regularly and not develop certain routine ways of doing things that express dramatically the ideas they hold about the nature of their communion. In the process a ritual has been established, a meaningful ritual that is excellent material for an anthropological analysis.

This certainly applies to the Protestant service, which is, in fact, very rich in symbolic meaning and can be shown to be part of the same system of transformations that includes the other phenomena I have explored until now. While I stressed in the preceding pages the diversity of certain aspects of religious symbolic behavior for purposes of differentiating church from church and subgroup from subgroup in the town, I also implied many times that these differences were quite superficial and in fact had to be so to play their role. There is, indeed, enough uniformity of ritual behavior among Protestant churches to permit an observer to recognize at once that he is in a Protestant and not a Catholic church, although he cannot guess so easily the denomination without looking at the bulletin given to him by an usher as he enters the building. It might even be difficult for him to decide whether the denomination is fundamentalist or not if he pays attention only to what is done and not to what is said.

As one walks into any Protestant church in Appleton on a Sunday morning, one is always welcomed at the door of the church by at least one couple with whom one exchanges everyday greetings such as "How are you?" or "The weather is beautiful today, isn't it?" If one is recognized as a visitor, somebody from another town or another church, the welcome will be more elaborate and somewhat inquisitive. Once inside the church, if it is of any size at all, one is taken in charge and led to a seat by ushers who distribute a bulletin on which is printed the order of worship and a few announcements.

Services always begin with a hymn and at least three other hymns are sung during the course of the service. The inner order of the service varies widely from church to church and sometimes also from Sunday to Sunday. A minister explained to me that this order of worship depends almost solely on the inspiration of the minister as long as it includes at least some of the various liturgical moments. These are:

1. Invocation. Always at the beginning, recited by the pastor or an elder. This is an improvised prayer to ask God's help that the service be fruitful.

2. Prayer of Confession (not found in all denominations). To ask for God's indulgence for one's sins.

3. Offerings. Consisting of a collection of money and a prayer over these.

4. Readings. Normally one from the Old Testament and one from the New Testament.

5. The saying of the only mechanical prayers recited in Protestant churches (except for the Episcopalian and Lutheran churches). They are the Doxology (Praise God from whom all blessings flow; Praise him, all creatures here below; Praise him above, ye heavenly host; Praise Father, Son and Holy Ghost. Amen), the Gloria Patri (Glory be to the Father, the Son and the Holy Ghost, as it was in the beginning, is now and ever shall be, world without end. Amen), and the Our Father. These prayers are used mainly as transitions from one part of the service to another.

6. Communion (not found in all denominations and in others only once a month). It consists (except among Lutherans and Episcopalians) of pieces of white bread and tiny glasses of grape juice. These are placed on trays and passed from hand to hand among the congregation, who remain seated in the pews. Everybody always partakes.

7. Sermon. "There can be a service without communion, but not without a sermon!" a minister once told me. It is the high point of the service, and all the rest (except perhaps for communion when it is placed after the sermon) is more an introduction to it than anything else.

8. Invitation (not in all denominations). The minister or leaders invites people who want to join the church to come forward and make a declaration to this effect.

9. Benediction. Always at the end, recited by the leader of the service for the congregation. This, too, is an improvised prayer. Like the improvised invocation, the formula may be very stereotyped and repetitive, depending on the personality of the minister.

People move out after the complete singing of a last hymn, and as they do, they pass in front of the pastor, who shakes everyone's hand with a word of greeting. The whole affair normally lasts exactly an hour.

These are the main elements of a Protestant Sunday morning service, and many are self-explanatory. Yet the unity of purpose might be lost if one were to look at each of them separately as the embodiment of certain theological choices. It could be noted that no church in Appleton used both a prayer of confession and an invitation, one of the rare regularities in the liturgical life. This could be related to two different views of salvation. On the one side were those (mainly moderates) who believed that salvation was a continuous process throughout life, with God continually forgiving sins. On the other side were those (mainly Fundamentalists) who maintained that salvation is a once-and-for-all event, that if it is real, there cannot be lapses. Thus Fundamentalists often added to the invitation to come forward and join the church: "and repent of your sins." In Pentecostal churches this is considered to be life's greatest moment. Once one has been saved, there is no further need for prayers of confession, and indeed these churches do not use them.

The necessity of offerings, or a collection of money, is not disputed by either party. Cynical observers might argue that its universality is symbolic of the essentially financial character of all churches. The amount of money spent by the congregations on their "religious" activities is indeed staggering: Protestants in Appleton spent at least half a million dollars a year, and sometimes more when building drives were under way. This averages about three hundred dollars per family, although not everybody contributed. On the other hand, to interpret this ritual moment in the service as the necessary "offerings one has to make to further God's work on earth" is just as valid, and certainly closer to the perception of the faithful. Without denying the importance of the economic aspect, it must be noted that the collection is not simply a practical necessity, for large gifts are more often made in the privacy of the donor's or the pastor's office. Indeed, from a practical point of view, it might be easier to make one's contribution once a year. But a service must include offerings.

The importance of the sermon is well documented in the literature on Protestantism, particularly American Protestantism. It is, of course, not by chance that a pastor is popularly referred to as a preacher. The remark about the necessity of a sermon to make a service complete was made to me by the Presbyterian minister, which shows that this point of view is shared by people of all allegiances. On that occasion he added somewhat cynically that "they all sleep through it." On another occasion, more seriously, he defined the role of the pastor as basically that of an organizer, a leader, and a preacher. According to him, one is not a pastor because of a special sacrament that sets its receiver apart as a different sort of human being, but because of certain capabilities given to an individual at birth, particularly the ability to speak inspiringly, much as one might be born with the talent to be a successful manager or a great painter. To many fundamentalists, even this would be a definition that sets the minister overly apart; they would argue that anybody can preach if he is "inspired by the Spirit" to do so. In these churches, "testimonies" from members of the congregation or visitors are frequent and particularly appreciated as religious experiences.

The central place of the sermon is the most striking symbol of the whole orientation of Protestantism. A sermon is addressed to individuals, and it calls for individual action, but only in the realm of morals. A sermon is normally an interpretation of the sacred myths, emphasizing their relevance to modern situations. Yet the directives that a pastor may abstract from his analysis of a passage in the Bible must not be for specific actions in the social world. That would threaten the freedom of the audience as individuals. A pastor can indicate only general principles by which to orient one's action. Thus a Presbyterian minister may attack "those in our modern world who, like the Pharisees, believe themselves to be true guardians of the faith because of their outward morality and great gifts of money" without raising the ire of his congregation, which contains many people who exactly fit this description. An individual who does might think: "I know that God does not like Pharisees, but He knows that I am not one, that deep inside I am really very modest." But to preach actual desegregation, for example, may be unforgivable because it offers more than a moral interpretation in that it enjoins a specific action. A minister of the Presbyterian church was fired in the early 1960s, soon after he started preaching such "engaged" sermons. Nobody told me explicitly that he was fired *because* of his preaching. Considering the general importance of preaching in this church to the present day, the parting of the ways between the minister and his congregation must certainly be related to it.

The other important character of the sermon as ritual is the demand of passivity it makes on the audience. I have emphasized that the same passivity is implied in the reading of a religious magazine. A sermon demands even more passivity, for while one must decide at each moment to go on reading a text, one has little choice but to sit through a sermon once the service has begun. One may or may not decide to make an effort to listen to the sermon, but one will have heard it.

The Meaning of Protestant Ritualism

One of the things that struck me most the first few times I attended services in Protestant churches was the uniformity of the congregation in matters of dress. In the winter (the summer heat is considered by many a good excuse for less formality) one would not find a man without a suit and tie (sports jackets are considered acceptable by some people, but the effect must never be sloppy), a woman without an elaborate dress or pantsuit and a hat. Even young children were dressed up. If they didn't want to wear a suit, they would be asked by their parents not to come to church at all for fear of embarrassment. Only once did I see members of the Presbyterian church in less than formal clothing. The occasion was the youth service I referred to earlier when a group of teenagers from the church symbolized their existence as a distinct subcommunity within the church. They chose the hymns, the musical instruments, and their (very informal, but still conforming within the mode they had chosen) dress—for the youth service, no youth came dressed formally.

The same formalism and striving for perfection of appearance can be recognized in the stark, abstract layout of the church building itself and also in the actual performance of the ritual. The impression, except in Pentecostal churches, is always that of a highly organized activity, perfectly timed, with almost no hesitation or blank moments. Each step is clearly indicated on the bulletin, announced by the pastor, and started by a trained member of the audience (the minister's wife or the ushers). Personal, individual rituals are totally ruled out, both by the absence of any slack moment in the service and by the impossibility of detaching oneself completely from the minister's doings.

All this is especially striking in contrast to a Catholic Mass, particularly before its recent transformations. In the Mass, the priest is the only person who has to be precise and exact, and the audience's participation in what he does is minimal. This gives a great amount of leeway for private acts of devotion, much more than can be found in any Protestant service. There, only group rituals are performed, all of which involve the whole audience as a body.

The Protestant Service begins only when everybody is in the church—there are very few, if any, late arrivals. Then the different choirs enter in procession, all dressed alike in long robes, while the whole congregation stands and sings a hymn. From then on, the only movements are sitting, standing, and the reciting or singing of prayers or hymns. At all times, except when the ritual of incorporation into the congregation is performed, the congregation is one body, acting in perfect unison. All this is done on signals from the pastor, whose role, apart from that of preacher, is mainly one of master of ceremonies and director. He is indeed the person who has planned the service, and he is responsible for its smooth progression. Some pastors included a minute of silent prayer in their services, but even this does not permit the individual to wander very far in private communion with God. No pastor would ever have to preach the sermons I have heard twice in Catholic churches, in France and in Chicago—sermons against old women entering the church during Mass and going about their private devotions to St. Theresa or St. Anthony without acknowledging that a Mass was going on. Yet some Catholic priests used to advise people to recite the rosary during Mass, something that is not a collective activity nor one that is directly related to the religious performance in progress. In fact, to say the rosary is but a mental version of the same activity for which the old women were criticized. All this would be unthinkable in Protestant churches.

In short, what is symbolized in Protestant ritualism is unanimity, one-mindedness, overarching community in which the participating individuals fully divest themselves of the qualities, symbolic and otherwise, that make them individuals. This is expressed most starkly in the ritual of communion. Not only is it considered to be nothing more than a sign of the togetherness of the congregation, it is also something that the congregation does together, as a whole: everybody partakes. Conversely, in Catholic theology, the reality of the Church as a community is never in doubt. What may be in doubt is the state of the individual, i.e., he may be in a state of sin. The onus is thus ritually put on him. He must actively decide to partake. And, until recently, many people did not partake, thereby affirming their individuality within the service itself.

Louis Dumont has shown how in the extremely hierarchical Indian culture, individualism, which is totally denied in the social structure, is permitted to flourish in religious rituals and doctrine and in the lives of saints; that is, of persons outside the social structure.[4] In America, the reverse happens. In a culture that emphasizes individualism, the religious rituals stress group activity. During the church service, the participants cease to be individuals. They form a disciplined society that effectively denies any individual freedom. This might be surprising to people who expect a direct relationship between the traditional interpretations of Protestantism and its rituals. In my preliminary analysis of religious ideas in Appleton, I indeed stressed the individualism to be found at their core. It would thus seem that the surrender of individualism during Protestant rituals (to generalize and encompass both public rituals such as the service, and private ones such as the reading of inspirational literature) does not depend on religious doctrine per se but on broader cultural principles.

In India, the caste system is derived from a *religious* definition of the world based on order and hierarchy. But it is in religion, and only in religion, that one can escape that very social order, either through renunciation of the world, and particularly of one's social place in it, or through participation in certain sects or *bhakti* movements that insist on a direct relationship between the God and the individual during the ritual.[5] In fact, these rituals are organized along caste lines, and the sects soon become new castes as they get institutionalized. These types of reversal and apparent paradoxes have been well documented in the mythology and religion of numerous cultures. Lévi-Strauss has argued that this may be a general process and that, in any event, one must not expect a direct relationship between a myth, the social structure of the mythical society in which its hero moves, and the actual structure of the society in which the myth is told.[6] The contradictions are not absolute. They derive from the attempts made by native philosophers and theologians to deal with irreducible aspects of the human experience denied in certain ways by the culture. Thus, because the social ideas and the most abstract religious ideas of Indian culture, and not simply of Hinduism, deny the very reality of the individual, it became necessary to somehow deal with individualism—the fact that human beings, being distinct from each other, do not always fit their social definition as well as the social doctrine they may believe in would have them do.

In Appleton, it is evident that the Protestant service is but a more formal, more rigid, and more consciously acted out expression of the desire for uniformity among small groups that I analyzed at length in Chapter 4. Even such an apparently unimportant rite as the welcoming couple of the Sunday service in moderate Protestant churches expresses the same structural principle. A welcome implies two things: something to be welcomed into, and somebody with a desire to get into that thing; it implies a social unit and people outside of it. It implies both integration and segregation, even though most people would see it only as a means of integrating newcomers, of proving that the congregation is friendly, that is, well integrated and universally integrating.

Like social life in general, religion in Appleton is thus both individualistic and the pretext for the creation of communities and, perhaps, the expression of the inescapable fact that men are not islands unto themselves. Protestantism is individualistic in its definition of its domain, the relation of man to a certain transcendence; it is social-minded in its practices and rituals. It is thus another actualization, obviously more formal and consciously performed, of the same cultural structure that generated the interpretative behavior of John's group. In both cases the legitimacy of the group is based on an individual movement by each member; in both cases the result of an integration based on such principles is similar segregative tendencies, a similar stress on one-mindedness during the meetings of the group, and the same fragility.

There is a very real difference, of course, between a party and a church service, a difference that goes beyond the necessity of differentiating group from group. In the meetings of the smaller groups, I could refer in my analysis only to a certain atmosphere, to certain modes of behavior. I could not refer to specific ritual acts such as communion as symbolic of the unity of the congregation. I was able to show only that the small group *was* a unit of some sort even in the absence of formal rituals. I could have argued that the passing around of a "joint" expressed the same underlying idea as the passing around of trays with crumbs of bread and small glasses of grape juice in church; indeed, getting drunk or high in a group is but the use of an artificial means of achieving the "good" feeling that is supposed to be characteristic of a "true" community. I believe this is overinterpretation. Similarly, and however tempting it may be, such an habitual act in John's group as having coffee in a public place after a party always held in a private home cannot really be interpreted as a ritual of "reintegration" into the wider world after a period of symbolic separation and limited communion. It may have such a function, yet the absence of any specific ritual structure obliges the analyst to say that it belongs to a different sort of social reality from the service. For the people who attend them, parties are occasions when one has some fun. Passing around a joint is considered to depend solely on the practical necessity of holding one's breath for some time after having taken a puff, and not wasting an expensive commodity by letting it burn into the air. Similarly, coffee is considered to have sobering virtues and nothing else.

In contrast, welcoming couples and communion are considered by churchgoing people to be primarily symbolic acts expressing a sometimes elusive feeling of community. For while small groups can often be shown to be actually experiencing one-mindedness, really to practice mutual help or in general to live the life prescribed by the cultural definitions, most churches, particularly the larger ones, such as all the moderate ones in Appleton, are formed of nothing more than an uneasy alliance of many subgroups and cliques, plus a few unattached persons. This makes their definition as "communities" very artificial, even from the point of view of the natives. Small fundamentalist churches often come close to an actual incarnation of the ideal: there it is the whole congregation that surrounds the newcomer on his first visit, knowledge of each other's lives goes beyond gossip, and mutual help beyond bake sales.

In larger churches, people know that they are divided and are forever planning activities to "further the sense of community among us"to little avail, of course. Yet the ideal remains, and the people continue to perform the ritual acts that they believe to be effective means to their ends. As an anthropologist, I must say that these acts, like all ritual acts, are *not* effective in themselves, or only insofar as people believe in their effectiveness. Yet there is a definite difference between acts that refer to ends different from their direct practicality—for example, communion in Protestantism has nothing to do with nourishment—and acts that refer directly to their practical ends—like sharing a joint. The distinction is often not absolute, but it is real enough for me to maintain that the former acts are basically ritual in character, while the latter are simply, and more generally, cultural; that is, typical of a certain society and its way of doing things.

At a more general level, both sets of acts can be considered to be "texts" produced by the culture, and, as such, it is not surprising that they should be structured in similar ways. Yet they have to be distinguished, for one pertains to an existential state of the members of the society and the other to a symbolization of this existential state. This can be restated in Victor Turner's terms: John and his friends were a "communitas"; most churches were "communities."[7] The former found ritual irrelevant; the latter could not escape it, in spite of their theological commitment to nonritualism.

This distinction is quite important in the context of American culture because it points to a little-noted structural characteristic: an inverse relationship between ritualism and the existential realization of ideals. Americans, it is well known, claim to be impatient with any type of ritual performance, and they will easily discount foreign customs as empty ritualism. Yet American life has a great deal of ritualism—in church activities, of course, but even more in everything that touches the political system, as I will show in chapter 6. Except for critics, this is not considered to be empty ritualism but a meaningful symbolization of an actual state of affairs. It is easy enough, of course, to show that affairs are not in the prescribed state, and also that the more disunity exists in a group whose unity is postulated, the more exactingly precise the rituals become. The atmosphere surrounding the flag as a symbol of the whole nation is the perfect case in point.

The unstressed character of ritual on those occasions which allow for the more complete existential actualization of the structure is a direct corollary of that very structure. Ritual in its very nature is a mode of behavior that reifies a certain ideology *outside* the involvement of individuals. Parliamentary procedures, for example, must be followed to the letter by governing boards for their decisions to be legal. The members of the board have no freedom to improvise, a requirement that directly contradicts individualism.

And yet it is not possible for the society as a whole to escape a measure of ritualism. While the smallest communities are built on the cultural model, the larger ones cannot be. They could not segregate effectively, and their integration was always doubtful. And yet on all the occasions when they had to be symbolized, and insofar as they were not experiential entities, ritual had to be used, a ritual structured obviously by the same principles as those which structure social situations that would be recognized as real communities.

The Catholic Church in Appleton: Enculturation and Ethnicity

There is a huge Catholic church in Appleton, with a large membership, many wealthy and powerful parishioners, and a parochial school that, though in financial difficulties, was responsible for the education of a majority of the Catholic youth in the town. It is thus an important social force, even though most members of the church are recent immigrants to the United States from non-Anglo-Saxon parts of Europe—Ireland, Italy, and Poland, particularly. It is not possible to discard the experience of these people with the easy affirmation that their way of being is a mere survival bound to be melted into the main Protestant stream of American culture. This denies the fact that an identification with Catholicism remains widespread in America beyond the first generations after immigration, and that Catholicism has remained a variation on Christianity that opposes itself to all Protestant churches rather than to some of them.

This is true even though the recent changes that have occurred in the Catholic Church have made Catholicism appear outwardly to have become more Protestant than it was. For example, the new Catholic church building in Appleton looks very much like the

Protestant buildings: it has the same abstract and stark atmosphere, with few of the nooks and corners and small side altars that permit private devotions. But the very way these changes were implemented, through decrees and decisions taken by the hierarchy and imposed on sometimes unwilling congregations, is but one example of the fact that the very structure of the religion remains what it has always been.

I am not going to analyze Catholicism in detail; I am just going to consider some of the basic traits that differentiate it most from American Protestantism to see how these are being interpreted by the faithful in their Protestant environment. For however different Catholicism may be, it is made to fit within the social organization of the town. How?

The universalistic appeal of Protestantism, the fact that it is open to "everybody," regardless of social position, race, color, or former "creed," is, in fact, severely limited in practice: the actual congregations are generally restricted to one social position, race, or color—and, indeed, creed. In theory, Catholicism, too, is universalistic in its appeal, and its basis is individualistic. Yet in its European incarnation, Catholicism denies a person—by opposition to the individual as a category—the possibility of a choice. Choice is not a social reality in Europe; converts are a rare sight, and religious diversity, in the few places where it does occur, often leads to serious tensions. In the last century a limited possibility of religious choice has appeared as it has become socially possible to reject the Church. But, in fact, most of the people who make this choice have been baptized in the Catholic tradition, which is enough for the Church. In American Protestantism, even if many members of a church do end up as members of denominations very close to their parents', a conscious choice must be made: individual freedom must mean personal freedom.

Sociologically, the Catholic Church is organized into social units defined by the wider culture and society and not by the active will of the persons involved. Thus there is one church per town, or per parish if the town is larger than a parish should be, and everybody who is born into that town, after being baptized, is a member of the parish and of the Church in general. The sacrament of baptism is something that cannot be eradicated by whatever actions the person concerned may do in his life; it marks the receiver as a Christian for all eternity, anywhere in the world—a special type of Christian, of course, a Catholic with all the duties and rights attached to this status. Obviously, such an interpretation of individualism is not at all congruent with the American version. Society stands first, and a person is not given much choice. He may conform or rebel, but he cannot create. In practice, in the modern world where sociological pressures force people out of their original social position, in space or rank, the doctrine often leads to a useless bureaucracy, as the following case exemplifies.

In a meeting of the Appleton Catholic church parish council, a man once rose and, pointing an accusing finger at the pastor, said: "This man refused to baptize my child! A little crying baby! What if it had died?" The pastor explained that the man worked and resided in another town and that the child had to be baptized in that town. The pastor in bureaucratic fashion had decided that this man was a member of a certain social unit, that other town, by examination of certain criteria—work and residence. This disregarded the fact that the man did not define his social self in that way. Many Catholic priests do not take quite so seriously their role in the Church's bureaucracy. However, a Protestant minister wouldn't even have considered handling a request about baptism in such a way.

I will not go into the religious duties of a Catholic; they are too many, and their interpretation is too much tied with sociological ideas irrelevant to American thought. I will deal at more length with one of the basic rights of a Catholic, a right that explains the peculiar character of the congregation of the Catholic church in Appleton by comparison with the Protestant churches. Membership in the Catholic Church is universal; one is not simply a member of a specific congregation. If one moves one's residence, one is entitled by right to membership in the local parish, and the congregation has no say. In fact, the phrase "membership in the local parish" is not appropriate; at most, one can be on the "mailing list" after one has registered with the parish administration. The process is bureaucratic, and only the pastor needs to know a new parishioner has been added to the congregation, and he may often not learn of it for a long time. Indeed, one of the most typical symbols of American Protestantism, the "welcoming couple," is not present in the Catholic Church, and I went for weeks to Mass without anybody coming to ask me who I was.

In Catholic thought, both the Church as a whole and the local congregation are direct reflections of a sociological reality and exist not as voluntary associations of individuals but as a unit that includes all the baptized men and women born into an area that encompasses all the individuals who may live in it. As such, it does not demand any specific showing of one-minded unity inside the congregation, since the members have no say as to their existence as a unit. The unity of the society is considered to come from a higher order: divine or political. The result of this absence of individually grounded unity has led to a much greater diversity in the social constituency of the Catholic church than found in any of the other churches in Appleton, excepting perhaps the Lutherans. The richest and most powerful families in Appleton, the owners and managers of the larger industries that were the industrial basis of the town, were Catholics, and so were many of the poorest families. The bulk of the congregation was, of course, middle income, since the social characteristics of Catholics in Appleton are very close to those of the population at large. Symbolically, this is expressed by a greater diversity in the outward appearance of the congregation. Even at the most formal of the Masses, the eleven o'clock Mass on Sunday morning, outdoor jackets, open shirts, corduroy pants, or even jeans were possible ways of dressing and could be found in the congregation. Many might disapprove of this, but they could not reject the culprit the way a Protestant congregation could.

The Mass itself, even in its post–Vatican II form, is a dramatic performance staged by a priest for an audience. The priest is still set apart, he is not merely a "leader." One can still find some faithful reciting the rosary, a private and individualistic form of prayer, during the Mass. Even though there is much less time nowadays for private prayers than there used to be during Mass, the amount of time left for such prayers is still disproportionate to that found in Protestant services. The latter are, in fact, also dramatic performances, but in them the split between actor and audience has been abolished: the play is not performed *for* the congregation but *by* it. Tillich said that in Protestantism there are no priests, but neither is there a laity, for participation is total. Perhaps we should thus turn Tillich's formula around and say that in Protestantism there are no laymen, only priests.

I am not going to get into any more details about each of these social and ritual characteristics of the Catholic church in Appleton, since the contrasts to what I said about the characteristics of Protestant churches are evident. Thus it is not surprising that what the Catholic pastor first tried to impress upon me was how divided the congregation was, how there was a constant battle between the "seven ethnic groups" that composed it. As the pastor explained to me, only three are really important and account for most of the power struggles inside the congregation: the Irish, the Polish, and the Italians, in the historical order of their establishment in Appleton from the end of the nineteenth century to the middle of the twentieth. The four others play minor roles and are not so readily identifiable; the pastor had to count on his fingers. They are "the Croatians, the Slavs, the Germans, and the French-Canadians." Among the subgroups that divided the church, one could probably add all those who rejected the relevance of an ethnic identification, a growing group as individual enculturation becomes widespread among Catholics.

In the consciousness of many people, both in and outside the ethnic groups, the ethnic groups represent an actual force, organic wholes with interests of their own that one expects them to defend (in the same way farmers or blue-collar workers are supposed to do). The three main groups, particularly, possess a certain amount of cohesion expressed by the activity of national organizations such as the Polish National Alliance and the maintenance of strong kinship and business links between Appleton and the ethnic colonies of Chicago and Detroit. Self-identification is probably strongest among the Polish, among whom one can find continued resistance to the total encroachment of the English language: confessions were still being heard in Polish in Appleton two or three times a year (but not in Italian). The Italians, insofar as there are still in their ranks a high proportion of actual immigrants born in the "old country," possess a certain empirical reality, though the process of enculturation is particularly fast for them. The Irish are almost indistinguishable from the rest of the town population, except in relation to other ethnic groups inside the Catholic church.

Yet to talk of ethnic groups implies certain traits from a sociological point of view that these groups, if they had them to begin with, are losing very fast, and indeed for the most part have already lost. The term implies mainly a social unit that would transcend the individuals inside the groups; it implies that all persons who are born of an Italian father and mother will identify themselves as Italian, will want to marry inside the group if at all possible, and will participate in specifically Italian activities, culturally and politically.

In fact there is only a statistical tendency for people to marry inside their original ethnic group, which can easily be explained if one considers that very often a young boy or girl will meet only other boys or girls of the same nationality, not because of choice but because of residence patterns in large cities. When choice is possible, exogamy is frequent, and, in Appleton at least, couples in which both man and woman belong to the same group are becoming rare. National ethnic movements appeal only to a minority of all those who could justify membership in them. Finally, at the level of consciousness of an ethnic identification, no objective criteria can be found—in Appleton, at least; a man with only one grandfather from Italy may decide that for certain occasions he is Italian, while another will never claim membership, although he may have more right to the title.

All this points to the transformation of these once social ethnic groups—nationality in Europe is something from which one cannot escape—into basically voluntary associations at the same level of social organization as the Protestant churches. Many of these, formerly, or still today, had or have an ethnic flavor. Lutheranism is associated with Germans, Episcopalianism with English, Presbyterianism with Scots. There are many Dutch Reformed churches in parts of the Midwest. And so on. As time passed, native American religious sects were created, from Unitarianism to Adventism, and the ethnic identification of old churches subsided. But while it lasted—while it lasts, as ethnic identification is still very strong in many areas of American society—it did not create a social structural problem. The melting pot really worked, not by transforming all immigrants into archetypal Americans but by making them fit into the social structure whether they had changed their cultural ways *personally* or not.

The Catholic congregation in Appleton differed both from what it would have been in a European parish and from the Protestant congregations in Appleton. The latter are each formed of *one* voluntary association defined as being a social unit, though it often may not be so. The former is formed of *several* voluntary associations defined in the same way as the others and with the same social limits (the Italians are a unit only for ritual and mythological purposes; social differences among them are great and are the source for many subgroups and cliques). Thus the Catholic church in Appleton belongs to a different level of social organization than the Protestant churches, a difference that could be shown in the accompanying diagram.

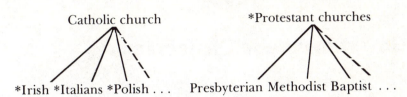

Catholic church   *Protestant churches

*Irish *Italians *Polish . . .   Presbyterian Methodist Baptist . . .

An asterisk indicates that the unit does not exist specifically as a religious unit in Appleton; inside the Catholic church the subunits are ethnic,[8] and the church is supposed to include all the groups that may be found inside it. The Protestant churches level exists as the "town," but each church is supposed to be one independent unit.

In terms of enculturation, it is interesting that the Catholic church has not systematically broken down into its constituent parts and adopted a more Protestant or voluntary structure. Some ethnically typified parishes can be found in other parts of America, and many groups are formed to worship in alternate ways, but all this remains very limited and not, I believe, the beginning of a trend. It is not simply that Catholics are particularly conservative or disciplined. They are perfectly prepared to reject the orders of the Roman hierarchy when they dislike them (the papal directives against artificial means of birth control and their dismissal by most of the faithful and many priests is a good example). There must be structural mechanisms, and I believe that these lie precisely in the definition of the congregation as an involuntary association. In Europe this mechanism allowed the members of intractably hostile clans in a small village to worship in the same church, to make no attempt whatsoever at pretending to unanimity, and still to define themselves as belonging to the same social unit (I dare not say "community," since the unit may well hold together through hate rather than through love).

Transported to America, this structure allowed voluntary associations to be built along specifically American social-structural rules within the church itself without threatening its existence. Even the Church's ritual formalisms can come to be interpreted as appropriate for the abstract level of community that is the Catholic Church's and to parallel the formalism of the rituals that express the unity of the town as a democratic unit. And thus, with little change in practice, the cultural reality of Catholicism will have changed and come to fit within America.

CHAPTER 6
Government and Democracy

The multiplicity of churches in Appleton is the direct product, I have argued, of deep structural principles that proceed from the articulation of individualism and community in American culture and the concomitant articulation of the efficient and the authentic or meaningful. The same principles applied to another domain of social action, government, have also produced a myriad of government agencies constituted ad hoc for the resolution of specific problems as they arose. Just as there is no overarching organization of the various sects that are represented in Appleton, there is no overarching bureaucracy, only narrow agencies fighting among themselves to preserve absolute jurisdiction of the domain given them. Thus the people who are the subject of this book depended on many government agencies, each with its special area, its special boundaries both geographic and administrative, and its special taxing powers.

There is the town council, in charge of the administration of the area lying within the limits of the town, supervising street maintenance, police, zoning, sewers, water, and electricity. There is the township, in charge of basically the same things in unincorporated areas (I met and interviewed people from five townships). There is the school district, in charge of administering the schools; its very irregularly bounded area extended over parts of four townships but the totality of none. There is the hospital board, in charge of the community hospital; the hospital district covered an even wider area of the county. The administrative independence of each of these agencies is complete. The school board has nothing to say in the administration of Appleton township, the Appleton Town Council cannot regulate any aspect of school activities.

A little more abstract and not so obvious is the fact that these agencies are also independent of such other agencies as the county, state, and even national governments. In general, even though most local agencies have to follow the laws and regulations spelled out for them by wider agencies, these also have to follow local ordinances or decisions when the occasion arises. More importantly, the wider agencies can issue only guidelines, not specific administrative decisions. In practice, this may be changing fast as state and national regulations become more and more precise and all-encompassing. Yet there is no sign of a formal change in the structure; at most what may be happening is a narrowing of the administrative areas in which the local agency is all-powerful.

The nonhierarchical nature of the American administrative structure has been well documented by Morton Grodzins, and my experience in Appleton can only confirm his analysis.[1] He stresses mostly the vertical independence of local agencies from wider agencies dealing with basically the same problems on a larger scale. The most striking example is that of the police forces. The people in Appleton routinely come in contact with three police forces, the town police, the sheriff's force, and the state police. Two other forces they might have contact with are the township police and the Federal Bureau of Investigation, neither of which is very much in evidence, the former being too small—in fact, barely existent—the latter too large to be routinely experienced.

The town police are supposed to deal with any crime that takes place wholly within the city limits; the sheriff, with crimes inside the county but outside towns with substantial police forces; and the state police, with implementing state regulations, particularly with regard to traffic on state roads, and with statewide crime. They also supplement the local police in cases of emergency. In theory, no police force should infringe on another's territory at the initial stage of an inquiry. In practice, a certain amount of cooperation exists, mainly because the facilities and experiences of wider forces are much greater than those of smaller forces, but no law compels cooperation in most cases, and competition between departments is as much in evidence as cooperation, as I was often told.

Even more interesting is the horizontal independence of, say, the school administration from that of the town or of the hospital. In practice as well as in theory, this independence endured: board and council members knew each other, sometimes they were friends, they certainly shared similar ideological outlooks, they had similar incomes and similar business interests, yet in spite of, or probably from their point of view *because* of, this general similarity in their social backgrounds, neither group would have dared invade the other's administrative domain. In most cases there was no need for it, but even in cases of conflict neither agency could have claimed authority over the other.

For example, the decision to let or not to let high-school students go outside the buildings for lunch rested only with the school board, and the town council could do nothing, officially, about the throngs of teenagers who got out of school at noon, except enforce loitering ordinances if it so wished. Council members could complain to board members, but only as private citizens in informal situations such as the businessmen's coffee hour, which I will discuss presently. This often worked, and if the students were prohibited from driving their cars into town during lunch hour, it was avowedly because the town was afraid of the traffic jams that could ensue.

But there is no official coordinating agency or office, and this has led, at least partially, to the establishment of alternate and informal structures where problems that interest more than one agency are discussed informally—"off the record"—by members of the different boards, councils, and committees.

From a strictly administrative point of view, this independence may not appear to be the most efficient way to deal with the government of a town if one views a town as an organic unit in which different functions such as water distribution, sewage treatment, education, and health services are functionally interrelated. This view may be correct from an abstract sociological point of view: a society could not exist if it did not deal with all these problems in a systematic way. It may also be the view held by most bureaucrats in Europe, where it corresponds probably to a deeply held belief in an organic definition of society. In America in general, and in Appleton in particular, society is not viewed as organic, if it is "viewed" at all, which sometimes appears doubtful.

Thus the administration of a town is treated as an empirical problem rather than a logical one. Every time a new area of general interest arises, a special ad hoc committee is formed that may become a formal council or board if the problem endures. For example, a few years ago the federal government instituted a program heavily subsidizing low-income housing for the elderly. Inspiration for such a development had to come from local communities, the federal government providing only guidelines and finances. Strictly speaking, public housing was nobody's business in the administrative organization of the town, and Appleton, like many other towns, could have let pass the opportunity to benefit from this program if some members of the town council had not decided that it was somewhat closer to their area of interest than to anybody else's. Yet they did not appropriate the planning of the housing development; instead, they organized an ad hoc housing commission with volunteer members who were put in charge of administering the project and of taking responsibility for its completion. Now that the building stands and is being occupied, it is not clear whether the commission will be disbanded or formally invested. If the latter alternative is chosen, it will probably have to be based on an elective process, which will be the last stage in the formation of a new independent agency.

The functions of all other agencies must be understood in the same way. The hospital board is a recent creation, and its formation followed the same general pattern as that of the housing commission. Even the town council in its present form, and the school board, the creation of which goes back to the foundation of the town, are the products of similar processes. Both are organized to deal with a definite set of problems, but neither can pretend to be the expression of the town in all its attributes and or in a holistic way. I have stressed many times that no group, at any level of the social organization of Appleton, is a holistic group in Louis Dumont's terminology.[2] The town, as such, is no exception. It is thus not surprising that there never was a felt need for the election of a man who would represent it symbolically to itself and to the national society. There is little relationship, from the point of view of the structure, between the president of the town council of Appleton—who is sometimes given the title of mayor—and the mayor of even the smallest French town, who could be said to play in relation to the central government of France the same role the Catholic priest plays in relation to God.

In political and administrative rhetoric, the "town" refers to all the people in the geographical area; it is an aggregate of persons, each of whom must have a say. It is a universalistic unit rather than a holistic one: "all the people (who happen to be living) in the town." And it is all these people who make the decisions and elect representatives. A member of the town council once gave me the following explanation of the government structure couched in historical and practical terms: "It used to be that the whole town, assembled in a town meeting, made all the decisions and elected a few officers to take care of everyday business. But nowadays the town has become too large, and a full assembly would be impossible to rule. So people elect representatives who act in their names."

Historically, it is not clear whether Appleton ever had a town meeting. Culturally, the interpretative structure ought to be familiar by now, for it is the same one that governed the telling of the Farm Bureau creation myth, and indeed the establishment of churches. The same rhetoric used for the organization of churches, the rhetoric that is largely experienced in very small groups, is also used in programmatic statements or speeches about the town. In this rhetoric, the town is—or should be, according to the occasion—a community with all the implications the term carries of equality, mutual help, participation, and one-mindedness.

The Limits of a Democracy

What I have just described is, of course, a "democracy" as the natives would call it. The idea is ritually performed that if men are left free to develop themselves naturally, they will come together and base their voluntary association on equality and, indeed, love. This was an accepted principle even among those who recognized that the town was, in fact, far from being an ideal democracy. What I never found were people who saw that whatever they considered "wrong" with Appleton as a social environment—for example, that it was profoundly divided into many hostile subcommunities, that a group of merchants appeared to subvert the town government, and that most people did not participate in the political process— was a direct consequence of the fact that it *was* a democracy and thus that no revivalistic movement that placed itself within the rhetoric of democracy could solve the apparent problems.

The recognition that Appleton was not an ideal democracy was widespread not only among the young critics of the town but also among adults, conservative and established citizens. The difference is that while the former were much more sweeping in their criticisms and in their willingness to make them openly in all situations, the latter uttered them mostly in contexts emphasizing a revival of old values, a return to age-old virtues, or in private. The signs people would point to as showing that Appleton was far from being what they considered an ideal democracy were numerous. One of the most flagrant was the fact that in January 1971, for the annual election of a third of the town council, only 118 people bothered to vote out of the 900 who had voted the preceding November in state and national elections and out of about 1,700 people eligible to do so.

Local elections are held once a year, in early January for the town council and in spring for the school board. They are announced several weeks in advance, and the newspaper editor often writes an editorial pointing out that if one does not vote, "one should not gripe" about the government. On the other hand, the elections are almost never contested, the candidates are picked by former and still-influential members of the council, and many people feel that it would be impossible even to get nominated if one were not somewhat close to the small group of merchants and professional men who form a sort of ruling clique with normally uncontested authority over routine government activities. Finally, people will often say that the activities of the town council, those of the hospital board, or even those of the school board are not terribly relevant to their lives, that they are intrinsically bureaucratic, routine, and do not allow for the development of imaginative programs or innovations. One will even hear it said that all the affairs dealt with by the local politicians are downright boring. It is often quite difficult to get people to serve on boards, and a few offices remain empty.

Poor voter turnout, clique control of the nominating process, and lack of interest in the actual work performed are all closely interrelated, and it is impossible to give an easy answer to the question of determining which is the main factor that gives rise to the other aspects of political (in)activity. Clique control is often cited by critics of small (and even large) town politics as the most important factor. A. Vidich and J. Bensman, for example, saw this as structuring all political activity in the small town they studied.[3] In this perspective, the self-interest of merchants who in most cases, and particularly in Appleton, form the core of the ruling clique is considered to be the primary motive for the establishment of such cliques. It is indeed easy to find specific cases where an administrative decision by the council can be shown to profit one or several merchants directly. In Appleton, merchants often asked for favors from the town. They asked for the blacktopping of parking lots behind their stores or the capping of parking meters during the Christmas season.

They openly admitted that these favors would profit them, but they argued that they would in fact help the whole town, something that the council accepted without discussion, though the ratio of tax money spent to tax money regained through increased sales was never made precise. In all fairness to the council, it must be said that they had not yet blacktopped most of the parking lots but they had appropriated money for leaf removal to cut down on air pollution in the fall. This may simply be another indication that the informal influences on government policies had shifted from the merchants who had traditionally held it to the suburban-oriented, upper-income people who had recently moved to Appleton for its rural and "slow-moving" character rather than for the "progressive" image that small towns used to want to display to the outside world. As I was proudly told several times: "We don't permit polluting industries here." People were conscious it would mean less growth, but that was precisely what they wanted. In any event, and in most cases, the merchants and professionals involved in the ruling cliques held their power purely because of a political vacuum, as much because of the lack of interest in town affairs by the rest of the population as because of any legal or even customary rights to power. Where there is interest, the hold of the clique on power suddenly becomes very weak.

In a neighboring town a few miles from Appleton, the traditional Republican-oriented clique was challenged by a coalition of a few disgruntled merchants, many blue-collar workers, poor whites, and blacks who united under the Democratic label and eventually took most political offices for the area away from the old clique. This happened because of strong campaigning by the opposition to get large voter turnouts, with the result that in the last few years town elections there have been attended with as much interest as national ones.

In Appleton itself, the school board was dominated when I arrived by people very close to the main ruling clique. Yet it already included a minority with strongly diverging opinions; at the annual elections, two candidates presented themselves, and the candidate who would have been more palatable to the core of the clique was defeated, and the majority shifted. In this case the opposition was based not so much on policial grounds as on matters of school policy, curriculum, educational quality, and taxation. The opposition came, in fact, from people who were friends of members of the clique. But the fact that such friendships existed did not mean that the usual people would be left to run the schools in ways that an organized opposition did not like. Thus, when a political vacuum is filled, when an issue of widely recognized importance is to be set-tled, or when a large enough group of interested individuals dis-satisfied with the status quo can be found, the dominance of the normal ruling clique may cease.

It must also be said that even though having administrative power did somewhat profit the merchants and professionals as a group—something that in any event should not be overemphasized—the individual merchants who actually did ac-cept or volunteer to be members of a government agency per-formed a job that was often very onerous for them. They had to give to it a certain amount of time and energy, easily ten hours a week taken off from their leisure time and for which they were not paid. One merchant had to resign from the school board because he felt he could not give it all the attention the job needed without endangering his own economic position. This situation should re-mind us of what I said much earlier about Mr. Howard: his partici-pation in the Farm Bureau possibly helped farming in general, but it almost killed him. Thus, the advantages that the merchants de-rive from their dominance of the political life of Appleton are not so obvious as may appear at first sight. From the point of view of an individual merchant, they may even be nonexistent. They see themselves, somewhat vainly, perhaps, as public-minded citizens who "sacrifice" themselves for the welfare of their fellow-citizens, and though the language may be extreme, it certainly corresponds to a certain reality.

The creation of a ruling clique in Appleton is not a simple matter of economic interest. It is not directly inscribed in the social structure. It is certainly related to it, however, but in a complex manner that must be elucidated carefully in order to go beyond the moralistic atmosphere that surrounds most sociological evaluations of American democracy.

In my discussion of the internal social organization of the churches, I argued that the character of a church is given to it by the doings of a small, active group that dominates the rest of the congregation by virtue of its interest in the activities of the church, the availability of its members, and thus their holding of all major lay positions. The town is but a wider church in which continuously active persons identify themselves, or are identified with, the town. From the point of view of the participants in the clique, the political organization is not extraordinary. In fact, it exactly duplicates their total social experience. Their belief in their own representativeness may be "false consciousness," but it is certainly not hypocritical, as it is sometimes made to seem. The closer they try to get to the "real" configuration of ideal American society, which is not simply absolute equality but also and just as importantly "love for one another"—that is, essential one-mindedness—the more they reinforce the present type of social organization.

These limits of hypocrisy must be drawn for us to understand that the people inside the cliques are not totally unconscious of their existence as a ruling clique, as the following case study will show. A few weeks after my arrival in Appleton, I was told that one of the most important institutions in the town was the businessmen's coffee hour at Lucille's, one of the three coffee shops closest to the center of the business area of Appleton. "Every day at ten o'clock," I was told, "you won't find anybody in their shops or their offices. *Everybody* is having coffee and discussing the affairs of the town." The owners of the main shops came, and one or two doctors and dentists, a few lawyers, the newspaper editor, the superintendent of schools, the Presbyterian minister, the Catholic pastor, one judge, the chief of police, and a few others. The regular and longest-standing members of this coffee hour even had their own coffee cups with their names inscribed on them. Following is the piece written by the newspaper editor on the occasion of the razing of Lucille's, a few weeks after my departure from Appleton:

Now don't get me wrong. I'm all for progress. And the more the merrier.

But, with progress there always results a bit of the past slipping away. And it often touches a tender spot in those of us who still admit to possessing what many scoff at as "sentimentality."

Because of this, it was with certain pangs of nostalgia, that I heard they were going to tear down Lucille's. That's like reporting that they are going to raze the Lincoln Memorial to build a parking lot.

Granted, Lucille's would never have won an architectural prize. It looks more like a trolley car than a building. But, it does provide a certain amount of contrast along Appleton's main drag.

However, in Lucille's case, looks were unimportant. It's the purpose it served that counts.

Some wives and co-workers look upon Lucille's as a place for their spouses and co-workers to goof off. Not so.

I'll admit that it was a good place to hide from unwelcome visitors or the pressures of business life a couple of times a day, under the guise of "a coffee break."

But that is all window dressing. The real importance of Lucille's was that it served as the hub of Appleton business, legal, social and governmental activity for many decades.

Some days, more business was transacted over a cup of java there than in the stock exchange during a bullish session.

The Jackson County Courthouse may be the seat of the judicial system in this area, but many a court case was settled in Lucille's booths before it ever saw the inside of a legal chamber.

And the problems of the world could always find ready solutions in the steamy confines of Lucille's. Few of those solutions ever reached the floor of the UN, but that's the whole world's loss.

Some of the nation's greatest quarterbacks have frequented Lucille's. Few of them have even set foot on the turf of a gridiron but they didn't have to. Didn't they see all the dumb calls and glaring mistakes the pros made Sunday on television? In Lucille's you didn't have to perform, you just had to be able to talk a good game.

Elections were won or lost in the booths of Lucille's. Bond issues failed or passed. Candidates were nominated and rejected. Local political parties were formed or disbanded.

It was not a place for physical action. There wasn't enough room. But, as a stimulator of intellectual activity, Lucille's had no peer.

But, Lucille's will be gone soon. And when you say you're going out for coffee, they'll have to ask you "Where?"

I wonder if there's an abandoned trolley car sitting around in some vacant field that has aspirations of becoming a seat of learning, a judicial chamber, a stock exchange without ticker tape and a community social room.

If so, the opportunity awaits.

Little more has to be said on the subject except that at the same moment across the street from Lucille's some members of the radically oriented young adults of the town were having their own coffee hour and a similar column could have been written about them. I analyzed the organization of the latter group, and the organization of the businessmen's ruling clique differs little from it. In particular, the cohesiveness of this clique should not be overemphasized. On certain issues serious splits did occur among members; distastes between members and potential members might go to the extreme of the sending of anonymous threatening letters. At a more important level, the businessmen are probably even more internally stratified than the radical groups, both horizontally and vertically. They are unified only from the point of view of being the ad hoc group that participates in the coffee hour. Many of the participants can even look at it with critical eyes, and they will say that this is not where their allegiance stands.

Furthermore, it seems that at the time of my presence in Appleton no one or two persons possessed absolute authority over the group. The situation thus seems to be different from that in "Springdale," Vidich and Bensman's town, where two brokers could be identified. The notion that such could exist was not absent, however; I could make informants discuss among themselves the possibility that such dominant men might be present in certain towns.

The businessmen's group does not exist by right, and it certainly does not possess any reality outside of the people who participate in it. The businessmen and professional people who discussed with determination the political problems of the town at Lucille's did so as independent individuals whose allegiances were, first, to their own small group—which in many cases was not the businessmen—and then to Appleton in general as it impinged on their survival and that of their group. It is in this second role that they had coffee at Lucille's "so that they could know what was going on."

By adopting such a line of argument, I am putting myself at odds with a popular interpretation of small-town government in the United States. I do not believe that what the businessmen's coffee hour reveals is the existence of a cohesive underground government that would, willy-nilly, subvert the principles of democracy. The businessmen/professionals, first, are not cohesive except in very abstract terms. Secondly, they did not govern from Lucille's except insofar as information gained about the intentions of other government agencies implies policy decisions. And, finally, the people who had coffee at Lucille's every morning did not subvert democracy, since it is democracy itself, with its emphasis on maintaining the separateness or independence of the units constituting the administration of the town and, more generally, of the body politic, that obliged them to meet in that fashion.

There are very few occasions in the life of Appleton when communication between groups as such and their official representatives is made possible. There are no easy mechanisms by which the town council can inform the school board of its reaction to a proposed action. For example, the students in the high school requested the right to drive their cars away from school at lunch time. This would have meant a noticeable alteration of the traffic patterns in the town at noon. But the official procedure for notification of the council was cumbersome, and school-board members preferred to speak informally about the thing with council members over a cup of coffee.

A businessmen's coffee hour has no place in the symbolic structure of the town, though it has to appear in order to fill a sociological deficiency in this structure. This deficiency is sometimes recognized consciously by some people in Appleton. Recently, the ecumenical movement in religion has led to the development of "community services" in which several churches participate. These attempts at ecumenism are, however, not understood as a mechanism to coordinate church activities. They are seen, rather, as a way to negate sectarian atomization: during the services absolute unanimity is maintained in outward appearances. The service is planned carefully so that each minister has a chance to participate, and nobody is slighted. But this participation has to be patterned so as not to include any inkling of the theological differences that are known to exist among the churches. If one feels these differences cannot be glossed over, one does not participate.

But while ecumenism is at least thinkable in religion, any similar movement of townwide unification of government agencies would be anathema to most of my informants, even those who might agree that to centralize all services under one administration would be more efficient. It would be anathema because it would lead to a radical transformation of the symbolic expression of the nature of the town. In the place of a difficult union that has to be continually recreated—rhetorically by appeals to togetherness, and practically by informal coffee hours—it would become an entity that stood by itself, "faceless" and "inhuman," since participants would suddenly find themselves irrelevant to its survival.

The Rituals of a Democracy

Nobody has experienced a time when Appleton was an actual community, and it is doubtful that it ever was historically, since it arose spontaneously as a crossroads town rather than as a utopian adventure. At present it possesses none of the characteristics of a community. It is only defined as such, and the only way to maintain this fiction is to affirm it symbolically and ritually in the only activity in which it is a working unit, administration and government.

Some of the easiest things to observe in Appleton, because they are specifically intended for and open to everybody, are the governing agencies at work during their official meetings. After my fourth or fifth evening spent listening to administrative decisions being taken, I came to realize that no actual work was done during these meetings, that nothing was seriously discussed apart from certain points of clarification requested by a member of the board or sometimes by a person in the always very sparse audience. After the normal sentences uttered by the president to open the meeting, the reading of the minutes of the preceding one, and the motion to accept them, the sessions consisted mainly of the reading of proposed motions by the president of the committee involved and the vote on these motions normally without even the brief discussion that sometimes occurred. This pattern routinely prevailed, and it was a very rare case when substantive exchanges could be heard. Negative votes were almost as rare, and if one was not careful one could have come out with the impression that the administration of a town or a county was a very smooth process where unity prevailed. One might also come out dissatisfied, a common feeling among native observers who do not happen to know board members personally.

The second impression is certainly understandable. Administration is not such a simple process, particularly when large amounts of money are concerned. When the administrative unit is relatively large and thus very diverse, far-reaching choices have to be made, and, in fact, sharp disagreements often arise among board members. But all this is buried in private or committee sessions and does not surface in public. Calm and composure are necessary, and if disagreement does occur, the tone remains as subdued in public as it may be violent in private. In private sessions, passions may burst out, direct accusations may be uttered, resignations may be theatrically offered. Very harsh discussions are permitted, and in fact, often occur, as many board members take their responsibilities seriously and can be very picky about the propositions of fellow-members. Even routine decisions are first discussed in private sessions, and the minds of all members are scanned so that the person proposing the motion may be sure that it will be supported. Some critics in Appleton accuse boards of making decisions in private, a very illegal procedure that the boards vehemently deny ever using. In practice, decisions *are* made in private and are simply confirmed and rendered legal in the public meetings.

Administrators are somewhat conscious of this way of proceeding, though they would insist that they are not being evil or hypocritical because they feel there is a need for private and committee sessions. They will say that "problems are so complex that solutions must be discussed at length in a relaxed atmosphere so that one can put one's mind solely to the problem. In public sessions one has to be careful of what one says, and one must spend more time explaining to the audience than doing substantive work. Most people have little knowledge of what it takes to administer any type of agency."

The mayor of a large city close to Appleton once wrote: "It seems to me that, very often, government is more in spite of the people than by the people." The defense of all these administrators is that they never actually make decisions during private meetings, they simply inform themselves on a subject that is supposed to be formally discussed in a public meeting. They are not, nor do they want to be, conscious of the fact that in most cases information means decision.

The real need for a distinction between private and public sessions does not come from anything internal to the process of administration, particularly in the smaller towns. Rather, it is dependent on certain cultural definitions pertaining to the nature of the ritual expression of democracy. The main difference between public and private sessions is that the former are highly ritualized, almost empty of administrative content, though legally compulsory, while the latter are not ritualized, confront problems squarely, and are not compulsory. The relevant distinction that makes the other ones necessary is that strife is common in private but avoided in public. Public unanimity is one of the strongest values one can recognize in local politics. It even overrides substantive matters, and a lot of effort will be spent to assure that it will not be breached even if it implies the covering up of important issues or at least the postponement of their solutions. This distinction between unanimity in public and permissible disputes in private was particularly striking for me because of my experiences in France, where, even in the smallest towns, public meetings of town councils are occasions when differences are stressed, and disunity and segmentation are symbolically enacted.

During the year I spent in Appleton, the school system was deeply split on the subject of the superintendent of schools, whom the teachers thoroughly disliked. A minority on the school board somewhat agreed that even though he was a good administrator he was not a very good leader in educational matters and sometimes might even be an actual hindrance to the establishment of worthwhile programs. This had led to the discussion of whether to ask for his resignation at the end of the first year of the three-year contract he had been given, a decision that was eventually rejected. Little of all this surfaced in public meetings of the school board, particularly nothing on the subject of what amounted to an attempt at firing the superintendent, a very portentous decision.

Troubles continued to brew, and one day the teachers decided through their union to make their grievances public in a particularly sharply worded public letter. This procedure aroused the ire of many people, particularly the newspaper editor, who felt that he had to write the following editorial under the title "The Power Play":

> Collective bargaining in our schools is now an established fact. You may not like it because it disrupts school management and removes teachers from the ranks of the professional. But, it is with us because the state has declared it legal.
>
> Under the collective bargaining procedure there are certain rules you must play by . . . tough, unrelenting rules. Bricklayers, carpenters and yes, even teachers, must play by these rules because they have chosen to play in that kind of ball game.
>
> This week the Appleton Education Association, collective bargaining unit for the teachers, made it plain that they do not intend to play by anybody's rules.
>
> They have apparently chosen, instead, to negotiate by newspaper.
>
> At dinner time Monday, the AEA hand-delivered to us a copy of a resolution denouncing Supt. A. K. and calling

for an investigation of "the educational merits of the decisions and practices of the office of the superintendent."

Tuesday afternoon we were again hand-delivered a follow-up statement from AEA president S. P. containing a long series of charges against the superintendent, some vicious, some vague.

The statement also, in a condescending manner, reported that the teachers "do not appear to have any conflict with the school board," in an all-too-obvious ploy to divide the board from the superintendent and thereby conquer . . . . And this after the AEA's long history of grievances, court suits and charges of unfair labor practices aimed at the board of education! . . .

It is significant to note that this public power play by the teachers' union was not made until Supt. K. had left the community to attend the national school administrators' convention at Atlantic City and would not be here to immediately answer the charges.

It makes the AEA's "unfair practices" charges almost laughable.

We will not defend Supt. K. against the AEA charges. We feel he is perfectly capable of answering them himself . . . when he has the opportunity.

What we are attempting to do here is to chastise a group of probably well-meaning, but ill-advised labor union members that they are not playing the game by the rules.

Their blatantly unethical and blatantly obvious struggle for power can only further damage the public's opinion of the teachers' union and cause serious and irreparable damage to the Appleton school system and the community.

We do not deny the teachers' rights to negotiate for higher salaries, shorter hours, better working conditions, or almost anything . . . but the right to run the school. This is the prerogative of the community, through the school board, and or the superintendent.

The labor union movement is based on two elements—labor and management. Nowhere does it suppose that labor will run the institution and give its orders to the management . . . in this case, the people of the school district.

Even if professionalism went out the window when

collective bargaining came in the school door, there are still certain ethical rules to be followed.

Attempting to negotiate through the newspapers for the power to run the school is certainly not only a violation of those rules, but a trampling of common decency.

Some of these grievances were settled in court, often to the advantage of the teachers. The specifics never surfaced publicly, even though one day it was announced that the school board had accepted the resignation of the superintendent. The paper carried the following story:

Supt. A. F. K. and the Appleton Board of Education have agreed to go their separate ways . . . but the agreement will cost the Appleton School District $15,000. . . .

The meeting, called by School Board President J. O. L. . . . was a well kept secret. The only public notice was a small type-written notice taped to the door of the high school building. . . .

After the meeting was called to order, the board immediately went into executive session for twenty minutes.

When the public session resumed, acting secretary F. W. read an agreement reached between the board and Supt. K., granting him the immediate payment of $15,000 in return for his resignation.

K. immediately submitted a prepared resignation, effective August 1. . . .

In the prepared agreement, the board acknowledged "that no cause, within the meaning of any contractual relationship between the parties exists for the discharge" of Supt. K.

"It is in no way," the board statement said, "caused by doubts or questions as to the professional competence, moral character or integrity" of Supt. K.

"Certain problems have arisen . . . between the parties in their day-to-day relations which have led both parties to conclude that the relationship should terminate."

After the board approved the agreement unanimously, K. submitted a prepared resignation.

"Please know," K. wrote, "that this resignation is submitted only after careful consideration and deliberation on

my part, said resignation being for reasons which I desire
to remain personal between myself and you as members of
the Board of Education."

What this story failed to stress is that the school board actually fired
the superintendent and did not give a valid reason for it.

The reaction of the newspaper to the teachers' complaints is
typical, though certainly more violent in this case than most people
appear to be when they talk about the need for unanimity. Yet in
this case the breach had already occurred, and those who were
responsible for it had to be castigated for the fact that they protested rather than because their complaints were unjustified. The
teachers insisted that they were resorting to this tactic only because
they felt all other avenues were closed to them. What they apparently had not realized is how precarious the superintendent's position had been for a long time before they stated publicly their
opposition to him, a probable result of the discretion with which
the case had been handled until then. The school board members
who opposed the superintendent were content to remain publicly
silent as long as it was clear that they did not have a majority on the
board. They, in fact, believed in the need for unanimity as much as
anybody else, even though the question was portentous, wide-
ranging, and probably worth a public debate. Similarly, once the
majority had shifted, the desire for unanimity remained as strong
as ever on the part of the new minority. In the fall of 1971, the
board had decided "unanimously" to extend the superintendent's
contract for two years. Nine months later, it decided, "unanimously" again, to fire him, not because anybody had changed
his mind but because the majority had shifted after the election of
one new member.

Where did unanimity have to prevail in this case? First, it is
evident that on the substantive matter of knowing whether or not
to fire the superintendent there was great dissent within the school
board, within the school administration—teachers, principals, and
superintendent—and within the town at large. The editor-owner
of the local newspaper was personally rather close to the superintendent and to those on the school board who were on his side. As
his editorial proves, he was very much opposed to the position
taken by the teachers. The people at large had only a very vague
notion that anything was going on. There was a vague dissatisfaction on the part of some of my informants with "the quality of our

schools" and "the way they are run." This was normally related to the fact that in the previous ten years several superintendents had been hired and then fired. For my informants this meant either incompetence on the part of the school-board members, who seemed to be unable to find good candidates, or serious splits within the community, something they did not like to contemplate.

All this was circulated by word-of-mouth, and the different cliques were never formally identified. In other words, the dispute never became a partisan one. The people had no idea of the history of the teachers' formal grievances or their nature, for the teachers accepted the idea that to discuss them was "divisive." But the teachers felt trapped by the hostility of the press and their inability to make their points known. The people had no direct information, either, of the process that led to the dismissal of the superintendent. They learned about it after the fact, and the reasons were never publicly advertised.

Unanimity in government works in two contexts only. First, it is clearly valued by the people involved. They are disturbed by proofs of disunity, and they seem to feel it is a negative reflection on their moral worth as individuals. The other use of unanimity, as I showed earlier, is in the public sessions of governing boards. The goal there is as many unanimous votes as possible, and members of boards are ready to verge on illegality by polling their views informally in private sessions rather than see their disagreements explode in public.

Seen in a wider cultural context, this overwhelming need for public unanimity represents a symbolic enactment of the one-mindedness that I have taken to be typical of the organization of social units in Appleton. The governing boards speak for the people, represent them first and mainly by behaving symbolically according to the proper cultural definition of their roles and of the type of unit they are supposed to represent. It is not enough for an elected official to be a good administrator, he must also be able to recite the myths properly. Thus, even though the town of Appleton is not a "community" at the level of its social organization, the behavior of the boards corresponds to the more general behavior of the people of Appleton in their daily social interaction. The formal organization of government, the makeup of the boards and the rites they perform—all are transformations into different media of the same structure that produces a certain way of telling one's history or a peculiar organization of supportive groups.

Parliamentary Procedure and Civil Religion

Robert Bellah, in his article "Civil Religion in America," points out that the rhetoric surrounding such national occasions as inaugurations or such myths and sacred texts as the Constitution and the writings of the famous figures of American politics implies the existence of what he calls, after Rousseau's definition, a "civil religion." Bellah insists justly that the constant references to God, the "Laws of Nature and of Nature's God," and the transcendent character attributed to the American historical experience cannot be dismissed as having only "ceremonial significance." He points out: "We know enough about the function of ceremony and ritual in various societies to make us suspicious of dismissing something as unimportant because it is 'only a ritual.' What people say on solemn occasions need not be taken at face value, but it is often indicative of deep-seated values and commitments that are not made explicit in the course of everyday life."[4]

It is immediately evident to an observer of America that its political life and ideology probably include a larger element of behavior directly recognizable as "religious" than could be found in most other modern Western nations. This religiosity, in fact, goes beyond references to God or Christianity, for it is "America" itself as an idea that is worshiped. In modern days, among non-Christians or people who have adopted a posture of anticlericalism, the word "God" can easily be replaced by "love" without really changing anything as to the central place given to America as the real transcendental element. But saying this does not detract from the religious quality of the American ideology and its government, or from the value of Bellah's article.

Indeed, Bellah does not go far enough. From an anthropological point of view, a religion is not simply a group of theological beliefs. It is also a set of rituals, and Bellah does not refer to the definite ritual aspect of all *public* governmental activities in the United States. Public meetings are rituals, not only because of their relative uselessness as far as day-to-day government is concerned but also because of their internal structure, their legal character, and the sacred atmosphere that surrounds them.

If the meetings of John's groups are not consciously structured, and if the services of the Protestant churches, though always structured, do vary from church to church and from Sunday to Sunday, the public meetings of government boards are rigidly codified by a set of rules from which no deviation is allowed if the actions taken during the meeting are to be legal, that is, binding on people represented by the board members but not present at the meeting or necessarily personally involved in their existential community. These rules are those which were codified in the nineteenth century by H. M. Robert in his *Rules of Order*. The first edition dates from 1876. There were several revised editions; one of the most recent is by R. Vitman. On the back cover it says that the book deals with "all the problems of running a *successful* meeting *smoothly* and *fairly* [my emphasis]"—another short statement of the ideological attitudes that I have analyzed in the preceding pages. Colloquially, to follow these rules is to use "parliamentary procedures."[5] According to these rules, a proposal first has to be spelled out in a formal manner and in unequivocal language, it has to have the active support of at least one other member apart from the one originating it, a set time is given to a public discussion of the matter so that differences may be aired and considered by uninformed members, and finally the matter is submitted to a majority decision. The keeping of minutes and the fact that a vote has to be taken on the way they are going to be entered in the formal records permits members to check that their feelings or votes have not been distorted by the secretary for his own purposes. Finally, the necessity for a vote to be taken on adjournment implies that the president cannot prevent certain business from being discussed simply by not allowing time to do so. The development of this complex procedure can be seen as a way of ordering unruly debates in large crowds so that everybody can be heard. In smaller groups it may be useful to prevent a minority holding the presidency from illegally imposing its will on the majority. In Appleton, on all the occasions that I observed parliamentary procedure being used, it was useless. In fact, I often had the impression that private sessions when it was not used ran more smoothly, insofar as in public sessions more time was often spent discussing procedural matters than substantive ones. And certainly the absence of parliamentary procedure never prevented anybody from talking.

The real necessity for its use lies somewhere else. It has become indispensable from a symbolic point of view. Even apart from the legal aspect of the matter, parliamentary procedure is used widely in Appleton, not only by governing agencies but also by private clubs, church groups, the Farm Bureau community group, and so on, even when the business dealt with is as unimportant as the next bake sale of the Methodist senior youth group. Parliamentary procedure is symbolic of "democracy"; that is, of the equal participation of all people as individuals. It is another case pointing to the essential isomorphism between the definition of democracy and the definition of the relationship of man to God in the domain of religion, narrowly defined. In both domains I recognize the same dual character of the structure. First, there is an absolute individualism at the level of the definition of the social units, an individualism expressed in politics by the rituals that stress the right of anybody and everybody to participate and particularly to express dissenting viewpoints. It could be said that in American democratic doctrine the individual is considered to be in direct relationship to the whole of society; there is no king or other symbol of the nation whom one must address when one has a grievance or a request. Secondly, there is unanimity and harmony at the level of the definition of the behavior proper among cultural units when they meet.

The use of democratic parliamentary procedure is required by law: no decision of a governing body is binding if it has not been taken in a public meeting ruled by the proper procedure. It is not sufficient that an elected official make a decision; election by itself is not enough. It allows the incumbent to speak in the name of his electorate, but it does not anoint him with an intrinsic power except that of casting a vote in a public meeting. Political decisions receive transcendental existence only through the *united* action of the elected officials. It is the board that possesses the real power; the community, not the individual members. Here again is found the duality between the individualistic definition of the constituent unit and the definition of what makes social action legitimate—a unanimous union. Public meetings are thus a rite, not only because of their practical uselessness—it is possible to administer a complex industrial society by other means—but also because they are symbolic performances.

If parliamentary procedure is used in such unlikely places as church youth groups or the meetings of a Farm Bureau community group or even by a newly formed radical gay liberation group that one of my informants joined, it is not simply because of uninformed sentimentalism or because it is the most efficient way to run meetings. Through parliamentary procedure, individualism is exorcised at the same moment it is glorified. Everybody is assured the possibility to speak his mind, but all must also bow to the decision of the majority after the vote. At this moment atomism has been transcended and—if not "real"—at least actual community established.

CHAPTER 7
Community

Robert Redfield said that social scientists have often seen in communities "integral entities," "units" appropriate for study.[1] From my experience in Appleton, I have to say that whatever substantive definition of community one wishes to adopt, it is evident that this town is not one. The smaller groups of friends and the smaller churches might seem the likeliest candidates for the title of community, but this is stretching the term, since it is generally used to refer to groups larger than a dozen persons or families. And even in the small groups the boundary problems are overwhelming: Where does one community stop and another start? What about unattached individuals? *Appleton is not a community to explore or map out.* Nor is it an aggregate of communities of the sort that could be explored or mapped out. The social organization of the town and its area could best be described using terms other than the traditional ones.

Nor is community or communalism or conformity—whatever one wishes to call it—a value, properly speaking. In many contexts my informants would state that they indeed liked being with their friends, that one feels good at a reunion or party, and that being without friends is the unhappiest of states and/or a negative reflection on the one's character. In other contexts, however, the same informants would say that they "couldn't stand" one or several of the persons seemingly closest to them, that they "didn't know what had gotten into them" or why "they couldn't accept everybody on their own merits." In other words, while community is often valued, it is only insofar as participation in one does not demand a complete overhaul of one's personality. And at the wider levels (the school district, the town, and so forth), where the word "community" is most often used in the loudest and most rhetorical manner in descriptive speeches or to chastise opponents, it is privately accepted that it cannot be achieved anymore (real community is then often projected into the golden age of early frontier days or seventeenth-century New England) because of the influx of strangers "who are not interested in what we are trying to do" or because of "bureaucratic intervention."

It is not simply that the values of community and individualism involve an irreducible tension between agency and responsibility, "doing your own thing" and "caring for your neighbor," so that any choice between alternative courses of action will be an either/or thing or at least more-one-thing-than-the-other. As I pointed out earlier, I believe that, in fact, there is no such opposition between the two ideas.

First, it must be noted that individualism is itself ambiguous. As with community, people often make statements in its favor, generally on the most solemn occasions (sermons, political speeches), but they also recognize that they are not such great individualists, that it is only on very rare occasions that they actually go their own way in the face of universal opposition. The reticence among those I would consider my most reflective informants to boast that they had achieved their ideals might be attributed to modesty. A more cynical interpretation of the evidence might be that what I observed is not individualism and community but rather egoism and conformity. ("My profit comes first, and to ensure it, let's not rock the boat.")

I am not a philosopher or a moralist prepared to settle this issue. Indeed, it is not an issue that can be settled empirically. Nor is it possible to settle empirically which is the primary value: individualism or community. One might devise a method to determine whether a specific choice by a person was oriented to the good of the self (individualism or egoism) or the good of one's neighbor (community or conformism), then count which choice was more prevalent in a person or group of persons and eventually make a statistical statement about the prevalence of one value over the other. But this operation would not determine the nature of American culture unless one were to argue that the method of determining the quality of an act had universal validity, so that only the rate of prevalence could indicate cultural sameness or difference (as it has, indeed, been argued—operationally, at least—by a lot of the research into value-orientation; for example, in the work of Florence Kluckhohn and Fred Strodtbeck).[2]

To argue for the universality of any scale of value-orientation is to go against what I consider to be the fundamental experiences that make the concept of culture necessary in any account of human action: the arbitrariness of symbols and their integration into systems. Any question or series of questions that attempts to determine whether an act is individualistic are meaningful only in the context of a culture where the notion is operative in precisely the way it is operative in the theory that is the basis for the test. If there is no isomorphism between the values of the researcher and the values of the population, the final statement can tell us only how far the population is from the researchers, not what it is in its own terms. What can be established is the fact that there is a difference. What cannot be established is the nature of the difference. Furthermore, insofar as the process of testing assumes the universality of demonstrably arbitrary symbols, it often can help hide the nature of these symbols and foster a false consciousness of their structure and meaning.

No test, then, can determine whether American *culture* is or is not individualistic or whatever. At most a test drawn a priori can tell us how certain Americans behave or think in relation to a certain set of ideals, but a consideration of the wording of the test itself would tell us more about the culture than the responses to it. The test is a total statement, while the responses to it (particularly if it is highly structured) are partial. The test may have been written by only a few persons, but insofar as it is meaningful to their peers, it is of very general validity and an excellent text from which to abstract a structure.

The fact that Appleton is not, at any level, a community never led my informants to doubt the usefulness of the concept or even its fundamental realism. The schools were community schools, the hospital a community hospital. I was introduced in the local newspaper as "someone conducting a year's study of the Appleton community." The word itself was used most frequently where it was most patently obvious that the referent was *not* a community. It was generally used as a synonym for town, and I have shown how the town is really only a location, a place in which people live, but not a unit, voluntary or otherwise. The community of the schools is even more abstract. The town is only a part of the school district (though townspeople have a tendency to see it as the dominant part) that includes large rural areas that are in conflict with the town and its merchants. As for the hospital district, it exists only for its administrators.

The churches would not label themselves community

churches. It is only when several joined together that a service could be called a community celebration. Each church would consider its congregation to be a "community," and yet a distinction is made. Being a community—and many churches are more communities than the town—is not the same thing as being a community organization. What is behind the distinction is a difference in the inclusiveness of the unit, a difference in the referent of the "everybody" who is the community. Everybody is taxed to support the school, the hospital, the town. Everybody is expected to contribute to the support of the Methodist church, and everybody is invited to the dances that the group of friends I investigated put on once a year.

Obviously the everybodies referred to are not the same: the boundaries of the districts vary geographically (the town, school, and hospital districts do not cover the same areas) and hierarchically (the church congregations are subsets of the geographical districts). The geographical variations are not considered relevant. There is a community to the hospital as there is to the school, and the fact that the former includes many more people than the latter is not marked symbolically. The town is even smaller in comparison, but it is not a subset. It is not even, as it would be in France, for example, a synecdoche of the area—that part of a whole used to represent that whole in a poetic metaphor.

The town, school, and hospital districts stand side by side as units of the same order. What they share is the literal manner in which the word "everybody" is taken: everybody (over twenty-one at the time of my study) may vote, everybody is taxed (according to ability, as measured by property or income)—*all* human organisms. The "community" is the sum of all these organisms. It is because it is a sum that variation in geographical area is irrelevant. As long as literally everybody is made to participate in an activity, however small the number of persons involved (as in the Johnson Community) or however large (the federal government is a community organization—theoretically at least!), then one can talk of a community institution.

The fact that the universality of these communities is enforced by the law—that is, everybody may vote and everybody must pay—gives them a character different from that of other institutions where freedom of participation is the rule. Some would argue that the town was, like the nation, "conceived in liberty and dedicated to the proposition that all men are created equal." But that was "fourscore and seven years ago," in the Golden Age. Others would argue cantankerously that those who didn't like the town could always leave it. A few did. But the nature of participation in this level of community remains, and there, obviously, lies the fundamental difference between it and the other levels.

The next level is consciously seen as consisting of subsets of the other communities. It is the level of the recognized voluntary associations (churches and clubs, mostly). They are not officially recognized as communities, since they exist only in the interstices of the polity. They concern those areas of one's life where one is still free to choose the people with whom one wants to associate after one has made the more fundamental choice of living in Appleton. The lower levels, those of friendships and family, are not recognized as communities in the same manner.

Yet, as I have tried to demonstrate, it is only at these lower levels that the ideal is lived, that the reality of the social experience is closest to the structure of the native interpretation of this world: John's group *was* "conceived in liberty." This is where the culture is least a matter of mere ritual, because the socioeconomic pressures are weakest and the people can act on their lives to make them fit their ideology. This is why, to me, these voluntary and noninstitutionalized associations are paradigmatic of the American experience. There can be seen the structure of the culture in behavior as clearly as one can see it in the ritual and mythical statements of broader units.

Furthermore, the broader units are structured in the same manner, even though they are not what my informants would consider "real" communities—even if they were so named—and beyond the fact that the dialectic of universality and segregation is handled differently there from the way it is handled in the smaller units. The town and the school district do not possess anything else than the ad hoc reality that resides in the fact that all people with Appleton addresses are members of the same administrative unit, have to obey the same rules and regulations, and have to deal with the same bureaucrats. The intermediate groups I talked about earlier possess the same type of ad hoc reality. The structure does not require that these particular groups exist, and it does not change whatever actual groups are present in any particular place.

The business/professional men (who are mostly moderate Protestants), the fundamentalists, the Polish, the hippies, and so on exist side by side but not in relation to one another, and this is probably why such a very wide diversity of life-styles and ideologies can, in fact, be found in the town. The businessmen may "rule" it, but they do not hold their power by virtue of their social position. They rule because the ideological definitions used by the other groups to account for themselves do not include participation in community affairs. Not far from Appleton, in a university town, radical youths decided they would become involved. They succeeded in having some of their own number elected and passed an ordinance lowering penalties for marijuana possession or smoking that went even beyond the state statutes. Thus, one could say that the businessmen who happened to dominate Appleton when I was there did not have real power but only a semblance of power that was given to them provisionally and that could be taken from them. In particular, whatever political power the businessmen may have had, they certainly had no ideological power. Fundamentalist Protestants on the one hand and hippies on the other (to quote only those groups who were most equal with the ruling clique) were not simply antiestablishment, oppressed minorities, they were also strong and defiant and flaunted their alternate life-styles with what amounted to total impunity. The ruling clique could at best shake their heads in disapproval and mourn.

In Appleton—and, I suspect, in any town of the same size or larger—the absence of culturally defined norms as to the proper composition of society leads to the possibility of small groups adopting ideological positions from an indefinite range. Because American culture *is* one, each new group will organize itself along similar structural lines: individualism, one-mindedness, diffuse and enduring solidarity. The famous paradox of what is called the "diversity" of the United States and the fact that it is almost impossible to distinguish town from town or church from church can probably be resolved following this approach to the problem. What is "the same" is not a certain ideology or religious faith, not the Protestant ethic, democracy, rugged individualism, inner- or other-direction, but a certain manner of perceiving how relationships between human beings are ordered. What is different and diverse is the *content* of these relations.

Furthermore, groups are defined in much the same way human beings are, with a stress on their independence, uniqueness, and differences. I showed in the first part of this book how the human situation is considered to be basically nonsocial, human beings not being defined as existing in relation to other human beings but in themselves, substantively. Thus the humanity of man is a natural quality, while his joining society is problematic, has to be consciously organized, and thus is a cultural process. Similarly, the identity of any group, at whatever level of the social organization of the town, is not defined as depending on its relationships with other groups. Groups are independent of one another, and the little amount of real communication that exists between them can be seen as a corollary of this independence. In practice, groups have to actually interrelate with other groups, if only symbolically, to establish their uniqueness. They do not, however, consider that they exist *because* of these interrelationships, and in that sense they remain simply aggregated one to the other, independent and thus individualistic.

The larger groups in Appleton had little interactional existence. Like categories of kin, such groups as the farmers, the professionals, the teenagers often had a cultural reality as a part of the way the world is, but they were not used as an integral part of the code or model that a person would use to pattern his interactions with others. The model is that of freedom of choice. Which is why, in spite of characteristics that make the social structure look like a segmentary one, or even a caste system, endogamous and closed, it must be understood as precisely the reverse. The categories have no reality. They are necessary, however, to give the illusion of movement. They are there to be transcended, not to be used as a framework for action. There are no interaction rules concerning what each group must do; no prescriptive, preferential or prohibitive rules of marriage, for example, no formalized patterns of exchange.

Indeed, when there are rules, in the legal system, for example, they are intended to assure that the independence of the units is preserved and that mutual contracts entered into by units are drawn around the needs of the business to be accomplished and not the nature of the units. In actual situations, when the nature of the units cannot help but enter into the process of interaction, the pragmatic solution is to limit interaction. If there is no interaction, there will be no unpleasantness. This is another way to deny that there is an inescapable content to community, that it is not simply human beings together, but certain human beings doing certain things. Without interaction, the fiction of universality is maintained.

Of course, the fact that persons, as individuals, choose their friends and the activities to be used in the definition of their selves does not mean that there are no socioeconomic biases in the determination of whom to like or what to do. It is not really a matter of chance if the majority in John's group have an ethnic bacground and hold white-collar jobs or if all the members of the school board were at one point drawn from the business and professional ranks. I could indeed agree with Marxist critics of American life that the type of individualism I have been describing increases the possibility of the creation of groups along sociological lines.[3] What my analysis does challenge is the idea that socioeconomic determinisms are the primary motors of the cultural perception of stratification in the United States, when it is so clear that the motors are psychological. Very often, in fact, political or religious ideas play a more important role than socioeconomic ones to create a sort of horizontal stratification within the traditionally identified vertical strata.

The model behind the empirical social relationships observed in Appleton in particular, and probably the United States in general, is thus made up of the freedom of the person to join other persons with whom to exchange equally at a chosen level. In native terms, "individuals" create "communities" by congregating with other individuals whom they decide to consider as similar to themselves. One of the clearest statements I have found of that structure is by John Dewey, who, when he succinctly summarized what he perceived to be the structure of all societies, expressed what I feel is the central organizing theme in the *American* perception of society:

> Men live in communities in virtue of the things which they
> have in common; and communication is the way they come
> to possess things in common. What they have in common in
> order to form a community or society are aims, beliefs,
> aspirations, knowledge, a common understanding, like-
> mindedness as the sociologists say."[4]

Dewey restates here in an abstract manner the process that I believe to have been followed by John and his friends, by the Farm Bureau, and by the social organization that resulted from it. None but a very few of my informants had any knowledge of American social thought beyond what they had learned, and quickly forgotten, in high school. And yet they lived this structure in all its implications. Dewey, as a twentieth-century philosopher, felt he had to invoke science and refer to what "sociologists say" to ground his insight. What they say, according to him, is that society is a purposeful, individualistic process. This is a controversial issue. In traditional, or at least continental, European sociology, the relation would be reversed: men have aims, beliefs, aspirations in common because they live in a community. Society is greater than its parts, as Durkheim said.

It is not necessary to decide who is "right," metaphysically speaking, Dewey or Durkheim. What is interesting to me here is the fact that a difference is possible and that it is easier to understand American social structure when it is seen as a result of voluntary choice. The statistically visible segmentation of the society into such things as ethnic groups or social classes is more the *result* of passivity and indifference than of activity and discrimination. If I were to draw a visual model of the social structure of the town, it would look something like the accompanying diagram.

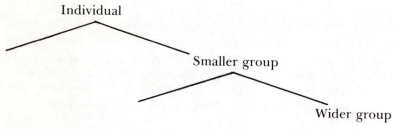

It is the individuals who create the smaller groups, and the smaller groups who generate larger groupings or identifications. Individuals, then, are in hierarchically superior positions to groups, communities, and societies, large or small.

To say this is to speak about something somewhat different and more precise than freedom of choice, as I have often referred to it, partially because this is what many natives call it. It is not necessarily that individuals are free in a metaphysical sense. It is rather that no boundary is set by the culture on the movements that they may make or may try to make—since final acceptance depends on others—within the society. Freedom is also aimlessness—*"nothing* to lose," as the popular song says, because one has nothing to begin with. There is a distinct irony here, for this form of freedom cannot be escaped. The very attempt to escape from it would be considered to be itself a "free" movement. It therefore comes very close to being one of the most extreme forms of authoritarianism.

Community, then, refers to a certain way of perceiving the relationship between human beings, a peculiar manner of defining society that is itself dependent on a certain definition of the units involved. I emphasized at the end of the first part of this book how defining the fundamental unit of society as the individual organism begs the question of the constitution of society: Will self-interest always lead people to accept any order imposed from the outside? Community refers to the type of order that they do accept, when they do.

Thus community and individualism are not in conflict; they are intimately integrated into one system of unit-definition and relationship-definition. Each implies the other; each is, in a certain sense, a restatement of the other. Indeed, community does not answer the question I asked. It is the result of the coming together of the individuals, but it does not bridge the gap. Is there something that mediates between the individuals and the actual groups that they form when they get together, something that partakes of both without being subsumed under either? I believe I have found this mediating term in notions that I will summarize under the heading of "love."

Individualism, Community, and Love

Enduring, diffuse solidarity, or love . . . is doing what is good or right for the other person, without regard for its effects on the doer.
—David M. Schneider, *American Kinship: A*
                                          Cultural Account

"Love is a Many-Splendored Thing"
—title of a television soap opera,

Introduction

"A dream! a Dream! I don't want to be alone! I want to know that I am loved!" Allen Ginsberg's cry in his poem "Who Be Kind To" echoes precisely the main themes of American culture: individualism, freedom, loneliness.[1] The first two elements can be positively stressed until a voice is raised arguing that total reliance on them leads to a third element, loneliness, a dreaded plight to be exorcised by almost whatever means, particularly the relinquishment of the very freedom one was born with, the melting of one's individuality into a group, a society, a community. *A* society, not Society; the difference is portentous. The individuality of the human person, however, is only apparently rejected by the call for friendship. The very word friendship is significant with all its implications of personal involvement with another person. In a community, one is face-to-face with a few other concrete persons. There is no possibility for the sort of abstract involvement that can remained detached from actual intercourse that is possible when the responsibility an individual carries to "care" is translated into participation in political reform movements. To distance oneself from intercourse is to be cold, hard, ruthless, and to cast suspicion on the sincerity of the effort.

Not that political action or the mere contribution of money to charitable causes (another form of care) is a negligible aspect of human life. But with such actions must go the actualized recognition that the person next door, the neighbor in the Christian sense, needs a friend to survive. He needs a friend now, personally, and his problems are not going to be solved by the actions of any men on society as a whole. Political involvement or charitable contributions do not solve the tragedy of the human situation. What is needed is private help; two or three friends or simply a boy or a girl to love. And insofar as everybody needs friends, there is a con-

163

comitant and quasi-religious responsibility for every person to offer friendship, to become personally involved with lonely people, to love them.

Allen Ginsberg's poem follows just this pattern. The narrator of "Who Be Kind To" offers first a grim picture of a world of abstract suffering and distant machines to whom we are asked to "be kind" until the cry for personal love, which I quoted, makes it clear that it is not really possible to do so, that we by ourselves will not have enough strength to succeed in being kind to this world. We cannot relate directly to the world, because it leaves us alone, in need of someone to love and to be loved by. To cope with the world, one needs to enter into a direct relation with one other person and exchange equally, communicate. What "I," the narrator of the poem, need and want is "our" flesh, "desire given and returned," in a sexual embrace.

By way of comparison, in Jean-Paul Sartre's *Nausea*, the disgust of the hero is caused by an observation of *human* society, not in its material or technological aspects but in its strictly human—I might say cultural—aspects. By the end of the book the hero has destroyed his last two links with society, his historical study and a long-standing affair with a girl in Paris. Both of these, like all other forms of social behavior he observed, were meaningless. He is finally alone, the apparent solution since no other is offered than total withdrawal from interpersonal relationships, not only from Society but also from any small-scale personal society, or community. The individual stands alone, in a gesture that reminds one of Lucien's challenge to Paris at the end of Balzac's *Le Père Goriot: "À nous deux maintenant!"* Lucien, at this stage of his career, is more optimistic than Roquentin at the end of *Nausea,* but his solution to his problem is the same. It is not grounded in the building of an alternate society. It is grounded in action, confrontation, whatever the dangers of personal destruction might be.

For someone like Sartre, Society (and I must capitalize the word) is the enemy. A voluntary society, a community, might be even more dangerous since involvement in such a society must be total and thus destructive of what for him would be "true" individualism. For my informants this was not a problem. The problem was: How do we maintain our fragile communion with our friends? They may have more experience of voluntary societies and know how difficult it is, in fact, to maintain them through time. Thus the emphasis on the search for truer communion and the importance of an understanding of "love" and concomitant concepts in any work on American culture.

Surprisingly, this has not yet been widely recognized in American sociology. David M. Schneider is still the only one to have systematically studied the concept, and only in relation to the domain in which it is most obviously relevant, kinship. But his work has certainly opened the door to further analyses of the concept, the central place of which should be evident to any observer of American culture who is willing to go beyond the boundaries artificially assigned to scholarly social science. It would indeed be remiss of me not to talk about such subjects as happiness, fun, or love, which came up so often in the conversations I overheard or had with my informants. A description that calls itself anthropological implies something about totality, at whatever level this totality is made to work. My informants created texts in many domains other than social organization, religion, or politics, which are the main staples of sociological discourse about America.

I am going to proceed with my discussion in the same manner I have used for the first two parts of the book and start with an example of the way in which one particular love story developed in Appleton. This should offer evidence that definitions that might appear to operate only at very abstract levels relate also to actual behavior that is intensively lived by many people most of the time.

The love story is that of John Lawrence and Sue Elliott, members of the small group of friends whose organization I explored in chapter 4. After having followed the intricacies of this drama, I will generalize their experience. This will lead us to review certain aspects of the social organization of the town that I glossed over before.

CHAPTER 8
An American Love Story

James Boon stated in a recent article on the concept of culture:

> Analysing ritual and symbolic behavior does not necessarily reveal the specific "needs" of the participants. They might just generally need "to get away from it all" or to feel near the "source" of it all (cf. Durkheim's "sacred"), whatever *it* is—vague "action-values" indeed! It is difficult to be sure if participants are in fact infused with meaning at such times. But we can analyse their forms to detect what sorts of meaning they might be infused with if they were.[1]

Indeed, one would agree that it is easier, and certainly morally less controversial, to analyze "empty" but structured ritual forms somewhat formally and coldly than it is to do the same in situations where one cannot deny that the participants are involved with the whole of their beings, when it is evident that they are at the breaking point of their personal lives.

How can one avoid being embarrassed about using information that was gathered in the most difficult moments of the participants' lives, when their defenses were at their weakest? And how can one pretend not to be personally involved at such moments? I was, of course, deeply involved in the situation I am going to describe. It was a difficult situation for the four main protagonists, since they were playing the fundamental drama of their culture: the assertion of the individuality of a grown-up child through a break with one community and the creation of a new one. In more concrete terms, this is the story of the departure from home of the third daughter and last child of a farm couple, and of her marriage to a man her parents did not like.

Eventually I am going to analyze the situation in terms of the structure of the symbols manipulated. I will try to show, as Lévi-

Strauss would say, "behind the manifestations of affective life, the indirect effect of alterations that took place in the normal course of the operations of the intellect [my translation]."[2] The situation, however, had strong affective overtones. So I will first give a history of the tragedy, soap opera, or love story, using the participants' own words as much as possible to give the flavor, rather than the structure, of this slice of Appleton life. Let this stand, then, as my apology to those who, with Gaston Bachelard, do not believe that one can "measure the diameter of life" without killing it.[3]

In Love

The story begins in June 1970, on a night when John Lawrence, completely drunk, was roaming through town with some of his friends in search of something or someone. He had by then "reached bottom" after having drifted further and further into the hippie and drug culture. ("I tried anything that did not need a needle.") He had been divorced the year before and had quit a well-paying, high-prestige job as personnel manager of an aluminum-casting factory ("I had more than a hundred people under me") because "I was getting crazy, just could not stand the pressure anymore." Since then, he had just been drifting, mostly out of work or in menial, unskilled, blue-collar jobs. ("It was one coninual party at my place, and we were constantly high.") However, John said: "I was getting more and more tired of one-night girls, but there seemed to be no hope."

One night he happened to pass Sue Elliott and decided with drunken determination that "I want to know this girl." So he and his friends asked around town to find out who she was and discovered that she worked as a nurse's aide in the hospital. They went there to pick her up. "By that time," said John, "I was completely scared, so I sent Cathy, one of the girls whom we were with, into the hospital—we were all drunk—to ask Sue if she wanted to go to a party." Cathy said: "I can still remember walking into the reception room of the hospital—you know, the nurse looked at me as if I was mad and asked me not to speak so loud. But she went and got Sue." Sue accepted the invitation. ("I thought, Why not? It might be fun.") And she was picked up at the end of her shift.

The details of the party are of no consequence, but John's attitude is: "I was just gross, treated her like dirt. I did not know what I was doing. The next morning I realized it, and I was sure she would not want to see me anymore, but I thought I should call and apologize for my behavior. That is what I did." Later he went to the Elliott's farm to talk with Sue and see how "she really felt." Sue remembers the disapproval in her father's voice when he told her there was somebody outside who wanted to talk to her but did not want to come in. She and John talked for more than an hour in his car: "John apologized, asked me to go out with him again, and said that nothing like this would happen again. I was dubious, but I accepted."

Sue and John soon started to see a lot of each other, and somehow her parents learned of it. They decided at first that John was a "good influence on Sue." This impression probably derived from the fact that she decided to go back to school. Mr. Elliott had his first long talk with John. John's interpretation, in a moment of depression, was: "At that time I was the good guy, they could use me, I was going to straighten out their daughter for them and disappear." Mr. Elliott told me, one of the first times we talked about John, that "John has a really nice personality, he is very sensitive to other people and very likable. And he also has had some painful experiences. He has been a good influence on Sue, but they both have a lot more growing up to do."

Mr. Elliott had learned almost at once, long before Sue had the courage to tell him, that John was divorced from his first wife, by whom he had two children, and perhaps he had also found out about the rather wild life John had been leading. At least he believed that John had some "psychological problems" and that he needed professional help. Sue herself had been seeing a psychologist. Nobody in the family would say they "really believed in psychotherapy," but it was the first solution that came to mind when they were confronted by a personal problem that would not go away. The romance progressed, with ups and downs. By November, Sue had gotten to the point of seeing John every night or so after work, and perhaps she was already seeing him every morning "to have coffee," as I later discovered they were doing.

It was at this time that John confided in me for the first time. We were driving out to the Elliotts' to pick Sue up, and I expressed my admiration for the way Sue had spent Christmas Day sewing two dresses she was going to give as presents (one to a friend and the other to her sister-in-law). It had been one of those occasions that prove the uselessness and danger of statistical classification: Was Sue conservative, radical, liberal? On that day, not only would she have warmed the heart of a conservative by giving proof that the traditional values of America were still alive, but she also presented a deliciously quaint picture, with her long blond hair flowing over the pieces of material she was sewing, framed by a background of bright sun on fresh snow.

I risked saying to John that she would make a good wife, even though the subject had never been discussed before in front of me. John looked even more thoughtful than he had before, and he said: "I guess she would. . . . We have talked about it several times, she would like for us to marry, but I am not sure I ready to make the jump . . . I want to be completely straightened out before I commit myself again. . . . I do not want to cause pain to Sue, and I think I would if we married soon. . . ." He was worried and serious, quite a different person from the life-of-the-party John that I knew best.

On that Christmas Day, John had been invited by the Elliotts to share their holiday meal. He had called to say that he was feeling sick—which everybody understood to be an excuse—and the atmosphere was somber. Suddenly Mrs. Elliott told me: "Sue is sad, and I think it is because John is not here. Why don't you take your car and go ask John to come? Do not say anything to anybody else, so that they can think he did it on his own." In his apartment, John was just lying on his couch, alone, watching TV, apparently very depressed, and I had no difficulty convincing him to go with me. I came to talk about his relationship with Sue as we were driving back. The rest of the evening appeared relaxed enough, but soon afterward, the crisis exploded as the tensions became too great to be concealed under the veil of politeness that had hidden them up to that time.

During the following week, I had long talks with both Mr. Elliott and John about their fears. Mr. Elliott elaborated on the theme: "I do not want John to think I have anything against him *personally*. In fact, I like him very much, he is very sensitive and understands people very well. But I think that Sue sees John too often, and if it goes on like this, it will end with an early marriage."

Mrs. Elliott had a slightly different interpretation. "John is a nice guy, but he is not up to Sue. He is not intellectual like we are, and his friends are not, are they? I do not understand why Sue keeps falling for guys like that. She has such great abilities to learn, and if she just wanted to try, she would succeed better than Cathryn. But she always had an inferiority complex towards her sister and wants to believe she cannot do as well. It was like this in high school, but she always brought back the most incredible people. I know she is unhappy at home and wants to punish us to prove her independence. She does not really like these guys, she just wants to get out of here. That is why she is always with John and doing things for him. She wants somebody to mother. That is all it is. But guys do not like that, and one day he will just throw her out like that other guy did, and she will be unhappy."

The Elliotts were hurt. John and Sue were hurt. It could be said that communication had broken down between Sue and her parents. From another point of view, the amazing thing to me was the amount of communication that was going on. Father/daughter, mother/daughter, father/mother, daughter/boyfriend, even father/boyfriend—all of them were continually talking to each other, each rationally trying to explain his or her point of view to the other and, for the time of the exchange, banding together against the absent ones with a pretense of objectivity and confidentiality.

I myself was an appreciated interlocutor, and all the people involved (Mr. Elliott and John, particularly; Mrs. Elliott and Sue more rarely) explained their positions to me! I might have acted in a more conscientiously professional manner if I had not intervened, but this was not humanly possible. Without my intervention, the affair might have ended differently. However, I do not believe that this intervention prevented my informants from handling the situation in their own way. So although I was not present at their private conversations, I have an idea of how they proceeded. They always followed the same quasi-ritual form. They would take place in the kitchen after a meal, or any other place where the participants could be "naturally" alone; that is, without a conscious decision on their part, which, I guess, would have been embarrassing.

When the participants wanted to confide in me, conversations would remain general for a while—we would talk about the weather, cars, politics—then there would be a long silence during which I would start to leave, only to be brought back by an apparently innocent question, such as "How do you think John has been feeling lately?" This would be followed by another silence and a cautious statement on my part: "Well, I don't know. He has been looking kind of depressed, but. . . ." Quite an understatement!

At first I was not at all sure how much I could disclose of what had been told to me under the understanding that, of course, I would not repeat it. But I soon found that (1) respecting this injunction would lead me to cut myself off completely from one side; (2) everybody else usually broke these understandings; (3) my giving a favorable interpretation of the other side's point of view helped dissipate some of the misunderstandings.

On the day that Mr. Elliott realized that John would break down if he and his wife insisted that the couple stop seeing each other, and also that John would become even more set against them than he already was, Mr. Elliott said: "I do not know what to do to make it clear to him that I have nothing against him, that I like him." In many implicit and explicit statements he showed that he disagreed with his wife on the subject of intellectualism. He did not really consider it important whether Sue finished college or went into an academic discipline. He differed on this quite significantly from Mrs. Elliott, whose main objection against John was that he had no college education and that he would prevent Sue from getting one.

A few months went by, with periods of peace interspersed with periods of tension, and in the background the interminable conversations continued. John and Sue decided that they would get married soon, and one day Sue tried to tell her parents about it. There was no outburst, but she did not have the courage to tell them the contemplated date, probably using the rationalization that it was not completely settled between John and herself. Her parents said: "All right, if that is what you want. But we want to be sure you are sure. Why don't you wait a couple of years, and if you still want to get married then, we won't be opposed. But we think it would be a serious mistake for you to marry soon. In the meantime, you should meet other boys and widen your experiences." None of them had moved an inch from the positions they had held at the beginning of the winter, and there was no solution in sight. John and Sue continued to talk of the end of June for their wedding, although they had not made any actual preparations.

Before going into the next act, I should give some background of the situation at the time. Sue was all but living at John's place, waking him up in the morning before going to work, and staying with him in the evening from the time she came back from work until ten or eleven o'clock. ("I have to leave now, my parents are going to worry." "Why don't you stay a little longer?" A daily battle.) Sometime during this period, John left the job he then had at a cement factory, and decided to try laying tile and redecorating bathrooms as a business, something that appeared feasible at the time. He appeared calmer and more balanced, less prone to wild and desperate acts; in particular, he had stopped experimenting with hard drugs and limited himself to smoking pot or hash when it was offered to him. This was partly due to Sue's influence; though she agreed to smoke, she said she disliked the idea. ("Why is it we *have* to do it? People do not give you a choice.") It was accepted by John that after their marriage there would be no drugs "because you cannot have both."

John and Sue decided that they would elope; that is, not say anything to anybody, though afterward it developed that this was mostly to prevent John's family from making a big affair of it, which would shame the Elliotts. The couple knew that the Elliotts would be difficult, and they thought it best not to mix the two families, their different styles, and their different opinions concerning the marriage, too soon. John's family liked Sue, thought she would be a good influence on John, and left it at that, from what I understood; I did not gather good information on them.

Everybody else (Sue's and John's everybody; that is, the friends in the group) knew about the contemplated move. They were told that John and Sue wanted the wedding to be completely private, except for their closest friends, who agreed because "everybody is free to do whatever they like. If you do and say what you really feel, if you are honest about it, there is no reason to be mad about what the other guy does." Sue and John passed the medical examination, applied for the marriage license, and asked the district court judge to perform the marriage in his office. They both regarded this judge very highly, considering him "fair," "open-minded," "intelligent," and "antiestablishment." The first of Sue's dresses was hung in John's closet.

The wedding date approached. At the last minute, John and Sue decided that they would tell her parents about it the night before. At 8:00 P.M. that night, they stopped at my apartment, solemn, nervous, and worried. The time for joking had passed; they were gathering all their courage, felt they were going to have a very hard time, but were determined to go through with it. Sue summarized her feelings with particular sharpness: "I wish they would not take it like that." She had no doubts as to the way they were going to take it, and she was right. Two hours later, Mrs. Elliott knocked on my door, more tense than I had ever seen her, and speaking very quickly about the weather—even in this circumstance, she would not violate the code according to which one never starts a conversation with the business one is really on. She sat on the couch, asked me: "You know about it, don't you? John and Sue are getting married tomorrow." And she started to cry.

"I do not understand why Sue does things like this, She is bright, and she could get the best, but she is always punishing herself. She does not love John. It is just like that other guy she thought she loved. Mitch. While they were going together, it was Mitch and only Mitch, the great love. When he left her, she forgot him right away. If she just waited, it would be the same thing with John. No, she does not love John [I tried to interrupt], she cannot love him. She just wants to punish us and to punish herself. You cannot convince me that it is anything else." She went on like this for twenty minutes and then left.

Ten minutes later, John and Sue arrived, depressed and almost as much in need of comforting as Mrs. Elliott had been. At first they were too stunned to say anything, then I slowly got the story. ("It was just horrible.") They had first gone into the house where Mrs. Elliott was alone—Mr. Elliott was in the barn, milking—and announced it to her. Apparently she did not say much, just started crying. Sue said: "She made me feel so bad for doing something like that to her." Mrs. Elliott went to her room, telling John and Sue to tell her husband, she could not. So John and Sue went to the barn—one can imagine the state they were in. They told Mr. Elliott, which started a storm. ("I've never seen my father so mad, he was throwing buckets around, shaking his fist.") John said: "I thought he was going to hit me, and I did not know what I would do, I just tried to stay out of his way."

Sue said: "He started by saying 'I give up on all you kids!' and then went on to recapitulate how all of us had somehow or other not turned out to be what he expected, and to have repeatedly gone against his will and to have fought with our mother." John said: "He also went back again to his own marriage, and the mistakes he had made, the frictions with his wife. I don't understand why he brings that up all the time." Mr. Elliott went on for more than an hour and concluded: "You ask me to give my blessing to this marriage. Well, I do not. But you go ahead and do whatever you please, you do not need my blessing."

The following day, John and Sue were married. Mrs. Elliott was present—and she cried. For a short while afterward, communication was completely broken. But soon the parents came to John and Sue's apartment; they offered their help, which was accepted, and almost daily intercourse was resumed (through telephone calls, dropping in, Sunday dinners, and so on), and it has continued for the last years.

A Time to Destroy and a Time to Create

The preceding is a sort of drama improvised by four persons. It is an essentially unique performance, like all improvisations, and yet it is revealing of a style and can be analyzed to reveal the mechanisms that make this style distinctive. What are the elements of this style? How are they interrelated?

"Why can't my parents let me be who I am?" "Why can't she see that he is not like us?" The struggle is over the location of the "I" of Sue. Her parents see her as "us," a member of their community. Without their daughter, they know, their life will not be the same. They have lost their other children to marriage and education. Informants generally emphasize the positive characteristics of freedom of choice in community building, but joining a new group implies having left another group, and this original group may not wish the old member to be gone. It is necessary for the new group to accept the prospective member. But the old group may be hurt by the person's departure and be unwilling to let him go, particularly if the person is considered constitutive of the character of the group, as parents almost always consider their children to be.

The Elliotts did not want Sue to leave them, and they were hurt that she should try to do so. However, they could not argue that she belonged to them by right or duty. They could say only that she was more like them than she was like John, and thus, rationally speaking, ought to continue participating in *their* community. Sue, on her part, was ambivalent. She was not sure she was that different from her parents, but she knew that in an indefinable manner she was close enough to John to want to participate in *his* community. For John there was no dilemma, but there was a fear that Sue would accept her parents' arguments and abandon him, even though he felt he needed her to make his community complete. To this extent he was in the same structural position as Sue's parents: he depended on Sue to complete his self.

Neither the Elliotts nor John could see themselves as complete without Sue. But they were all staying put and thus were not confronted by the dilemma that confronted Sue: she was moving and responsible. But she was not simply moving *away from*; she was also moving *to*. She could not remain alone. It was either her parents or John (or, of course, any other man). It could not be either community or noncommunity. She wanted to be herself, but she did not want to do this by herself.

In other words, though the units of society are individuals, and though society is seen as involving a constant "free choice" on their part, individuals cannot remain alone. Smoking pot and dressing like a hippie may be immature or evil, but these activities are not so pathological, abnormal, or dangerous as living by oneself alone in the woods. Many anthropologists have argued that the dangerous can easily be transformed into the sacred; Thoreau's famed year in the woods by Walden Pond is a sacred moment in the history of individualism, even though it is not a proper model for life. Indeed, Thoreau himself soon moved back to the town he visited regularly during his symbolic retreat.

It could be said that individuals are dependent. But this is not the way the protagonists in the drama put it. Individuals *love and take care of*. They are concerned *for*; they are turned *toward* the other person; they give. However, as anthropologists have known since Marcel Mauss, a gift, however altruistically given, always coerces the receiver into accepting and later returning it. Mr. Elliott's angry reaction "I give up on all you kids" can be understood only in the context of a gift not accepted. Mrs. Elliott, for her part, felt the gifts had been returned but in a grotesquely inverted manner. ("Sue is bright, she does so well in school, we'd support her through her years in school, as far as she would want to go," but "she punishes herself and punishes us.") Even in her marriage, Sue does not simply *do*, she does *to* (herself and her parents).

Society is indeed the product of the movement of free agents toward other free agents. It is this movement toward—love, as I will refer to it—that I will explore in the following pages.

CHAPTER 9
Happiness and Fun: A Further Analysis of John and Sue's Love Story

In the preceding pages, I have introduced a mode of interpretation of such an event as John and Sue's marriage that probably demands further elucidation. I will argue that John, Sue, and her parents, at the very moment when they felt most in control of their own lives—though, of course, not of the lives of the other protagonists—were also most determined by that type of sociological force that I am calling cultural. They were improvising a play they had never performed before. But if they were free to articulate the incidents of the drama in whatever fashion they thought appropriate, the theme of the drama, the structure of its plot, and the very need to perform it was imposed on them. They could not escape living this particular experience. And yet this experience does not derive in any simple way from biological determinisms, though it is obviously also about puberty and sex. Nor does it derive from narrowly defined sociological pressures, though it was certainly also about status and economic survival. It is rather an aspect of the peculiar definitions of society and marriage that American culture imposes on the people who live it.

One might wonder, of course, what the exact relevance of the case is. I would not argue that it is typical—few families of my acquaintance were so intensely introspective as the Elliotts. I might argue that it is "tautological"; that is, that all the elements that make situations meaningful in American culture are present in the drama. I hope that this will be more convincing after I have explored in more detail the correspondences that exist between this situation and others. Initially, it is of interest to me because it is an elaborate text improvised by the participants in a sort of extended jam session. That they are virtuosi in the performance of their culture does not detract from the relevance of the text; on the contrary.

The Relevance of Social Organizational Pressures on Marriage Choice

In my rejection of biological determinisms as the fundamental structuring process in the unfolding of the love drama, I am placing myself quite obviously squarely within the anthropological tradition inaugurated with Margaret Mead's work on the cultural relativity of puberty crises and of definitions of adolescence. In rejecting social organizational determinisms, on the contrary, I put myself at odds with much work on the subject of marriage and the choice of a partner in Western cultures. I would like—briefly—to make explicit how I differ from, say, W. Lloyd Warner and his school or a simplistic use of Marxist principles and why I believe this is legitimate given my approach and the data I examine.

A simplistic Marxist analysis would be the most superficial. On the one hand, independent farmers—in America as in Europe—do not possess the amount of power that their apparent control of the means of production would imply they have. The real power is in the hands of the processing and distributing firms and of the banks, to whose whims the farmers are totally subject. I have heard many complaints in the Farm Bureau about it. On the other hand, John does not identify at all with blue-collar workers; he feels that he chose his present menial work and that he could go back to management whenever he wants. More importantly, perhaps, he is the grandson of one of those food-processing industrialists who, in economic terms, stand above the Elliotts; and John is a grandson in very good standing.

In Warner's analysis—which is based on social and cultural data such as the style of house lived in, the choice of leisure-time activities, religion, and so on—income, job, or economic status are given a secondary place as a criterion determining someone's place on the social ladder, with much mention being given to who meets whom in what situation. Even though I suspect that Warner chose his "up-and-down" terminology because he expected a certain congruence would always exist between social status and economic/political power, his scale was based on a complex of criteria, only a few of which were of a purely economic nature, rather than on a unique criterion considered to possess overriding importance. Thus, according to Warner and many of the sociologists who followed him, if such a middle-middle-class family as the Elliotts considered the marriage of their daughter to a second-generation

Italian objectionable, it meant that John, because of this very rejection and the fact that at the time of the study he was behaving in ways typical of the lower class, should be classified as no more than lower-middle class, if not upper-lower class, and only possibly upwardly mobile.

But, in fact, is John upwardly mobile because he married Sue, or is he downwardly mobile because he abandoned the management job that had put him at the same level as his parents for blue-collar work? Why is it that two of his best friends are successful small businessmen and another is a barber? Why is it that John can bully the police in Appleton ("You don't think they would touch me!") in a way reminiscent of upper-class kids in Warner's "Yankee City"? But why does he live in such a crummy apartment? I could go on with these paradoxes for a long time—as a matter of fact, I can make a list almost as long for every person I know well. John's case is not unique. As for Sue, what is it she likes in John? His very difference, as she herself says?

A sociologist in the great tradition of Durkheim or Marx would argue—with reason—that the individual's perception of his actions is not a valid datum for the understanding of these actions in the context of his social system. Sociology may be able to describe the rate of suicide in a society and explain its variations across time periods and societies, but it is not equipped to explain why one person rather than another commits suicide or becomes a successful capitalist. Now, of course, the only data available to sociologists are individual acts, and it is out of such acts—which cannot, theoretically, be explained purely sociologically—that sociological theories must be built. There is a logical paradox here that has not yet been solved satisfactorily even by those who try to escape it by collecting large numbers of cases and analyzing them statistically. Sociological analysis must thus be evaluated by the way it jumps the chasm between the single act and the law or structure.

In chapter 6 of his book *Social Class in America,* Warner reveals how it does this. He gives long examples of the type of data on interpersonal relations that he gathered in his interviews, and of the analyses he made of the declarations of his informants. Let us examine briefly a clear-cut example: "Here are the Stocktons who don't [belong to the '400'] . . . . Mrs. H. Cross, she doesn't. Now, she is C. Stockton's sister, but she is not in. Now, there is the case of a girl who married down and stayed there."[1] Mrs. H. Cross was dropped because she behaved once and continued to behave in a way that displeased the speaker and, we can suppose, all her friends. Warner does not give more details on this case, but he has often said that most of his informants' classifications varied slightly according to the speaker. Indeed, all the other cases he offered as examples of the types of answers informants gave to his questions about social organization presented the same characteristics: the criteria for membership in all the classes were personal, individualistic, matters of likes and dislikes, perceptions and impressions.

Warner did not draw this somewhat obvious conclusion. What he did was to reify his informants' perceptions (and upper-class informants, at that) into a *social* system; that is, something that ought to be considered to transcend individual perception. He used his very fluid data as evidence for the existence of substantively real classes that were given primary explanatory power over most other social phenomena he observed. Warner was a student of Radcliffe-Brown and probably could not have escaped adopting a substantialist view of Yankee City's social structure. In the process he lost sight of the fact that the primary characteristic of his data was fluidity, with the concomitant importance of unranked segregative cliques.

But the level at which the principle generating these cliques operates is not the level of action Warner wanted to explore, and therein lies the crux of the matter. Though these were not his words, he was more interested in problems of infrastructure than superstructure, in problems of macrosociology than interpersonal relationships. His error was in not searching for the answers to these questions in the proper place and in assuming that individual perception necessarily reflects the structural forces he was after.

This does not mean that social scientists should not take into consideration the types of data provided by individual action or statement. There are matters of interest to a sociologist in a suicide note or in the unfolding of so personal a drama as the one played by John, Sue, and her parents. But the interest these matters carry for an anthropologist does not consist in the fact that they would reflect such things as class struggle, for the difference in level means that they do not in any direct fashion. There are intermediary levels between macrosociological forces and personality. They are, in particular, the levels at which communication processes operate: language, and, indeed, culture as I understand it. It is obvious that one cannot speak except in a language that is understandable to the intended audience. A suicide note, insofar as it wants to transmit something of the person's reasons, must use traditional forms, and to this extent it can be analyzed socio-logically.

What I can handle properly in John and Sue's love story is the patterning of the declarations of the participants and the response each made to the stimuli provided by the others. Mr. and Mrs. Elliott insisted that they had nothing against Catholics, Italians, blue-collar workers, or even people who do not have a college education. Their opposition was phrased in a different way. Mrs. Elliott said: "Sue is used to living in an intellectual atmosphere, with plenty of books and intelligent, substantive discussions shared by informed people. She does not find this type of thing with John, and she won't be happy with him." Mr. Elliott said: "I do not care about John's lack of education, but Sue is too young, she has known John for too short a time, she does not have enough experience, and if she gets married too early, she may have a bad experience and become very unhappy—I say 'she may,' not 'she will,' as my wife would say, but I would not be surprised."

What they talked about was happiness. All the arguments I heard for or against the marriage centered on the probability that one or the other protagonist would not achieve happiness. ("She is not happy at home, that is why she wants to leave us.") I was asked often: "Does she enjoy herself when she is with John and his friends? Is she happy? I don't believe she can be happy with him." Sue would say: "My parents believe that I am not happy at home and that is why I want to leave, don't they? They don't understand anything. I am happy with them, and I *love* them, but I am also happy with John!" John would say: "Sue and I are really happy together."

Happiness

Intriguingly, happiness is one of those words the participants would say "cannot be defined." ("I have no idea what happiness is, do you?" "One is happy, or one is not happy, you feel it. It is not scientific.") They meant, I think, that it is not measurable in any objective sense, and there is no necessary relationship between any situation and whether a person would or would not be happy as he experienced it. To recognize happiness, one cannot simply read a gauge.

What all this means, I believe, is that happiness is not a thing in and of itself, an object to be observed in a detached manner, but rather that it is a *relation*. In context, nobody in Appleton had difficulty discussing happiness and deciding whether he or she was happy; it was only when it was considered outside of any context that it became impossible to talk about it. Those who said that happiness did not exist were not wrong; what exists is a particular person who is being, or not being, happy.

I was present on many occasions that were later said to have been happy, or at which people had been happy or unhappy. Often the word itself was not used directly; people would say, at first: "It was a great party last night." "We really had a lot of fun." "I really enjoy spending an afternoon like that, lying in the sun, playing in the water with your family, John." It was only later, in a further analysis of the occasion, that the idea of happiness came more directly to the foreground. ("Did you think Jocelyn was really happy last night? She looked bad." "Jim told me that he is not happy with his parents.") Sometimes it appeared to me that the word happy was used more in negative or doubting sentences—I do not think because of a belief in the impossibility of happiness, but possibly because of a sort of superstition that makes the word too loaded to be used carelessly.

Happiness is generally recognized to exist in two main circumstances: (1) one is happy if one has married the right person; (2) one is happy when one is in tune with the group one happens to be in, when one likes what is going on and participates in a relaxed manner. Obviously the two circumstances are related, for marriage is a special case of community life. To delineate more fully the field of happiness, I will now analyze a situation of happiness.

The situation is a gathering of the Matrone family, an Italian family in which almost everybody married a spouse of non-Italian descent. The grandfather, who had immigrated from Italy fifty years before, married a girl from Tennessee. His son and two daughters all married "out," and so did the two grandchildren, John Lawrence and his sister. Most of them have jobs as small businessmen, managers, or in public administration, and all enjoy a standard of living that places them in an average- or above-average-income category. Most of them are devout Catholics and conservative Democrats. In all this they are very different from the Elliotts and most of my other informants. The most important difference, and one that has cultural overtones, is the apparent strength of their family bond, which reveals how close they still are to their European background.

Yet too much significance should not be given to this if only because it was not clear to me whether the enthusiasm of the children and grandchildren for their grandfather was the result of their deep belief in what has been called familism or of the fact that he owned a piece of property on a lake where one could swim, water-ski, or just sit around in a private setting. But whether family reunions were frequent because the grandfather liked them and had strong enough incentives to hold them or because they corresponded to something in his children's cultural makeup that would lead them to continue them after his disappearance is not very relevant to my present analysis. What is, is the fact that the younger Matrones spoke about happiness in contexts very similar to the ones in which the Elliotts, for example, used it. In fact, this could be a clearer criterion for acculturation than a belief in familism, which would be very difficult to measure.

Toni Matrone, the grandfather, never seemed to worry about members of his family beyond their physical and material well-being (which reminded me strongly of my own grandparents in France) while John's mother—Toni's daughter—John's sister, and of course, John himself would treat these things matter-of-factly and discuss at length whether somebody was happy. My data about happiness come from conversations with the younger generation.

I was invited to several of the family gatherings that took place in the grandfather's small lot at the beach on a nearby lake. Present at one time or another were Toni Matrone and his wife, John's mother with her second husband and his daughter, John's sister with her husband and their three children, John and Sue, one or two children of neighbors or friends, and I. The lot itself was nothing very impressive—a small wooden cabin and the barbecue pit were the only permanent structures. It was well shaded, but the most important and relevant aspect of the place was the beach, with two boats for water-skiing, and a raft lying a hundred feet out on the lake. It was a very nice place indeed! When I arrived, around 1:30 P.M., most of the adults were at a picnic table laden with all types of food. They were eating, drinking beer, or just sitting. The others played in the water, swam or fought playfully on the raft, or sunbathed.

Conversation was general and continuous. Nothing substantive was said most of the time; small talk was more typical—about the weather, the houses, the neighbors, the children. There was no apparent structure to this talk. Often two or three dialogues went on at the same time; people switched interlocutors in the middle of a sentence; nobody cared about interrupting—even the children did it without being censured. Even the segregation by sex or age usual on such occasions was not particularly noticeable. What was noticeable was the ease with which friends, neighbors, or even foreigners like me were accepted and integrated without formality. I was treated just like everybody else, which also meant that nobody took particular notice of me.

This informality toward outsiders reveals that the boundaries between outside and inside were not narrowly based on kinship. There *were* boundaries, of course. This unit, as seen by the younger generation who invited me, like other communities in Appleton, was based on similarities in interest and behavior. Certain neighbors were never invited, and one branch of the family never participated in the more informal gatherings. Conversely, the only requirement for integration was the approval of at least one member of the group. Once one was inside the group, equality and freedom were stressed. ("Just go ahead and do whatever you please!") It didn't matter whether one sat on the ground or on a chair, had a beer or a Coke or nothing, swam or just sunbathed, and so on. There was freedom of dress: this is what a sentence like "Take your tie off, you don't need to wear it here!" was intended to communicate. The implication was that wearing a tie is something that is necessarily imposed by an authoritarian world on reluctant subjects whose only wish is to take it off. In this very assumption, a boundary is, in fact, reached. Someone who would insist on wearing a tie would probably be rejected as being in some sort of way "different" and unacceptable. At the other extreme, informality in dress and behavior could not have been carried to any play of an obviously sexual nature. Freedom existed only within a range of variations bounded at each end by behavior that would lead to exclusion from the group.

But that afternoon nobody went far beyond these limits. There was only one minor incident, involving John's brother-in-law and his grandmother, about disciplining the children. The brother-in-law got violently angry for a minute because the grandmother had criticized the manner in which he spoke to one of his children after a minor misbehavior. Sue told me afterward that she was shocked both by his attitudes toward his children and by the way he talked to the grandmother, and she added: "Everybody was shocked." But this was a very minor incident that, from the way Sue told the story, appeared to have been more surprising than really shocking.

The general reaction at the end of the day was that it had been a particularly good afternoon, that everybody had had "a lot of fun," that everybody had been happy. Having been present at several such afternoons, at the Matrones' and elsewhere, I must say that it was not in any way extraordinary. Many people in Appleton would question whether it had been happy at all. (Another informant told me about one of his own family gatherings: "They were not happy, they were just pretending to be. In fact, it was a terribly boring afternoon. Everybody thought so, but nobody had the guts to say it.")

That very same day, John and Sue were worried about the teenage daughter of his mother's second husband, who "didn't seem happy." They spent some time deciding that it was so and searching for the causes, which they thought they found in the daughter's relationship with her father. One could also have wondered about Sue herself, whose family reunions possessed a palpably different atmosphere that was almost as WASPish as the Matrones' was Italian. Was Sue happy? She would have maintained stubbornly that she was. Indeed, she expressed happiness in her behavior at the gathering and verbally many times to John and to her parents. The former was doubtful sometimes. The latter were certain that she did not know herself, since "she cannot be happy in such an atmosphere."

To be happy is not, however, an easy thing to be. The Elliotts, for example, displayed a particularly strong tendency to torture themselves by turning any situation that they themselves would agree was typical of what any happy situation should be (and that I, with my simpler definition of happiness, would have classified as indeed really happy) into a family drama à la T. S. Eliot. Henry James, or Arthur Miller when they started analyzing it.

Another example of unhappiness is that of Harvey Segala and John O'Connell, who were known in John Lawrence's group as being unhappy. Their problem sprang from emotional failures. Harvey's wife had left him just before I arrived in Appleton, and he had not been able to attach himself to another woman. John O'Connell might have had some real, though slight, psychological problems preventing him from settling down. But both were liked by, and liked participating in, John's group, the core of which was formed by four couples who presented a picture of ideal love. Harvey and John contrasted with the others on this point. They could, of course, have moved their social allegiance to a group of single men—and I believe they did, eventually—but, for a few months at least, they participated regularly in the meetings of John's group. This decision was interpreted by the other members of the group to mean that they wished they could conform, were unable to do so, and were unhappy.

We are thus led back to the individual. It is never a situation that is happy, for the same situation can be a happy one for some, and an unhappy one for others. It is persons who are happy—persons-in-situation always, for happiness is not a concept to be used for someone staying by himself—but always persons. Indeed, even in the closest communities what was stressed was not the survival of the group as group but rather the psychological survival of the individual member, his happiness And this survival depended not on the group as such but rather on the actions of the other members. When individual survival is threatened, then changes must take place, either in that individual or in the people around him. If these changes do not occur, then social reorganization becomes necessary. That this might lead to the destruction of the group is irrelevant.

In other words, even though happiness is something that can exist only in community, it remains an individualistic concept. Indeed, it is not a constitutive aspect of the irreducible tension that exists between individualism and community but rather one of the concepts that, with the concept of love, form a bridge between the two poles of American culture by participating directly in both.

Why Sue married John: A Cultural Interpretation

Sue was caught in just such a social reorganization. I pointed out earlier the cultural insistence that the survival of society is a matter of active individual involvement, implying a period of separation even when the eventual "choice" is to return to the parents' life-style. Obviously, in Sue's case, her flight from her parents' community was not a flight from communities in general but simply the result of her desire to choose her own and to be an original member of a new one. To join her parents' community matter-of-factly would have been a more basic rebellion against their teachings than to attach herself to an ever-so-slightly rebellious community she had directly participated in creating.

This process, however normal, is a very difficult one to the extent that it is not grounded in any very consciously formulated sacred tradition but rather in a perceived psychological need. For Sue to leave her parents, she first had to be persuaded that she was not "happy" with them, or at least that her continued happiness was problematic. The Elliots participated directly in this process. They worried that she would not be "really" happy with John, thus implying that this was the ultimate yardstick. Sue, on her side, maintained stubbornly that she was happy with John, his friends, and her parents, and that, in any event, *she* knew best. Obviously, she had to search out in her own makeup the seeds of new relationships. And to do this, she first had to define herself by choosing what it was that would make her happy.

She did not make these choices fully consciously or rationally, but in most cases by default, not having been exposed to other possibilities. She accepted getting drunk or high, though never to the point of losing control of herself. She had nonplatonic relationships with her boyfriends. She preferred rock to classical music. She also always dressed with great care, cleaned up carefully after parties, enjoyed children, disapproved of pornography, and worked very hard at her job.

The mix of these traits is purely idiosyncratic. I have not met anybody else who exactly matches the choices she made. It would be necessary to go into her psychohistory to find the reasons that pushed her to make those particular choices and not those made by her brother and sister. Culturally speaking, these traits must be understood as constituting the diacritical signs that differentiated her and her communities from everybody else and from all other communities she would not participate in. These traits would, in particular, help her decide on her level of happiness in a certain social environment.

They symbolize her difference—her individuality. They are the basis on which she can measure her sameness with some of the people with whom she enters into contact—a sameness that can then become the "reason" that one is happy with them or that one wants to marry one certain person rather than another. Thus why Sue married John cannot be understood as a reflection of anything other than these processes of individual classification, processes that work in a way similar to those that generated the various characters of the churches. In these choices, the participants do not express, however indirectly, their sociological reality, but rather the cultural need to differentiate themselves, to break away and then to create.

Thus I cannot state the exact reasons that led Sue to make the specific choices she did make. The cultural structure does not prescribe the person one has to marry or even the group that person must come from. In the same manner that it does not prescribe what communities may exist in one place or the exact number or type of government agencies, it places on the individual the responsibility for deciding by himself or herself whether to marry, when to marry, and whom to marry. That other determinisms are thus allowed to reveal themselves—whether social, organizational, or psychological—is not surprising and certainly not at issue in my analysis. But when talking about the culture, it must be said that *its* structure consists in the refusal to set boundaries on individual action that I have documented many times—what the natives call freedom (rather inappropriately, in fact, since it refers to a way of perceiving human life that is definitely imposed on them from the outside by their environment).

I would insist, then, that the process Sue lived is very conservative. At no point did she behave in ways that were inconsistent with my understanding of American culture. She played with perfection the roles she had to play in a drama she never fully understood. Her parents did not understand that drama very well themselves. They had seen their three children leave them in the same sort of tragic rebellion against the solutions they had been at such pains to explain so that their children could appreciate and accept them. They had rejected the solutions their children had found in spite of the efforts the children had made to explain them. And they said to me as I was packing to leave at the end of my stay: "You are more our child than our three others are!" Had I not chosen them, and had they not chosen me? None of the participants truly wished a conflict to arise and a break to appear. All—in that family, at least—expressed the unhappiness they felt. This expression often took the form of guilt, as they felt responsible for the turn of events. But in fact the process escaped them. Their cultural environment had given them the theme for the drama they were to improvise; and *there*, they had no choice.

CHAPTER 10
Love

My discussion of love will draw mostly from the domains of kinship and religion. But to restrict the relevance of the concept to these two domains would be a mistake, as I hope to demonstrate. Love is a context for happiness—and vice versa, of course. Many of the things I will say about the former will throw light on aspects of the latter that are hidden because of the nature of the medium used to express in dialogue and behavior the reality of happiness. The philosophy of happiness is nowhere as developed as the theology of love. Conversely, what might be called the sociology of happiness is much richer than that of love. And yet the two notions are closely interrelated. I would even argue that here there is but one master symbol appearing under different names in different contexts. I will refer to that symbol as love, too, for lack of a better word and in order to avoid jargon.

Love and Kinship

One of the areas in which David M. Schneider's *American Kinship* breaks ground is in his treatment of love as an integral part of the American kinship system. Though in his disputes with the componential analysts of kinship terms, Schneider has not emphasized the fact, it is probably their failure—a failure imposed upon them by their theoretical and methodological approaches—to deal with love that makes their analyses incomplete. Kinship, for Americans, is not simply a matter of classifying relatives. It is also a matter of *relating* these people. Componential analysts, and many sociologists of the family, assume this relationship. Natives don't.

The interplay of blood, law, and sex constitutes the distinct domain of kinship. Kinship as a domain is an extremely rigid thing.

"Blood" is whatever geneticists say it is. "Sex" is simple enough. "Law," which ties people to people in the system, may even become "whatever psychologists say it is."

But, interestingly enough, as the scientific hardness of the distinctive features of kinship has increased—who would challenge genetics?—the natives have argued that, after all, families are not built to conform to the definition but rather to transcend it. As Schneider says, "the relative is a person." As a person, the speaker may or may not like any one of his relatives, may or may not wish to relate to him in an actual manner. In this manner, brothers, sisters, uncles, or aunts can be dropped, and the ex-husband of a divorced aunt may be retained by someone as an "uncle" (though that person's brother may chose not to do so). Indeed, totally unrelated friends may become identified as relatives. Finally, institutions such as schools or communes can come to be considered families. Schneider mentions the puzzling case of a student who insisted that her roommate was her sister. This is puzzling only until one notices the similar way certain churches have of insisting that they are families, or the way certain teachers insist that their classes are families. Some will not even say that their group is "like a family," but that it *is* a family, because family is a feeling, a way of relating, and does not have to correspond to any set of distinctive features.

In this manner the informants lead the observer away from kinship to more general principles that can be applied *to* kinship as much as to any other domain but do not constitute the essence of kinship. When informants say that a church or a classroom *is* a family, they are saying that the mode of relating among the people is fundamentally the same in all these environments.

I have introduced this exploration with a discussion of Schneider's contribution because it is central to the development of my decision to complete my analysis of American culture by dealing with love. Whatever may be one's objections to Schneider's analysis, nevertheless he has demonstrated that one cannot interpret American kinship without considering love as an integral part of the system. And, in the same way, one cannot deal with social structure—American ideas about society—without also dealing with that which ties the pieces together, which I have been referring to as love. That love is not a respectable, traditional sociological category is irrelevant. That societies are not created by their members and that they persist very well without active concern about their survival by their members is not the point, however valid these strictures are. My informants were worried about relationship, and in their search for an understanding of matters that so concerned them, they created a system of interpretation that, like any other attempt at intelligibility, created something that is quite independent from reality and thus somewhat arbitrary. And it is precisely because it is arbitrary that we, as social scientists, cannot assume that we know what our informants are saying.

Love and Sex

The relationship between blood and sex at the level of distinctive features is evident: without sex there would be no children and no relatives by blood. Furthermore, there cannot be sex except between two partners drawn from different bloodlines. Indeed, the prohibition of incest in American kinship might be understood structurally as deriving from the need to build relationships-in-law (communities) where there are none. "Marrying in" would be a denial of the creation myth of all groups, which emphasizes that integration is valid only after separation. Through the sexual act, law is established. Having sex makes law.

Sex is what ties blood and law. In a sense this is a transformation into the scientific realm of the structure of individualism and community mediated by love ("love makes community") that I have identified at the level of feeling, actions, and definitions that transcend the scientific realm. Sex and love are thus in the same position, which is probably why they are so difficult to distinguish, not only for the observer but also for the participants themselves.

Those who are the most puzzled by the ambiguities of love and sex are, for obvious reasons, adolescents. It is from statements made by high school students in their senior year that I will illustrate my argument. For the first time, adolescents are considered ready to make the choices on which American society is based: choices of friends, of mates. And yet often these cultural definitions have not yet come to be considered as natural as they are for adults. Adolescents are closer to apprehending the arbitrariness of the adult culture. As they grew up, each new experience was interpreted by the adults, who told them, with authority: "This is how it is"—even when obviously it was not so. Puberty may be the last of these "new" experiences that all people have to go through. And here again adolescents must learn the appropriate responses.

They have no choice but to learn, and most know it so well that one would not find more informed informants on the subject of sexual values than adolescents. To most of them, sex is an immediate issue and often an overwhelming one. The statements I will analyze were recorded on "natural" occasions—most of them during a twelfth-grade sociology class—and other situations where I overheard rather than inquired.

The sociology class was set up in seminar style, with a panel of three students who were supposed to lead a discussion among the students of the class with minimal interference on the part of the teacher. Participation by the students was probably just about as good as anybody could expect: two or three students dominated the debate, half a dozen intervened from time to time, and the other half of the class just sat there, too shy or too bored. Yet the point is not so much whether every student agreed in detail with what was being said but that the positions taken openly were popular.

The subject discussed that day was premarital sex: whether it is right or permissible for a boy and a girl to have sexual intercourse before marriage or whether one should remain a virgin until marriage. The discussion was opened by a highly negative exposition of the "double standard" by the three students in charge of the topic. ("People used to think that it was all right for a boy to have 'experiences' before he got married, but that it was completely forbidden for girls.") Nobody would defend this position. The first comments were along the following lines: "It is not logical. Where did the boy find the girl? Was any reason given why it should be so? What happened to the girls with whom the boys had made it? I just do not see how anybody could defend this, it is completely immoral. It should be permitted or forbidden to everybody without segregation." The girls were much more vocal in their opposition than the boys and, in fact, prevented one or two boys from voicing a general explanation. By contrast, Sue Elliott told me that three years before, on the same subject, several had argued in favor of girls remaining virgin until marriage because, they said: "We do not want somebody to come up to us and say about our wife, 'Wow, isn't she good!'"

The discussion shifted to the questions: "Why not? What is wrong with it? If we *really love* somebody, why not go all the way? When one is really in love, it does not matter, or it should not matter, what one or the other does or has done, physical or material things should not be considered. There is no reason why one should expect the partner to be a virgin at marriage if he or she is a good person. You do not even have to tell." (There were disagreements on this.) Such statements went on and on, and the only person who dared object openly had to take the almost untenable position that neither boy nor girl should have intercourse before marriage. He was almost hooted out of the room, and he had to retreat behind a "I do not know why, this is just how I feel." Nobody had the courage to say: "Because my church—or God—forbids it."

All this makes clear, I think, that what could be called the spiritual basis of love is something that transcends any specific acts or behavior. In one of the sessions of the sociology class following the one I just described, a film was shown that argued strongly in favor of virginity before marriage (though the argument was clearer and stronger for girls than for boys). This movie had been made in the late 1950s or early 1960s and depicted four college students, two boys and two girls, and their sentimental adventures.

Artistically, the movie was a terrible failure, and its message simplistic: one girl "gave everything" to her boyfriend, and he left her to marry a girl "back home whom he had not even touched." At the end, she was depicted sobbing brokenheartedly as she dropped out of school and left for the big city. ("I could not face my folks now.") The other girl refused herself to her boyfriend, who angrily abandoned her for a while but eventually came back to her and married her because he realized there were not many girls like that one.

At one level, it appears that this film depicts intercourse as intrinsically evil and life-destroying when it occurs outside of marriage. This is how it seems when the plot is summarized, but the makers of the film made important distinctions. When the second girl refused to give herself, she explained that if she did, her boyfriend "would not *respect* her anymore," and even if they got married, "it could not work" because "he would not have confidence in me." The same type of reasoning was used to account for the failure of the other girl; even though she did love her boyfriend, he did not marry her because if she had done it with him, there was a good chance she would do it with others.

What all this makes clear is that even though sexual intercourse is made to be a primary symbol of love, it is only as a *symbol* ɔf moral worth that it is powerful; it is not intrinsically powerful. And furthermore, love itself is defined in the movie in very much the same way as in the sociology class: love is not only a romantic feeling of happiness but also a matter of respect and trust. It is not a matter of prescription. This corresponds, of course, to the more general rule that in matters of "relationships" no prescription can be made. In their structure, the definitions given by the class and those given in the movie were the same, and it was the attempt of the film to make a specific act a touchstone of moral worth that was artificial.

Specific acts are meaningless. To me, this is fundamental even to the "old morality." Isn't there a clear structural relationship between the disjunction of sex and love that is typical of the so-called new morality and the old Calvinist idea that good works are no proof of salvation?

Love and Marriage

I discussed briefly in the last chapter why one could not speak of Sue and John's "choosing" each other. This is central to an understanding of love. Love is the domain par excellence ȯf subjectivity, the unconscious, the nonscientific: it cannot, it must not, be possible to explain "why" so-and-so fell in love with so-and-so. A favored comment is one that stresses the illogical character of the choices, the fact that the protagonists had little influence on themselves and that they started loving the other without realizing what was happening to them "until it was too late." This glorification of irrationality in marriage, this refusal of any rules, conscious or unconscious, is the same as the common perception of what holds together those small communities that are the backbone of the social structure of Appleton.

Yet irrationality in the formation of any community is not consciously expressed or used as the most basic distinctive feature ɔf the decision of a few friends to come together. In fact, I talked of ˙he pretense to *universality* of the group itself and its choices, with ts implication that anybody in his right senses would join the group f he knew about it, that joining it is a normal act. Yet this is an ˙bstract universality that applies only to situations or people who ˙ave not been directly experienced, which are known only through theoretical deduction. On the contrary, it is structurally necessary for each community to distinguish itself from all other communities with which it comes in direct contact. Thus, the supposed universality of the appeal of a particular community, which is taken as explaining why a few people did come together, and which at a certain level does explain to these people why they made that choice, is structurally equivalent to the transcendent irrationality on which the love between a man and a woman is supposed to be based. For the irrationality of love exists only, in the minds of my informants, with regard to the socially defined categories of mechanical rationality. It is not because one plus one equals two that John and Sue fell in love; it is against reasoning of this type that they would protest.

Conversely, they would agree that there are probably transcendent factors that brought them together. Furthermore, their moral acceptance of each other's habits and peculiarities implies the elevation of idiosyncratic choices to a universal level: "Everybody who would know John as I do would know that he is a good person"—and almost "would love him." The only real difference between conjugal love and community happiness is thus simply that the former refuses the logical extension "would love him if they knew him," which the latter makes, though with just as little result; in other words, in the same way that John and Sue do not expect anybody other than themselves to fall in love with them, members of a community do not actually expect the world to join them.

Love, then, is greater than what happens between boy and girl, for the way they are seen as coming together is the way society is seen as being formed. Boy and girl marry because they are in love. People live with people in communities because they love each other. If this last statement seems absurd, the first one must be seen as absurd, too. And if the first one seems somewhat more credible than the second, it is because, traditionally, what makes people come together into communities has been named only in the context of marriage. Even there the word is so powerful that it is very rarely used. One can say freely: "Wow, I loved that show," but John had to be completely drunk to go beyond: "You know, I really like Sue. We are really made for each other." I do not think I have ever heard Sue say of John: "I love him," and her parents always balked when I implied that love has its own rules, which do not yield to reason. Happiness is what is generally talked about in an in-love situation. If the word is so powerful that people hesitate to use it in the context of marriage, it is understandable that they would not use it in the context of community, where the evidence that the whole thing is artificial and arbitrary, anyway, is so much more glaring. So informants use paraphrases: they speak of the need for "establishing relationship," "maintaining communication," or "developing trust." In other words, whatever the words they use, they are searching for *personal* involvement, and if they don't find it, in frightened anger they may say: "America, love it or leave it!"

Love, Religion, and Mythology

In the preceding pages I have been led oftentimes to the borders of transcendental domains that would seem to fit best in a discussion of religion as an all-encompassing and self-contained domain. However, I have decided to steer away from the temptation to treat religious thought in such a way in this book.

Not only does love possess many traits of a transcendental and sacred nature in its usage in contexts traditionally considered to be profane, but it is also one of the central themes of religion in Appleton, particularly Protestantism. The concept is most widely used in churches with an evangelical bent. In these, it reappears in so many different contexts—sermons, songs, prayers, pamphlets, and so on—that one might be tempted to refuse to assign any meaning to it. It might appear to be just an empty word repeated over and over again through habit rather than conviction. But the amount of meaning that an individual person may put into a cultural concept is of only peripheral interest. It is sufficient that the concept exists and that it is inescapable.

Love possesses this type of inescapable reality in American thought. Even those people who do not get involved as much as they are supposed to in the substantive reality that the word expresses know very well how to use it and in what context. The feeling of meaningless repetition and uniformity that one may get is thus but an indication of the unity of the structure. Indeed, whatever pastor uses "love" in one of his sermons as the definition of the relationship between God and man or between man and man, the sermon will remain the same. Love is not simply the rallying point of Jesus freaks or Pentecostal revivalism, it is also the staple subject of sermons in the Presbyterian and Methodist churches of Appleton. And, furthermore, in all of these churches the complex of definitions that explain the concept vary only minimally, relative to the central theme that I am going to expound.

I found this theme presented most concisely in a letter to the editor of *Decision*, the monthly magazine of the Billy Graham Evangelical Association. The emphasis in the letter is mine. It goes like this:

> Dear Billy Graham,
>
> My name is Mark Patton and I am ten years old. I have donated a dollar and I would like some stikers. Last night I have just come to one of your crusades. It was the best show I have ever been to. Before this my sister and I would fight everyday. Now that I and her have given our lives to God, we are laughing together, playing together, *having fun together,* doing everything together. I thank you for your crusades and everybody else that helped. I am *a much happier person now.*
>
> *Love,* Mark Patton[1]

Fun, happiness, love—they are all here. I will leave aside the interesting fact that this letter was written by a ten-year-old. Even if the ideas expressed by this letter are not really the ideas held by this little boy, they are certainly a direct reflection of the ideas his parents (probably) and the Billy Graham literature (certainly) want to convey. Similarly, even though the Billy Graham Crusade is often regarded as the height of religious hypocrisy, faddism, and exploitation, it is interesting to note that such movements are popular in America, and that their message is framed in precisely this way.

The point of the letter is an account of how the "giving of lives to God" replaces disharmony and chaos by harmony and togetherness in interpersonal relationships. A pastor expounding on this example would say that the writer's recognition that God *loved* him personally permitted him to come to love his neighbor—to live with him peacefully and to do things together with him.

In another issue of the magazine the same point was made pictorially with a series of three photographs taken during the invocation at the end of a Billy Graham service. In the first we are shown a kindly, smiling woman approaching a frightened girl, in the second the woman is speaking seriously to the girl and has her hand on the girl's shoulder, and the third shows them embracing. The caption underneath the picture says: "What starts out in the counseling area as a formal dialogue (1), becomes more intimate as the counselor and the inquirer talk about the Lord (2), ends in a love feast (3)."[2] Love, in religious theory as in social theory, destroys the isolation of the human being and is a bridge between men. It is also the bridge between God and man. A universalistic religion such as Christianity, once it has dropped the necessity of a mediator between God and man, has to conclude that God is open equally and in the same fashion to all men, whatever their place in the social structure or their modes of life before conversion. There are no privileged channels; each man is responsible for his self.

This individualism has a reverse side. Heaven is yours only if *you* want it, if you make a positive commitment to God. ("God is helpless to save those who reject Christ.") God loves everybody personally, yet a person can reap the rewards of this love only through a personal commitment to God. Love, in religion as in marriage, is a two-way tie that demands commitment from both sides. If one side reneges on the contract, the other cannot do anything about the rupture. The Spanish Inquisition could believe that someone who confessed his doctrinal errors through torture was saved, whether the person made a real personal commitment or not. This is as much anathema to an American Baptist in the field of religious doctrine as the idea that a marriage between a man and a woman is not necessarily based on a personal commitment would be to any native American, religiously bent or not.

It could be argued that the opposition between traditional Catholic and modern Protestant thought on love is not so great, that the latter view is already present in the former's theology. For someone like Denis de Rougemont, for example, the significant opposition is between Christianity and the "pagan religions," by which he meant mostly Manichaeism. In his great book *Love in the Western World,* he traced the last struggles inside Western thought between Manichaean tendencies traceable in such things as the Albigensian heresy, the poetry of the troubadours, or the myth of Tristam and Isolde, and the dominant Christian doctrine as expressed in the definitions of love and marriage. He summarized this doctrine in the following way:

> [In Christianity] the symbol of Love is no longer the infinite *passion* of a soul in quest of light, but the *marriage* of Christ and the Church. And in this way human love itself has been transformed. Whereas, according to the doctrine of mystical paganism, human love was sublimated so thoroughly as to be made into a god even while it was dedicated to death, Christianity has restored human love to

its proper place, and in this status has hallowed it by means of marriage [author's italics].[3]

Rougemont then goes on to show how the notion of love as passion survived for a long time in literature and drama, in tragedies such as Shakespeare's *Romeo and Juliet* or Racine's *Phèdre*, or in Wagner's operas. In these, as in the original myth of Tristam and Isolde, love is a direct threat to the society of the stricken lovers, who are taken by a force wholly exterior to themselves (symbolized by the magic philter in Tristam and Isolde) that carries them along paths they have not chosen and on which they would refuse to travel if they were in their right minds. Love, in these works of art, is madness and death, and associated with the powers of darkness.

Rougemont thus makes clear that when it is opposed to non-Christian philosophies, Western culture is a unit. Love, in Catholic as in Protestant thought, is associated with life and the very foundation of society. Yet in Rougemont's very summation of his argument can be recognized a view of the nature of God's love closer to what I consider to be a Catholic view than a "Protestant" one. He says that "the symbol of love is the marriage of *Christ with the Church*," in my terms of God with society. This view is "individualistic" insofar as it considers society to be *one*, and God unique. This is very clearly in opposition to Indian thought as interpreted by Louis Dumont, or even classical Indo-European thought as interpreted by Georges Dumézil. As Dumont says, Indian gods have no substance, they exist only as relations; similarly, though conversely, the Christian God is all substance and no relation.

While all this may appear a little abstract and removed from the everyday world of people not involved in theological discussion, there is a definite interplay between definitions of love and socioreligious ideas reflected in cultural performances. In India, for example, reform movements have used the symbol of love as a lever against the caste system.[4] From the point of view of that system it is thus obviously a threat and must be presented as evil. Similarly, love remained on the side of the forces of death in Western literature as long as the general emphasis of the social structure was on hierarchically organized groups where individuals had to bend to the higher good of their family, state, nation, or of the Church.

It is only relatively late in the mainstream of Western literature that the theme of love as a positive force appears. The first serious use of this new theme can be found in the works of Jane Austen. The lovers still have to bridge a substantive gap. They generally belong to different social classes. But they do not die, they triumph. The happy ending of a modern love story is not a degradation of the myth of Tristam and Isolde, as Rougemont says. It is, in fact, quite as necessary as the deaths of the tragic lovers in earlier times.

In India, as in classical and modern Europe, love was, if not an individualistic notion, at least a personal one. The close relationship of love with sex was always present, and sex remains purely a personal thing between two human beings whatever the cultural modalities. Particularly in cultures that effectively denied the reality of the human being as a unique person, it is necessary to recognize—properly inside religious and mythical thought—the irreducible biological and psychological uniqueness of men and women, which is what love did. Love then had to be repressed by being associated with the evil aspects of human life; the persons, finally very few, who insisted on putting their freedom first had to be ostracized or killed.

Conversely, a wholly individualistic society such as America could put only a positive value on love, and thus reward those people, who now had to be many, who based their lives on this psychological principle. In the same way that an Indian youth had to be coerced into accepting a hierarchical society by being shown the dangers of individualism, an American youth had to be coerced into accepting an individualistic society by positively stressing love and also, of course, by negatively stressing hierarchy.

These last remarks explain why myths about love have shifted from a dominant place in the higher spheres of literature and philosophy to a minor place, from an area of limited popular appeal to one of extreme popular appeal. Conversely, the critical slot that these myths occupied in classical literature is now occupied to a large extent by different types of critical texts, particularly those that can be classified under the general label of existentialism and that deal with the problems raised, and not fully answered, by the necessity of individualism in a world that is not fully individualized, however much the definitions and organizations of the different domains of social life may reinforce this cultural choice.

Love and Charity

This rather long and yet very rapid digression into comparative mythology and literature is intended to offer a background against which to contrast more effectively what I am saying about love in America. The notion is so very close to the center of our preoccupations as natives of an individualistic society, and we are so ready to see in it something of universal meaning in time and space, that I felt I had to stress the variations that texts about love present cross-culturally and diachronically. The place of love has changed. Similarly, there have been shifts in what could be referred to as love.

The text I have chosen to illustrate one of these shifts is the translation of a key passage of the New Testament on which is grounded much of Western religious thought on love: Paul's first epistle to the Corinthians, Chapter 13. The last verse reads, in the original Greek:

$$\text{Νυνὶ δὲ μένει πίστις, ἐλπίς, ἀγάπη, τὰ τρία ταῦτα μείζων δὲ τούτων ἡ ἀγάπη.}$$

The Latin translation (Vulgate) reads:

> Nunc autem manent fides, spes, caritas, tria haec; maior autem horum est caritas.

The Protestant King James (seventeenth-century) translation reads:

> And now abideth faith, hope, charity, these three, but the greatest of these is charity.

The Catholic Douay (sixteenth-century) version reads:

> And now there remain faith, hope and charity, these three: but the greatest of these is charity.

The Protestant New English Bible (1960–70) reads:

> In a word there are three things that last forever: faith, hope and love; but the greatest of them is love.

The Catholic New American Bible (1970) reads:

> There are in the end three things that last: faith, hope and love, and the greatest of these is love.

The shift in the translation of the word ἀγάπη from charity to love is recent and well in keeping with modern tendencies. The latter translation was, of course, the one that was chosen by the composer of the folk song of the 1960s. "There Are But Three Things That Last—Faith, Hope, and Love."

Yet as late as 1948, L. Pirot and A. Clamer, French Catholic commentators on this passage who had chosen to translate ἀγάπη by *charité,* stressed what they considered to be an important difference between love and charity:

> The word "love" has a very general sense which the Greeks would translate by ἔρως , the love of egoist desire, of possessions, sensual and passionate, or φιλία, disinterested and benevolent love which applies mainly to relationships of friendship . . . . If St. Paul did not use this last term, which represented for his contemporaries the highest forms of affection, it was because it was still inadequate to express a predilection the new basis for which changed its origin, its content and its goal. In fact, it is God who is the center of Christian love. Charity is the gift of the Holy Spirit *par excellence* . . . and it permits us to answer the love which God feels for us. The Greek φιλία, preference grounded in nature and created by chance encounters, is addressed to a small circle of persons, but friendship "in Christ". . . has an unlimited extension and duration. While the Greek only sees a man in his neighbor, the Christian discovers God in him [my translation].[5]

What Pirot and Clamer are trying to maintain is the Greek distinction between ἀγάπη and φιλία . To them, it is the latter that would express in Greek what I have called in these pages "love"—a sentiment appropriate for the relationship between equals, between friends in a community. They emphasize that Christians do not love in this manner. Karl Rahner and Herbert Vogrimler, two more modern Catholic theologians, still enter both "love" and "charity" as different concepts in their *Theological Dictionary.* They give a larger role to love than to charity, but they insist that "charity is a fundamentally distinctive mode of love"[6] and, indeed, primordial, since "man's love for God depends on God's prodigal, condescending *agape* selflessly given to His lowly creatures"[7]; that is, His *charity.* The emphasis on the condescension of God to His lowly creatures shows that Rahner and Vorgrimler have not moved very far: God and man remain fundamentally unequal. It is not so surprising in this context that charity should also mean, in common parlance, almsgiving from the rich to the poor, from the superior to the inferior, where there cannot be any return. Since Mauss, we have known to what extent a gift lowers the recipient and enhances the prestige of the giver. Nonreciprocal services imply a hierarchical relationship in which the giver occupies the dominant position. This is indeed the position of God, and particularly Christ, vis-à-vis man in traditional Catholic thinking, and the concept corresponds closely to social structural realities prevalent when these arguments were first made.

The modern translation, whether it is accurate or not, is intended to stress something else that corresponds to new social structural realities: love implies equality, reciprocity, and individualism. Christ, in modern American Protestant thought, did not die for mankind, he is not supposed to have atoned for the original sin in a transcendent gift that men cannot return. He died for *YOU* personally. This was his gift to you, and his sacrifice will atone for the sins you have committed in your present life and it will be useful to you only if, in exchange for Christ's gift of his life, you "give your own life" to him in return. Original sin then becomes nothing more than a symbol of man's sinfulness; it is not something that stains a newborn baby in a literal sense and has to be eradicated as soon as possible through baptism. It is no longer necessary to baptize infants in modern Protestantism, for baptism has a new meaning. It is no longer the sacrament that transforms a person into a Christian. It is at most the symbol of integration into a community. What transforms a person into a true and full Christian is the experience of salvation, a personal, voluntary experience based on an equal exchange in which both Christ and the saved person give their lives to each other.

Love and Happiness

When my informants talked about love, they were freed from all infrastructural determinisms. If the preceding discussion appears abstract and somewhat irrelevant to everyday life, it is probably because we do not live in a world free from such determinisms. In love there are no barriers except those generated by the concept itself. In happiness—that is, the realization of love in interpersonal relationships—there is brought to the forefront the fact that to love is to love a particular person with all his or her idiosyncrasies, idiosyncrasies possibly unbearable for the subject who finds himself obliged to adopt a nonloving, segregative posture. If, as I pointed out, informants talked more about unhappiness than about happiness, it is probably because of the difficulties that prevent love from being actualized in everyday life.

Love, I might say, is a dream in relation to the reality of happiness and fun. I would rather say that love is a myth, the expression in ritual speech of a structure whose expression in behavior is happiness. What differentiates love from happiness, in other words, is the medium that the participants use to articulate what must be recognized as essentially the same culturally determined theme. For the performances in which love and happiness are dramatized, however different they may be in their superficial character, say the same thing within the greater dialogue that cultures hold with each other. These performances are part of the same system of transformation and exhibit a fundamental unity that cannot escape a foreign observer. Thus talk about love is not idle chatter, for the very fact that it is furthest removed from the realities of life makes it a privileged area in which to look for properly cultural structures.

CHAPTER 11
Individualism, Community, and Love

"Love each other in all that you do" says one of the numerous songs that became so popular in the 1960s. My argument is that this is indeed the fundamental precept underlying the organization of social interaction in Appleton as interpreted by my informants. It is one of the deepest and most general principles structuring their cultural statements.

Love is the total giving away of oneself to somebody else who must answer in kind and equally, and thereby "save" himself and the originator of the exchange. There is no love if it is not shared; love cannot exist in the abstract, it cannot be directed toward something or someone who does not answer. At the most elementary levels—the couple, the family, the small group of friends—this is interpreted literally to imply one-mindedness and an equal exchange of services. Differences have to be minimal in all aspects of behavior, though the only relevant domains are considered to be those pertaining to the psychology of the person: a social position, considered to be external to the person, can be transcended—even if it often is not. One-mindedness and the stress on the psyche as defining the true nature of a man are direct concomitants of the reciprocal and individualistic implications of the idea of love. Insofar as true humanity lies in the full psychological realization of a choice, it is belived that communication through exchange, on which small groups are based, demands full psychological—that is, in fact, ideological—similarity inside it. Thence the famous uniformity that critics resent so much in American small-community life and for which religious bodies forever pray because they are never satisfied with the degree of it that they possess.

It is indeed unachievable—for the same reason that the type of love Americans favor is unachievable. Unanimity, because it is grounded in the psychology of the person, is highly dependent on internal moods and idiosyncrasies. It is thus clear that the maintenance of a *social* group is very precarious: people change easily, and one-mindedness cannot be assumed necessarily to endure; it has to be continually reinforced. The pattern of intense segregation, very frequent interaction, and extreme demands on the loyalty of the individual all tend to make it a more traumatic experience to break away from the group. This is very often unsuccessful, and the larger the group, the more easily it disintegrates as internal diversity becomes so great that even the mildest and most insubstantial forms of superficial one-mindedness become impossible to maintain.

The notion of love also implies certain things about *universality*, another concomitant of its individualistic structure. Universality is defined in relation to a hierarchical view of the social world and in opposition to it. It says that the distinctive social features of a person must be rejected as a valid basis for planning interaction with him, and only his conduct must be considered. But since love is personal this universality must not be thought to mean that one actually loves everybody. To call the members of one's group "everybody" is only a trick. Love should be extended to somebody, anybody, whoever he or she is. And thus, because love must be extended to a real person instead of an abstract category, it cannot be for everybody, since there is no way one could get into direct contact with more than a few people. This creates a certain discomfort among some people because it puts limits on universality. Presented with a choice, though, somebody wins over everybody, and this is particularly clear at the level of social organization, where the numerical boundaries of love are soon reached—two dozen persons appear to be the outside limits of a viable unanimous community.

The reverse problem creates more social complexities. It is very difficult for most people to define exactly why it is that they do not like some other person, in what way that other person is so different from them that they cannot share with him, love him. This is particularly sharp the closer the person is to oneself in external social appearance. For it must be remembered that unanimity is something other than homogeneity. It doesn't matter whether the members of a community are objectively alike as long as they agree not to insist on expressing whatever differences may indeed exist. Conversely, apparently alike people often wish to separate themselves from their narrowly defined peers. It thus becomes necessary to invent ways of emphasizing or even creating differences. In other words, this way to disunity has the same structure as the way to unity and community. It is most important to achieve differentiation from people who are closest tó oneself and with whom one is in some contact. Identification with a certain socioideological reality is possible only in direct contradistinction with other possible realities of the same order. Thence comes the large number of potential realities offered to most people in Appleton. And since segregation must involve direct interaction, a universalistic link can then be established with people outside the nearest groups. This link does not totally satisfy the conditions of universal love, but it offers a very good substitute for, and hides the contradiction inherent in, the structure.

That groups and communities should evolve in any human society is considered a natural thing. These groups gain substantive reality and self-definition through interaction with other groups; that is, with units of the same nature and of equal standing. At the most elementary level—that of the person—the same dialectic is at work. A person is a natural unit because he is a biological one, but he does not exist as a human cultural unit until he has entered into relations with other individuals. At both levels, it is the *relation* between units that is problematic. Yet there is a central difference between groups and individuals. For while groups gain substance through interaction, the individual is supposed to lose his own substance. A baby at birth is all substance and no relation; a small group of friends is, at first, all relation and no substance. Later the child is supposed to lose his substance in a group, and this group is supposed to gain substance by differentiating itself from other groups. Thus, while a small community has to be one-minded, the wider society has to become—logically and historically—diverse; that is, many-minded. Thus can we solve the paradox that what seems to some the most conformist nation in the world is also the most diverse.

Furthermore, even though a group has natural aspects and the individual has cultural aspects, it is groups—communities—that are evidently cultural, and persons—individuals—who are natural. For individuals, however hard they may try, never lose their substance, and groups never gain any.

Individualism and community are thus two poles of the structure. They are integrated insofar as neither exists outside of the other. But this integration is achieved through dialectical opposition: where there is individualism, there cannot be community; and where community triumphs, individualism is destroyed. If any mediation is possible, it is achieved by love, an individual sentiment directed toward another person. Love pertains in this way to both individualism to community? How do we transcend our diversity? fundamental questions of American culture: How do we go from individualism to community? How do we transcend out diversity? How do we achieve *e pluribus unum*?

Love! I have no doubt that many readers will consider this an astonishing conclusion to reach after almost two centuries of writings by economists, sociologists, political scientists, or historians stressing the horror perpetrated on the human spirit by a complex capitalistic society that has been defended more because of its productive efficiency grounded in the natural egoism of human beings than in such a spiritual thing as love. I may be accused of making this statement more for its controversial ring than because of any scientific value it may have.

But why should a statement like this be controversial? Is it really because love is a mystical entity that cannot be measured, operated upon experimentally, and thus ought not to be handled scientifically? Or is it rather because it is so close to the very core of American culture and indeed to the core of the ideology of science, because the rationale for science is that it will help establish on this earth a more humanly grounded order, a nonalienating society with liberty and justice for all?

I have answered the first question many times throughout this book. I have tried to make scientific statements not about the underlying "reality" of love, whatever that may be, but about the fact that the concept and words that belong to the same paradigm are constantly being used and to this extent are events in the world susceptible to being objectified for a scientific analysis. But obviously it is precisely in that objectivization of notions that are so evidently subjective that lies the controversial nature of any analysis of love and the concomitant principles. For the question is not so much whether my statement is scientifically meaningful as it is whether it is humanly meaningful, particularly in a book addressed to the participants in that conversation of which Heidegger spoke. How can I tell, and what is the use of my telling, people who are in search of authenticity, freedom, real relationships, and love that they have already achieved these things in the very fact that they are searching for them, a search that cannot be completed and thus abandoned without radical change, and thus define their very reality?

The issue is a moral one and the simple fact of my foreignness does not solve it. I tell Americans that they have achieved love (and justice, and freedom). They tell me that it is obviously not so. I will say that it is in the search that they achieve it. And it is because I believe my work participates in that search that I will argue that it does have some value beyond the purely "scientific" value that will be relevant mostly to people outside the culture.

For Americans, the search for love, and all that it implies, has to be actualized to be fully appropriate. Acts cannot be "merely symbolic." They must not only express love, they must also work. The evaluation of the effectiveness of love has always been understood to be an objective thing. The development of science in so spiritual and mystical a culture as America would not be understandable otherwise. One has only to read Emerson to realize the ease with which the rhetoric of man becomes a rhetoric of science in American culture. It is not so much that science objectivizes the subjective as that it demonstrates that the subjective and the objective, man and the world, are but one thing.

Thus it is not surprising that most sociology on America by Americans has been framed in terms of the discovery of the real behind the ideal, an orientation justified by the need to ensure that political rhetoric not be mere lip service and be translated into objectively measurable reality. That this is also appropriate, particularly for a native, I do not deny. I, however, am not a native. I adopted the outsider's stance. I remained detached. I did not become involved in what bothered my informants to the point where I would cease to observe and report and start to calculate the real in terms of the ideal. Is America a free society? Is it an authentically human society? I did not try to evaluate in such a way what I observed, probably because the principles that generate my special anxiety are of a different sort, but also because I believe that as an outsider I am better equipped to explore the reality that underlies even lip service, a reality that must also be explored not because it is behind the ideal so much as it is in it.

By focusing on the ideal as expressed (both in deeply held belief and empty rhetoric), I could not measure its actualization. I do hope, however, that I can help others in the creation of a better yardstick. One of the dangers inherent in the activity of debunking such myths as "America is a democracy" lies in being forced into emphasizing details, parts of the whole, and in missing essential linkages between the parts. This is why the debunking activities themselves must be evaluated by checking whether they really accomplish what they set out to do or whether they, too, are mere lip service. The dialectic of the objective and the subjective is ever alive, since the taking of the objective stance is always a subjective action and thus in need of objectivization. Thus, insofar as most American activity—whether at the personal level, in churches and government, and indeed in science—is "in the name of love," love itself must become an object, and in the process killed perhaps, in the same way as innumerable rats, mice, cats, dogs, and monkeys were killed to build the medical knowledge we possess.

That we have to kill to live, objectify to develop our subjectivity, is a paradox that we will not solve. We can accept it and continue the search according to the rules set for us by our ancestors, or we can dismiss it by shifting to another culture and, I am sure, another unsolvable paradox. This will necessarily happen. But in the meantime we have to continue acting in our given context.

Objectively, then, American culture may be found in the intersection of individualism, community, and love. I promised at the outset that my picture of American life in Appleton would be surprising, that I would make the people strange, exotic. Part of the surprise may lie in the fact that there were no surprises, that what I discovered are the worn-out cliches of countless sermons and Memorial Day speeches. But maybe this is where the folk wisdom of American life lies and what constitutes its exotic beauty. The Farm Bureau Creed is an unbelievable document. It is unbelievable not because it is a mark of the distance between ideological lip service and real life but because it is uttered in real life. It is as real and exotic as New Guinean masks, dances, or rituals, and it just cannot be dismissed. Nor can we dismiss any of the other experiences I have explored.

However, it must also be realized that the structure provided by the interplay of the notions of individualism, community, and love does not provide, in any real sense, a solution to the problems the people of Appleton encounter. What are provided are questions, riddles. And perhaps it is in that constant questioning of themselves and their lives that the complexity and authenticity of the people I met in Appleton are to be found. They are real, round, multidimensional—people involved in a dilemma-fraught battle with their own ideology. The structure provides only the framework for action, the rule to follow to understand a situation and to justify to oneself and to the world the action that is taken. How to interpret a specific action and what action to take in response remains problematic. Americans have to decide whether this neighbor is one of *these* neighbors who form one's community.

They have to decide whether to interpret their children's life-style decisions as a rightful exercise in individual variation within a community or as a rejection of the parents' own choices. Can it be both? Neither? The culture does not provide any guidance except insofar as it poses the questions. But the questions have to be answered concretely and often painfully.

Thoreau at Walden Pond, the movie *Love Story,* and the practice of social work, for example, are three myths that sing of different aspects of the structure of individualism, love, and community. But none of these myths can be taken as *the* model of and for action because each cancels out the other. Thoreau is admired for his flight to the woods as a proof of his triumphant individualism; and yet the whole weight of the American educational system is intended to break the original aloneness of the child, to socialize him. In the movie *Love Story,* the lovers are depicted as alone and never with a group of friends; but we should not love in any ivory tower. Social work, service to the community, is often considered the height of moral worth; and yet one should not become so immersed in others as to lose one's own individuality.

These are not conflicts between the real and the ideal. They are conflicts within the ideal. Each statement apparently proper in itself becomes conflictive when it is put in its ideological context, as will necessarily happen when people start operating on it and then arguing within the very logic of the culture that the decision that has been taken according to that same logic is improper, as it must always be. Thence comes the intensity of life I encountered in Appleton and which I have tried to render in these pages.

I may not always have been successful in expressing the intensity of this anxiety as I emphasized the objective exploration of the sources of the unique style used by my informants to express their anxiety. In the process, I may not have reconstructed appropriately the life that I have so directly experienced. I simply hope that the reader will participate in reconstructing in his imagination the existential quality of the situations I have taken apart. To stress this I would like to close this book by quoting a song that was very popular among some of my informants. In it are expressed all the themes I have explored, and with it I can state one last time the uniqueness of American culture.

With a Little Help From My Friends

What would you do if I sang out of tune,
Would you stand up and walk out on me.

Lend me your ears and I'll sing you a song,
And I'll try not to sing out of key.

I get by with a little help from my friends,
I get high with a little help from my friends,
Going to try with a little help from my friends.

What do I do when my love is away
(Does it worry you to be alone)
How do I feel at the end of the day
(Are you sad because you are on your own)

No I get by with a little help from my friends,
Do you need anybody,
I need somebody to love.
Could it be anybody,
I want somebody to love.

Would you believe in a love at first sight,
Yes I'm certain that it happens all the time.
What do you see when you turn out the light,
I can't tell you but I know it's mine.
Oh I get by with a little help from my friends.

      (John Lennon and Paul McCartney)

Postface

*And so it is that in language, art or anything else,
communicability lies somewhere between
reproduction and randomness; therefore,
communicability cannot be exact, yet neither can
it be absent.*
*—James A. Boon, From Symbolism to
Structuralism: Lévi-Strauss in a Literary Tradition*

I chose as a last statement of what I take to be the fundamental themes of American culture a song written by two Englishmen. Musically this song is a transformation of a native American musical style (rock 'n' roll), which itself sprang from the encounter between West African and Western European folk forms. How can I say that this song is "American"? Conversely, while it was extremely popular for a while, it was far from being universally appreciated. Many Americans did not recognize themselves in it. Furthermore, it is *one* statement, unique. All the statements I have analyzed were unique, idiosyncratic. Whatever value they may have as illustrations of ways in which the themes are handled in everyday situations, they cannot be considered to be proof of my analysis. In what way, then, can I say that there is an American culture, and that my analysis is relevant to it? And if there is, how does one decide whether a performance one is watching is American? What are the signs, and how is one to account for them? Furthermore, how is one to understand the very term "culture"?

These questions are of obvious theoretical and methodological import. I cannot ignore them. During the course of the book, I have implicitly argued the point that what I was saying about the Howards, the Elliotts, and Appleton, I was also saying about American culture. I have not been explicit about my reasons for taking this step from the very particular to the very general, mostly because it would have led me away from my primary goal, which was to contribute to the ethnology of America and not to the theory of culture. However, for those who are interested in the question, I have decided to make my reasons more explicit.

The Universal and the Particular

The social sciences in general, and anthropology in particular, are rooted in a philosophic paradox, the two sides of which keep the discipline in an irreducible tension. The paradox lies in the dual search for those aspects of human behavior that can be shown to be universal and those aspects that are typical of one man, one social situation, one culture. For the very existence of the discipline is justifiable only insofar as it can be assumed, and then shown, that man is one. Yet social scientists know, both through their professional training and observations and through their existential experience as human beings, that universal statements about man, at whatever level, rob the situation about which they are made of an essential element of richness, depth, and, indeed, humanity. One can argue that something like the nuclear family is universal because it is the natural condition of procreation and nurturing for the human species, or that each culture is a whole in itself that an outsider can never wholly understand. Then one must struggle with the other side of the paradox, the evidence that different people have different ideas about what appears to be the "same thing" the world over, and the evidence that, in spite of the cultural gap between societies, it is still possible for people from different cultures to communicate, in an imperfect way perhaps, but in a definite way. Anthropologists and nonanthropologists alike are able to "learn" a culture in such a way that the natives come to recognize something of themselves in the other's behavior and may eventually accept the newcomer as one of them. Like a language learned late in life, the new member will have a recognizable accent, but he will be understood.

The paradox cannot be resolved empirically. The debate between partisans of the "psychic unity of mankind" and partisans of "cultural relativism" that raged in the early decades of the modern development of anthropology has quieted, not because it has been resolved but because a sort of gentlemen's agreement has been struck that it would not be fruitful to pursue it. It is not that anybody has been convinced of the immateriality of the debate or that everybody has been won to one side of the issue. From time to time, theoreticians take positions that identify them with one point of view or the other; for example, Lévi-Strauss reaffirms in his work a belief in something akin to the psychic unity of mankind, while Geertz leans toward almost absolute cultural relativism. What all this suggests is that the paradox belongs to the philosophic grounding of the discipline and that it is not part of its field of inquiry. Anthropology may eventually be able to trace in detail the relationship between ecology and social organization or to understand the working of the human mind as expressed in ideological behavior, but it will not be able to prove that human beings are either all the same or all different, because these are the very postulates on which all other theory is grounded.

This book has been about the differences among human beings. It is grounded in the culture shock that nonnatives experience when they encounter Americans. ("How can they be like this?" "What's going on?") Americans *are* different from Frenchmen, and from this perspective, "When you have seen one, you have seen them all." The stance I have taken is that *the differences that exist among Americans are not so relevant as the differences that exist between them and people from other cultures.* Having lived and listened to Americans for several years now, I know how shocking this is to many who are fond of the diversity that is supposedly typical of America. The unity of America in the context of other cultures is a fact, however, and cannot be dismissed out of hand. There are things in America that are characteristically American, a certain way of seeing the world and man's place in it, that one does not find elsewhere. This has been the focus of my analysis.

I believe, obviously, that I can analyze what is characteristically American, that it is not fully opaque to me. To those who think that "the natives know best," I can only suggest that they read Melville, Faulkner, or Updike. Even Henry James may have said in his novels more profound insider things about America than I or any other outsider may say. Yet I believe I have something to say that may be helpful even to insiders. This may be easier to accept if one is ready to see culture as an intellectual as well as an emotional thing. It is obviously easier for me to understand Americans intellectually than feel what Americans may have felt participating in the Bicentennial rejoicing, for example.

What is accessible to me of what is characteristically American, then, is a certain way of *thinking* about the world, not an emotional response to it. This is not a radical limitation, for it is because culture is *intelligible* that it can be taught to, and learned by, children and anthropologists.

Fundamentally, then, my stance is universalistic. All human beings are similar enough, I have assumed, for their communication systems to be mutually intelligible. And because my stance is universalistic, I believe it is also scientific.

Culture as Communicative Action

Culture, I have argued, is a proper area for scientific inquiry insofar as we can assume that it refers to a structured, or structurable, activity. What kind of activity?

That I should even ask such a question implies an a priori assumption: that human action can be analyzed fruitfully into subsystems, each of which is structured by different processes. This assumption is obviously Parsonian, and I must here recognize my debt to this school of thought. Culture, as I see it, is not a mere reflection of underlying social or economic forces, even though these certainly do participate in structuring behavior. On the other side there are the simplistic Marxists and functionalists for whom culture, the ideological superstructure of a society, doesn't say anything other than its infrastructure, and says it badly since true consciousness of the historical situation in which the subject finds himself is exceedingly difficult to gain. In fact, the very argument that there can be false consciousness implies that other processes, in certain contexts, override the simple unfolding of infrastructural determinisms.

I cannot demonstrate fully the relative independence of the superstructure from the infrastructure or, in Parsonian terms, of society from culture. I can only suggest by brief references to alternative ways that ideological or ritual theories about the world cannot be explained simplistically by reference to their infrastructural functionality. The need for ritual unanimity during public meetings of government boards, for example, does not derive from the capitalistic nature of the American economic system. In France the same economic system leads to the constant reemphasis of internal schisms within towns, within the ideology, even within the most united families. Native French analysts may interpret this symbolic recognition of conflict as a product of a class society. Their analysis is, in its turn, rendered doubtful by my observations in Appleton. In both France and America, something is involved in symbolic encounters other than a projection of social structure into consciousness.

This does not mean that economic pressures can be fully transcended by culture. On the contrary, it is evident that they provide the content of the interaction. The Farm Bureau was not created "because" of a desire on the part of some farmers to symbolize any sort of mystical communion. It developed, obviously, as a response to the economic transformation of the American economy beginning about 1910 and running through the 1920s and 1930s. Schools, hospitals, and the water supply must be administered in one way or another. And the very nature of the service to be delivered necessarily determines the choices that will eventually have to be made.

What the structure of the relationship between man and his environment through the means of production does *not* determine is the mapping of the semantic field. The telling of an autobiography is something other than the living of one's life, and it is not subject to the same rules. In the same manner, interpreting what it is that makes people come together is not the same thing as actually joining a group. Performing the rituals of the public meeting is not the same thing as making a decision.

In other words, I have not been dealing with "behavior," narrowly defined, or only insofar as one can argue that the structure of one's semantic system does feed back to one's nonsemantic behavior. The Sapir-Whorf hypothesis may have been too radical in this respect, but the recent work of Michael Cole and his associates would seem to indicate that the structure of one's culture is not completely powerless in determining noncultural behavior.[1] And after all, isn't talking a form of behavior?

In the emphasis I have put on seeing my data in quasi-linguistic terms as aspects of general communication between my informants about themselves and their world, I differentiate myself from the most orthodox Parsonian interpretations of culture. As late as 1972, Parsons still wrote that "the meaning of cultural patterns seen in the context of their relation to action is *always* in some degree and respect normative [author's emphasis]."[2] And he went on to stress the importance of "values." I have had little to say about

values in this book, for I do not feel I can assume that the performance of a particular cultural act necessarily implies the emotional
involvement that I think must be present if one is to assume that
something is valued. What struck me in Appleton was the extremely structured character of actions that were *not* valued, that
were performed mechanically without reference to any possible
sanction.

The activity I interpret as cultural is thus not necessarily
evaluative or normative. It is, if I may say so, intellectual; that is,
essentially neutral from the point of view of affectivity, though it
can be used to express emotions and also raise them. On this point I
follow Lévi-Strauss in trying to discern "behind the manifestations
of affective life, the indirect effect of alterations that took place in
the normal course of intellectual operation."[3]

This theoretical posture has definite practical implications in
terms of data and empirical validation of substantive analyses. It
grounds cultural anthropology in science by concretizing the data it
can use. What are these data?

Words. Sequences of words. Acts only to the extent that they
are interpretable. Acts that are not interpreted may be useful in the
process of analysis, particularly in a comparative context. They
often reveal central properties of the system (for example, my informants' lack of understanding of society as a self-regulating
process). Other absences may be highly significant (for example,
the absence of disagreement in public meetings of local government board). In short, what I studied was not the minds of my
informants but what they said. And while what they had in their
minds may be unreachable, what they said is directly observable
data, as concrete and empirical as one could wish. Culture may be
an abstraction, but it is a valid scientific abstraction when one can
argue that what one is saying about it is grounded in the observation of a definite concrete object in the phenomenological world.

To see culture as a concept that refers to certain types of empirical data is to ground cultural anthropology as a science. It is
a science that obviously shares a lot with linguistics, which is also
about words and sequences of words. Linguistics, however, operates at a different level. It is most properly the science of the process of communication of contents between different points (human
senders and receivers of messages) and using a certain medium
(the human body and brain). Cultural anthropology would then be
more properly the study of these contents—"meanings," we might
call them.

Some may not agree with my labels and would prefer to reserve the word "culture" for the conglomerate of everything human beings produce—material objects, technology, ecological adaptation, social structure, religion, ideology, and so on. It is, of course, fruitless to fight over labels. If someone wants to call "human ecology" "cultural ecology," isn't it his right? It probably is so long as it is clear what aspects of the world the term refers to. This is what I have tried to do in these pages. I believe that I have bounded a certain level of human action that possesses its own structuring processes. To this process I give the name "culture" to emphasize the tie binding me to the American tradition that goes from Kroeber and Benedict to Parsons, Schneider, and Geertz.

From Culture to Cultures

This position is influenced by what can be called, broadly speaking, French structuralism. My methodology and epistemology are direct outgrowths of my understanding of this structuralism. What I did in these pages is different, however, from what most practitioners of structuralism in France do, because of my interest in the "characteristically so-and-so." Structuralist tools have been used most often to analyze modern French forms in their arbitrariness (Foucault or Barthes) or to establish a science of intelligibility (Lévi-Strauss). There are very few structuralist ethnologies (except possibly the work of Dumont and Dumézil) and no full-fledged structuralist theory of the characteristic. This issue of the individuality of cultures has, on the contrary, been a central interest of American anthropology. If there is a strong perceived need to deal with a middle level between single myths or customs and universal categories or processes, the level of culture, it is to a large extent because of the work of American scholars, and to this extent my work is as "American" as it is "French."

What is the nature of this middle level? Ferdinand de Saussure in his epoch-making *Course in General Linguistics* made a fundamental distinction of possibly universal significance to all the social sciences. He distinguished between the individual speech act (*parole*) that is the concrete material on which the linguist works and the social, shared structure (*langue*) that the speech act must follow, however approximately, in order to be understood by an audience that has no insight into the speaker's meaning other than his verbal (or quasi-verbal) speech. To Saussure, *langue* was only "tongue."

But the distinction he makes between *parole* and *langue* is of more general relevance. He argues that *parole* is individual, accidental, and contingent from the point of view of *langue*. *Langue,* on the other hand, is social, arbitrary in relation to the world it organizes, certainly, but nevertheless restrictive on the person who must speak it to be understood. *Parole* emphasizes the content aspect of language; and *langue,* its form aspect.

Linguists have argued since Saussure made his distinction that a tongue is not an obvious object in the world. Even within the boundaries of mutual intelligibility, speech acts can be collected that do not conform in all respects to the grammar of the dominant tongue. To deal with this evidence, it is necessary to talk of dialects and subdialects characteristic of regions or social classes, and even of idiolects, the dialects of individual speakers. Saussure's division between what is social and what is individual in language thus cannot be taken literally: an individual can have a tongue that is all his own. But even at the level of the idiolect, the distinction between the necessary and the contingent, *langue* and *parole,* remains valid: an idiolect is a reconstruction from single speech acts; it has a grammar that the speaker follows quite as much as the reconstruction of the characteristic traits of a family of mutually unintelligible tongues has a unique grammar in relation to other such families of language. The criterion for acceptance of the grammar of an idiolect as a valid representation of its structure is still that it accounts for all speech acts the person may utter in whatever context. This grammar must, like any other grammar, be presented as form, as a set of rules to be followed, and not as content.

At the other extreme of generality, Saussure did not emphasize the universality of the *capacity* for language and the concomitant need to write grammars that produce not only recognizable speech with a certain tongue as the point of reference but also grammars that take the general capacity as their point of reference. From this point of view we might say that tongues are themselves "speech acts," individual and contingent, and the capacity, the "human mind," is the fundamental "tongue," arbitrary from the point of view of systems of animal communication but necessary for human beings who do not have the possibility of communicating the way ants and bees communicate but do, obviously, have the ability to learn each other's dialects.

This emphasis on the universality of the deepest structures of language has been made most strongly by Noam Chomsky. In the field of culture, Lévi-Strauss has made essentially the same point.

Myths or kinship systems must be understood, he has argued, as embodiments of universal principles of thinking in both their wild and constrained forms. In his attempt to make his point, he moves (in a way considered reckless by many) from the most individual speech acts—a single myth and its variants across "cultures"—to the most general without stopping at intermediate levels, either "idiocultures" (the individual styles of the authors or tellers of a myth) or subcultures (regional variations) or cultures (stylistic typifications of broader but not yet universal validity).

It is not, I believe, that Lévi-Strauss denies that systems of signification and intelligibility are organized at these intermediate levels. It is simply that he, like most influential French theorists, is not interested in exploring the mechanics of cultural activity in this way. This may very well be a product of French culture itself and its traditional interest in the working of the mind. The American fascination with cultural uniqueness may, conversely, be related to the themes of individualism and the relativity of value that organize the American perception of the world.

That these insights are grounded in the respective cultures does not make them less relevant, for each is telling us something. Each has perceived an aspect of the situation: men all think alike, but the hazards of history and of demography and the technological limits to communication that have thrust men apart into self-sufficient isolates have led the general structure to actualize itself into many different systems that start by being mutually unintelligible. It is one of the marvels of the human species and probably a central aspect of its great adaptability to various environments that the forms of the communication processes between individuals of the species are not fully determined by the general structure of these processes or by the content of the messages. There are constraints: our cultures and languages must be precise enough so that we can survive in our environment—in the short run, at least. But communicability does not require reproduction. It only requires a contract between the people, however few or many, who belong to a set. This contract produces mutually intelligible tongues, cultures (or simply dialects or street-corner subcultures) that have a theoretical reality that is not simply the creation of romantic or idealistic American anthropologists.

But ecological conditions change. New technologies are introduced and radically transform the demography and then the social-structural environment of a group. New tongues, new cultures develop. The value of the different items that enter into the total human situation change. But the function itself, in the mathematical sense, remains the same. New cultures can be learned by human beings. We are thus justified in hypothesizing with Lévi-Strauss and Chomsky that the capacity to interpret new situations is species-specific, that individual interpretations are all transformations of this general capacity, which can be conceived as the system of all these transformations, a structure, in Piaget's sense, not necessarily "of the mind" but certainly of our thinking processes.

The Scientific Study of Culture

It is rather easy to argue that there exists in the existential world a certain type of activity—culture—that cannot be subsumed under any other type. This activity, this force as we would say if we were dealing with a physical effect, is unmistakable. The difficulty lies in describing it precisely and unequivocally, in bounding its extension and in accounting for actual manifestations of it. The time has passed when anthropology could content itself with demonstrating the existence of culture. What must be done now is the difficult job of formalizing our insights without doing violence to either the reality we are studying or the rules of the scientific method.

The road to formalization is strewn with theoretical dangers, two of which have been particularly deleterious to past efforts: reification and idealization. It is difficult to realize concretely that while the concept of culture is useful and refers to something in the world, what one observes when one attends a Sunday service at the Methodist church is not Protestantism, religion, America, or culture. The concept of culture, or of a culture, is an abstraction, a construct. What an anthropologist in the field encounters are streams of behavior, both verbal and nonverbal, that involve interaction between different persons. This gets recorded in field notes, already crudely analyzed, inescapably, by the physical inability of the anthropologist to record everything, his own native biases as to what is important and not important in human behavior, and his professional training. This leaves a mass of heterogeneous data to be organized, "analyzed."

The initial temptation is to classify the odds and ends collected into the pigeonholes provided by the tradition of the discipline. One piece is kinship; another, religion. It has become more and more difficult to do this as it has been demonstrated that such categories have no universal validity. More or less formally, anthropology has been moving toward organizing its work in terms of models, structures, or processes. These concepts allow for more flexibility since the analyst is freed from a priori constraints, except the general requirement for cohesiveness. The advances in our understanding of American kinship were made possible, for example, when it became evident to David Schneider that there was no reason to consider it only in terms of the way it classifies kin.

The danger of reification remains, however, though in a transformed form. It no longer consists of substantivizing categories such as kinship, but in assuming that the models generated by the analysts have a life independent from the life that is given to it by the persons who operate on it. Of course, scientific models are valid only if they correspond to some reality outside of themselves. Thus, to gain scientific status, cultural anthropology must deal with concrete realities that can be encountered in the experiential world rather than with abstractions that it may think useful.

But the building of models is not an easy task, for a model is never built in a vacuum of absolutes. It is always built by a certain person with a certain experience, and it is intended to be relevant to a certain context. A model is always oriented, and thus unique. The model of America I have drawn is unique since it derives from my observations of a few idiosyncratic persons in nonreplicable situations and since I am myself an idiosyncratic person, a male in my late twenties trained at the University of Chicago and, above all, French. I am very conscious that my models are so oriented.

Some might call this orientation a bias. I would argue, though, that the idea of bias when used pejoratively implies the further idea that there is, or ought to be, a way of doing science without bias, that our ultimate goal is to develop models that would be unbiased, pure absolutes. Here lies the issue of idealism. For what could be more idealistic than this belief in absolute models or structures? One can imagine a scholar, many decades from now, taking all the models of American society and culture built by all sorts of people for all sorts of reasons and constructing an abstract model of America from their accounts. Would this model not be oriented? Or would it not simply be oriented toward a different goal starting from a different point? The second alternative appeals to me more.

Science is not simply the collection and description of substantively bounded entities. It consists rather in transforming the existential world into an intelligible thing apprehensible by the human mind, something that is not predicated on sampling procedures, because the discovered order is not in the things studied but in our operations on them. It is not that the world is not there. The inevitability of death reminds us that there is something outside of us. It is rather that we cannot be certain whether the theoretical elaborations of mathematics (and any other system of logic and reasoning that we use to make scientific statements) "fit nature's phenomena by virtue of a 'deep' structure of congruency which would be inscribed in the ontological reality of entities, and would link our operations with nature, or only by a surface articulation, the compatibility of which with the theoretical products is to be conceived of in terms of occasional harmony."[4]

There is a world out there, but we cannot apprehend its grammar directly. I am not contradicting what I said earlier. The models we build must be true to something outside us. But even a yearning for transcendental truth cannot blind us to the fact that what we encounter in the historical situation that is ours, as scientists as well as natives, are not absolute entities, crystallike wholes, substances to be discovered and then explored. What we encounter are single, particular, nonreplicable events, odds and ends. And we encounter them haphazardly.

Some will say that this encounter is anything but haphazard, that it is instead highly structured by our very position in the world. I do not dispute this, but I maintain the word to stress that we do not know *what* this position is, which means that we cannot fully deal with the fact of our being in-situation. I can stress that I am young, French, and so on. I can also stress that I see my work as a study in cultural anthropology, the comparative study of Indo-European ideologies, the distinction of an American culture in opposition to a French culture (rather than a European culture in opposition to an Indian culture, as Louis Dumont has been doing, or a Midwest culture versus a Southern culture within the United States, in which many Americans are more interested), and so on. All this says some things about my positions, but what exactly? Aren't there also many more such biases of which I am not fully aware? Probably. What are they? This question cannot be answered purely empirically, for any attempt to elucidate all my biases would be submitted to the same limitations as my study itself. A model cannot be evaluated by simple observation, but rather by manipulation. Whatever scientific order we find in the odds and ends we have encountered and collected is not (necessarily) the transcendentally real order of these things. It is always a *constructed* reality, a human reality.

The Analysis of Cultures: Explanation and Understanding

What Saussure did when he differentiated *langue* from *parole* was offer an escape from these fundamental limitations of the social sciences. For example, such a grammatical "fact" as that in English the third-person singular of regular verbs in the present tense is marked by an *s* added to the root is not a simple observational event: linguists cannot describe this *s* univocally in speech. In different contexts it can be pronounced [s], [z], [ez]. It is still the same significant unit in English in this and a few other contexts. Individual occurrences of this *s* might be described comprehensively, but such a description would not help arrive at a general theory of English. To do this, we must construct a phoneme /s/ that becomes the theoretical event to be manipulated.

In the social sciences, "facts" are always constructs and to this extent always dependent on the ever-changing position of the observer. In the relationship observer-observed there is no fixed point, everything is in continuous motion. The situation of the scientist is the same as that of the *bricoleur* in whom Lévi-Strauss sees the prototype of the human being in-(cultural)-situation. Like the *bricoleur*, the scientist starts with odds and ends, pieces of events, singular occurrences, and tries to make them intelligible by ordering them and then reordering them as they shift and disappear or as new ones appear.

This is most obviously true of anthropologists in a field situation. They cannot control their sample in any systematized manner. Their samples are never random, always haphazard. The whole about which they are trying to make a statement is thus always problematic. Strictly speaking, I have not described Appleton in this book. I have not even described the Howards, the Methodist church, John's group, or any of the other events to which I devoted many pages. To do this I would have had to (1) define the whole about which I wanted to make a descriptive statement strictly in time, space, and aspect, and (2) either describe "everything" or choose a sample (random or stratified).

I did not do any of the above because systematic sampling does not solve our problem. A survey is valid only for the short period of time during which it is taken. It is a flash picture. However many times one may take the picture, one still has nothing more than events whose generality beyond the time and space bounded a priori remains problematic. This does not have to do with the sophistication of the sampling so much as with the instantaneous and ultrafocused nature of the technique.

This is not to deny that as far as taking pictures is concerned, a method that tells us systematically what the field of the picture is, the point of view of the photographer, the type of lens, the point of focus, and so on, is more adequate than one that does not offer this information. Anthropological fieldwork just cannot compete with survey techniques in such endeavors. They have probably already co-opted the field of ethnography, except for those areas of the world where practical problems may preclude their use. Who could claim nowadays to have given a mimetic description of a human community without having listed all the variations in arrangement of individuals, attitudes, and the number of people in each category?

It remains that two essential aspects of the process of quantification cannot be handled in a purely quantitative manner and must depend on what is very inappropriately called "qualitative" thinking. One has to do with the definition of the unit to be counted, the other with the definition of the population. In the social world neither can be taken for granted. Are all female-headed families "broken homes"? How does one decide that a family is "female-headed"? Why, indeed, do we think that this is an interesting thing to count if not for theoretical reasons that do not have their source in the methodology itself? Furthermore, no theoretical discourse can be satisfied with the concreteness and singularity of the empirical world. We are then left with the constant questioning of the adequacy of the abstracting process in the two directions it takes: Does a concept usefully organize the existential "reality"? Is the operationalization of the concept appropriate? Neither of these questions can be answered empirically or by observation.

Similarly, the bounding of a population is dependent on a decision grounded outside the methodology. The decision can be political (as when a researcher accepts a census unit as his population) or it can be theoretical (as when a sample is stratified by "class"). In any event, the discovery of a population to sample and describe is a type of activity that demands a different form of logic, one that is, in fact, very similar to the one I used in this book.

Of course, survey techniques and statistical tools are used for more than mimetic description. Like any other operations of human behavior (or any other event in the world), additive, numerical statements show regularity. Correlations can be established; certain behaviors can be "explained" or—to speak more precisely—related to the occurrence of other behaviors or events; others can be "predicted." To this extent, statistical correlations *are* structures; they are sets of items related to each other in a systematic manner. They are, indeed, transformational sets, since it can be demonstrated that as certain properties of certain items change, other properties of these items also change. But this search for correlations is only one moment in the total process of the social sciences.

Statistical analysis is a branch of mathematics that deals with the probability that certain definable, discrete events occur in a bounded population. It is appropriate to use the method only if one can assume that the event is not changing radically as the different steps of the analysis proceed. For example, to compare divorce statistics in the United States, in, say, 1920 and 1970, one must assume methodologically and operationally, that divorce and marriage were defined and recorded in the same way at both times. One must also assume, *theoretically*, that divorce and marriage are the same in their nature at both points of time in spite of any other changes that may have occurred between the two surveys. What if one is led to believe that they are *not* the same? Then the comparison cannot proceed statistically.

In other words, to deal with large numbers is not to escape the fact that all human activity, including science, starts with unique, particular, idiosyncratic events. Nor is it to solve the problem of the theoretical generalization of these events. To collect many events is not enough, if only because survey data is never "raw" data, it is always data interpreted by the nature of the instrument used to collect them. Furthermore, the result of any survey is not a general statement but a new, unique event limited to the point of view of the operator, the type of questionnaire used, and so on. A survey is also limited by the instantaneous nature of the picture—synchrony at its extreme!

In other words, any attempt at exact description or measurement implies another step in the process of inquiry that is logically primary: one cannot describe or measure what one does not first understand, however culture-bound, "mytho"-logical rather than analytical, this understanding may be. Explanation is always secondary to understanding, theory always primary to observation

and correlation. There is no "grounded theory" in the strict induc-
tive sense advocated by Barney Glaser and Anselm Strauss.[5] And,
obviously, the methodological demands of a research oriented toward understanding or interpretation, as mine is, are quite different from those of a research oriented toward explanation.

To say that all observation is dependent on an a priori understanding doesn't mean that this understanding cannot change in
the encounter with the concrete world. Obviously, if the activity is
to be science, it must be susceptible to transformation as events,
even singular events, are encountered that in certain ways do not fit
the initial understanding. It is in this intellectual feedback that,
hopefully, we will move from a mythology to a science of human
behavior. But certainly we must not be naive. This process is not a
fast or easy one. Not to mention the fact that it is not an individual
thing but an historical one.

Understanding is not mimetic description. A statement fully
appropriate within the rules of understanding may not refer directly to any observable reality, though it must account for it. In
other words, understanding must be general and thus transcend
the particular events that it must account for and that have hopefully guided the development of its special character. To come back
to Saussure, an account of any *langue* must be more than a collection of *paroles,* however numerous and properly randomized this
collection may be.

The Analysis of Cultures: Data and Procedures

All this is necessary to introduce—and justify—the steps I took
in my analysis and presentation of my results, and the conclusions I
have reached. It must be noted first that I did not do anything that
is essentially so different from what other anthropologists have
done. I conducted fieldwork, which means that I lived for one year
in a town—with a family for a while, in an apartment in town, and
then in a house in the country. I talked a lot to people formally and
informally, I went to church twice every Sunday, to board meetings, to parties. I worked with a farmer for a month, in a factory for
ten days. And I took notes, I collected all types of literature. And
then I attempted to order these odds and ends in a way that would
not do violence to any of them.

At one level, my book is just one more community study. But I
have tried to do much more. Is another community study of an

American small town really needed? Is what I found so different from what Lloyd Warner and his team found in "Elmtown"/"Jonesville" or James West found in "Plainville"? Thirty years elapsed between their work and mine, but is this sufficient reason for a simple restudy? To try to duplicate their work would have been irrelevant, I believe. Their work represents one moment in the history of the discipline, and the discipline has evolved since they wrote. However one wants to look at it, I could not have done a restudy. In particular there has been the growing awareness that, in Geertz's phrase, "Anthropologists do not study villages . . . they study *in* villages."[6] This was paired in my mind with an interest in culture and ideology in historically characteristic manifestations. Finally there was my concern that references to "America" or "middle-class" culture were often made in sociological discourse with little understanding of the structure that generates this culture.

That there is an American culture, something that even some anthropologists of my acquaintance profess to doubt, was never an issue for me. From my first day in the United States, I have always felt that it is somehow different. It is this "somehow" that I have tried to explore and to understand. Culture-shock is a feeling that is triggered by something concrete. What is this something? What are the signs that make one notice that a performance is American and not French—or anything else? These signs are not, in a strict sense, the absence or presence of discrete items. There was no old aristocracy in Appleton, there were no hippies in Springdale; still, both are unmistakably American towns. I have not directly experienced Springdale, but both the image of the town I have after reading Vidich and Bensman and the very style of their description make me "feel" America. For example, they use the word "community" twenty times in the first three pages of the Preface to their book. We are told that there were "a number of sharp contradictions in the community's institutions and values" and that this was so striking that the basic question became: "What are the integrating psychological and institutional factors that make the community's social life possible?"[7] Couldn't communities "survive" in spite of conflict? Couldn't it be that conflict *is* the driving force of social life? I am sure that many Americans would consider the argument, and some might even agree with it. It remains that, particularly when the focus of the utterance is directed elsewhere, the theme of society—what is called community—as being something fragile in need of an integration based on psychological or institutional factors is pervasive, both in popular and in esoteric doctrine. Each occurrence is unique, and yet the structure is the same.

What I collected were incidents to analyze. I collected these incidents haphazardly. When I say that there is no old aristocracy in Appleton, I am saying that I never met anybody who would fit into such a category, and that nobody mentioned it either. Could I have missed it? Very possible. I did not even strive for completeness. What I looked for was a set of events to analyze, and I tried to maximize contextual variation in the belief that this would help me most to pinpoint structural properties.

The method would have been unacceptable if my aim had been mimetic description. It is, however, fully appropriate to reach intelligibility. To write a grammar, a linguist needs only a set of sentences and a few informants. I think this is all one needs to describe a culture, too. What I have attempted to do is reconstruct the equivalent at my level of what the linguists call phonemes at their level; that is, units that in their systemic interaction with other units of the same order allow for a speaker to transmit an intelligible message to an audience. To test such an analysis, one need not check the substantive reality of the unit postulated: the phoneme /s/ in English is not a substance. Similarly, love may have properties very different from the ones attributed to it by Americans. What one needs to check is the significance of the unit within a system, and the question to ask is: Is it necessary to postulate such a unit to account for the examples collected? Thus, what I have tried to do is not to describe individualism, community, or love, but to demonstrate that they are three significant units that function together to structure in a characteristic manner the semantic level of American speech.

There is one fundamental limitation to the approach I have chosen: there is no way I can ascertain from my data alone the extension in time and space of the culture I have outlined. Have I painted a network culture, a subregional or a national culture? The test of the extension of any culture is probably mutual intelligibility, though it is not enough for the grammarian of culture to ask of an informant whether he "understands" an utterance or even simply whether it is grammatical. One can often understand ungrammatical sentences, but their ungrammaticalness will stand out. With culture the situation is more delicate, since the participants can more easily project their meaning into an event that they could not have produced. The absence of a welcoming at the door of the Catholic church may go unnoticed by a Protestant visitor or it may lead him to say that Catholics are cold. This would be an interpretation from within American culture of something that is perfectly understandable in the context of the definition of the parish, the local congregation, and the Church (with an upper-case *C*) in Catholicism outside American culture. Conversely, parents of teenage rebels are wont to say that they can't understand their children anymore, even though it is possible to argue, as I have, that statements made by both parents and children proceed from the same structure while appearing mutually unintelligible.

The problem is that it is obvious, even to the linguistically unsophisticated, that language is form, structure, code, but not content. On the other hand, the reality of culture as a system of meanings that is also structure and code rather than emotional and political content is not so easily perceived. A statement like the Pledge of Allegiance is seen first as the mark of a certain political position. That it is written in English is accepted to be contingent to a fundamental meaning of universal significance. That it also consists of a certain arrangement of concepts such as I, pledge, me, nation, and so on, that is as arbitrary as the tongue in which it is said, and thus of anything but universal relevance, is rarely recognized.

Why this should be so is not mysterious. Ideologies, cultural codes are *used,* like tools, to make statements about the world. The objects they create are more important to the operator than they themselves are. The Pledge of Allegiance can thus be used by the various classes in their power struggles. But there is a logic to tools, and it is the logic of this special kind of tool, cultural interpretation, that I set out to discover.

Finally, my analysis is not in any way predictive, nor is it historical in the sense of indicating where the items I explored came from. For many this may be the most serious limitation of the approach. I will say simply that I in no way deny the value of *also* doing histories of cultures. It remains that historical knowledge cannot duplicate the knowledge one can gain from what is not so much a synchronic as an atemporal approach: the *bricoleur,* like the chess player who takes over a game after a number of plays, does not have to know where the pieces he is going to deal with come from in order to grasp the possibilities inherent in their immediate organization and start playing the game, telling his myths, or speaking his situation.

American Culture

I have argued that this book is about American culture. What do I mean by American? In the simplest way, I mean that on certain occasions all my informants referred to themselves in that way. This entitles me to so identify them, too. One difficulty lies in the fact that on other occasions they also referred to themselves as other things. Many of them were also farmers, Methodists, and/or Italians. But whatever else they were, which only a few of them were, they were all also American, which was the only label that possessed an all-encompassing quality. There was something else, however, for many of my informants saw themselves as being first and foremost human beings, their deepest reality in that it was also the most universal. For them, American referred to only one aspect of their identity, one that became relevant when reference was made to the non-American world and to what they themselves recognized were people of a different culture. But informants quickly added that, under their apparent diversity, all people, whether European, African, or even Russian, were also human beings and thus there was a fundamental unity between them, the people of Appleton, and people from all other parts of the world. In a way, this process of universalization is similar to the attempt to involve everybody in one's own small community.

Indeed, as the greatest universalism is reached, we come back to extreme atomization, since human beings are always, it is agreed, unique individuals and thus all different, however similar they may appear to be. The rebellion of many native sociologists (for example, all the theoreticians of the "new ethnicity": Nathan Glazer, Daniel Moynihan, Michael Novak, Andrew Greeley, and so on) against the idea that there could be a distinct American culture, against the idea that in some ways the melting pot *has* worked (though possibly not in the way the earlier versions of the theory thought it would work), may be a concomitant of notions of individualism. If ethnic variation is real and alternate life-styles take hold, then the lonely crowd is exorcised. For it is the lonely crowd, the other-directed individual, the attempt to keep up with the Joneses, the "ticky-tacky" life that are the ultimate evils. Americans were created equal, but they are all different. To argue otherwise is either to make a mistake or to offer the most radical criticism of the American way of life.

For apologists for the diversity of America, the word is a convenient term to refer to a geopolitical area where human beings are free to be themselves without external constraints. Furthermore, any human being who rebels against convention is potentially American and must be encouraged. On the earth there are human beings on one side; and on the other, political systems that prevent humanity from developing fully. America is in the interstices between these systems. Of course, radical natives of the United States argue that the United States government is just one of those political systems. But their movement away from imposed government to consensual human government is still essentially Puritan, Jeffersonian, American.

On the one hand then, I have informants arguing that "America" is not a substantive entity, but rather the place where there are no substantive entities above the individual, where the human spirit is free. On the other hand, I have my ordering mind, my skepticism, and particularly my anthropological relativism. From this point of view, could I accept at face value the attempt to deny the specificity of the American experience in which consists the attempt to transcend it by emphasizing that in America the fundamental units are individuals free to be whatever they wish and, in particular, not American? To accept this would be for me to "turn native," and to violate my experience in Appleton.

A culture is not something to be easily transcended, and even if the goal *is* to transcend it, the first step must be a confrontation with it as a reality. I decided to label this reality American. What else could I have called it? I could have been strict and called it the "culture of the people of Appleton." But beyond the fact that my informants did not see themselves as different from people in neighboring towns and states, I believe I have experienced the culture I encountered in Appleton in the other parts of the United States in which I have lived. Chicago, New York, many of the writings of popular figures and more arcane philosophers who are also referred to as "American"—all have reminded me of Appleton. I feel I have recognized it across social classes and certainly across regional provenance and history. I have also encountered institutions or groups who are truly different. I encountered one of them in Appleton itself: the Catholic Church, which was still organized in a European manner. Whatever their class identification, all Protestant churches are essentially voluntary associations. The Catholic Church is not.

In other words, when I talk about the unity of American culture, I am not talking about the diversity of the United States. I believe that what I have called American culture is the culture of authority and government in the United States, and it is probably the only one that is viable in the long run, but it is not the only one that is operative at present. Obviously not. However, I do not see the utility of denying the structural unity of an extremely large set of events that take place in the United States and inform its most salient productions either because that very structure denies its own existence or because all persons who live within the frontier of the country—from wetbacks just arrived from Mexico to a new Vietnamese immigrant to Hopi Indians—are not American.

Culture is not an individual thing. It is quite possible that many people who constantly use American forms do not completely believe in what they are saying. The best American philosophers often struggle with the argument that society is not created by the people who participate in it. Some may even rebel against individualism and the idea that society is perfectible. I am not thinking here of Thoreau—a quintessentially American figure—but rather of somebody like Reinhold Niebuhr in his fight against liberal Protestantism.

But the presence of alternate modes of interpretation within the territory of the United States cannot be taken as evidence for a theory of American culture that would see it as an amorphous conglomerate of conflicting values. Systems of communication must be structured, and to ignore this structuring process is to fall into a special form of false consciousness. There *are* ethnic groups within the United States whose culture is structured differently from the dominant one. But a true consciousness of the situation of these people must start with a proper delineation of the dominant culture. It is only if this is done that the operative differences between, say, American and Puerto Rican kinship patterns will become visible, something of obvious relevance to fields from education to mental health. And more importantly, perhaps, it is only by working on their own culture as I have done in these pages that Americans will confront a question that they themselves perceive as fundamental: not "Have we achieved what we started out to achieve?" but "Who are we?"

Notes

Introduction

1. F. Boas, *Race, language and culture* (New York: Free Press, 1940), p. v.
2. R. S. Lynd & H. M. Lynd, *Middletown: A study in modern American culture* (New York: Harcourt, Brace and World, 1929), p. 3.
3. *Ibid.*, p. 4.
4. H. J. Leichter (Ed.), *The family as educator* (New York: Teachers College Press, 1974).
5. D. M. Schneider, Kinship, nationality and religion in American culture: Toward a definition of kinship, in V. Turner (Ed.), *Forms of symbolic action* (Proceedings of the American Ethnological Association, 1969).
6. L. A. Cremin, *Public education* (New York: Basic Books, 1976).
7. I am referring here to a movement in modern cultural anthropology that has emerged recently. The basic statements are those of D. M. Schneider, What is kinship all about?, in P. Reining (Ed.), *Kinship studies in the Morgan centennial year* (Washington, D.C.: Society of Anthropology, 1972); and H. Geertz & C. Geertz, *Kinship in Bali* (Chicago and London: University of Chicago Press, 1975).
8. R. Redfield, *The little community* (Chicago: University of Chicago Press, 1956), p. 1.

Chapter 2

1. D. Schneider, *American kinship: A cultural account* (Englewood Cliffs, N.J.: Prentice-Hall, 1968).

234

2. I have dealt at more length with concomitant aspects of this theory of evaluation in two papers: H. Varenne, From grading and freedom of choice to ranking and segregation in an American high school, *Council on Anthropology and Education Quarterly* 5 (1974), pp. 9–15; H. Varenne & M. Kelly, Friendship and fairness: ideological tensions in an American high school, *Teachers College Record* 77 (1976), pp. 601–614.

Chapter 3

1. P. Tillich, *The Protestant era* (Chicago: University of Chicago Press, 1957), p. 174.
2. *Guideposts,* November 1971.
3. A. Gennep, *The rites of passage* (Chicago: University of Chicago Press, 1969; Trans. M. Vizedom & G. Gaffee); and V. Turner, *The ritual process: Structure and anti-structure* (Chicago: Aldine, 1969).

Chapter 4

1. The rites of passage of most societies involve a test by often physically painful trial of the ability of the child to withstand the rigors of adult life. In different ways, the rite is always related to the sociocultural life of the people involved. In America there is little physical pain involved in growing up from child to adult. But there certainly is psychological torture as the people who have always been closest to the child—his parents—begin telling him that the things his new reference group may define as normal are either illegal or, if legal, morally reprehensible or, at the very least, "immature," "irrelevant to real life," "not aesthetic," and so on. It would be interesting to investigate in detail the relationship that must exist between this type of rite of passage and the individualistic and moralistic nature of American culture.
2. For example, in H. Gans's *The Levittowners: Ways of life and politics in a new suburban community* (New York: Random House, 1967). See particularly Chapter 7, in which Gans summarizes his overview of the new town. However different his idiom may be from mine, the processes and outcomes he describes and his conclusions about the nature and functioning of small groups are very similar to my own.

Chapter 5

1. K. Rahner & H. Vorgrimler, *Theological dictionary* (New York: Herder and Herder, 1965), p. 415.
2. P. Tillich, *The Protestant era* (Chicago: University of Chicago Press, 1957), p. 174.
3. P. Tillich, *Systematic theology,* Vol. III (Chicago: University of Chicago Press, 1963), p. 236.
4. L. Dumont, World renunciation in Indian religion, in his *Religion, politics and history in India: Collected papers in Indian Sociology* (Paris: Mouton, 1970).
5. For an excellent, succinct discussion of this process, see M. Singer (Ed.), *Krishna: Myths, rites and attitudes* (Honolulu: East-West Center Press, 1966).
6. C. Lévi-Strauss. The story of Asdiwal, in E. Leach (Ed.), *The structural study of myth,* ASA Monograph No. 5 (London: Tavistock, 1967).
7. V. Turner, *The ritual process: Structure and anti-structure* (Chicago: Aldine, 1969).

Chapter 6

1. M. Grodzins, *The American system: A new view of government in the United States* (Chicago: Rand McNally, 1966; Ed. D.J. Elazar).
2. L. Dumont, *Homo hierarchicus: The caste system and its implications* (Chicago: University of Chicago Press, 1970; Trans. M. Sainsbury).
3. A. Vidich & J. Bensman, *Small town in mass society: Class, power and religion in a rural community* (Princeton, N.J.: Princeton University Press, 1968: rev. ed.).
4. R. Bellah, Civil religion in America, in his *Beyond belief: Essays on religion in a post-traditional world* (New York: Harper and Row, 1970), p. 170.
5. H. Robert, *Rules of order* (New York: Pyramid Books, 1967; R. Vixman, Ed.), back cover.

Chapter 7

1. R. Redfield, *The little community* (Chicago: University of Chicago Press, 1956).
2. F. Kluckhohn and E. Strodtbeck, *Variations in value orientations* (Evanston: Row, Peterson and Co., 1961).

3. For a brilliant summary articulation of this argument, see M. Merleau-Ponty, Around Marxism, in his *Sense and non-sense* (Evanston, Ill.: Northwestern University Press, 1964; Trans. H. Dreyfus and P. Dreyfus), pp. 99–124, particularly pp. 102–103.
4. J. Dewey, *Democracy and education: An introduction to the philosophy of education* (New York: Free Press, 1966), p. 4.

Part III: Introduction

1. A. Ginsberg, *Planet news: 1961-1967* (San Francisco: City Lights Books, 1968).

Chapter 8

1. J. Boon, Further operations of "culture" in anthropology: A synthesis of and for debate, *Social Science Quarterly* 52 (1972): 221–252, p. 241.
2. C. Lévi-Strauss, *Mythologiques IV: L'homme nu* (Paris: Plon, 1971), p. 596.
3. G. Bachelard, *The poetics of space* (Boston: Beacon Press, 1969; Trans. M. Jolas).

Chapter 9

1. W. Warner, *Social class in America: The evaluation of status* (Chicago: Science Research Associates, 1949), p. 103.

Chapter 10

1. *Decision*, December 1971, p. 11.
2. *Decision*, October 1971, pp. 10–11.
3. D. de Rougemont, *Love in the western world* (New York: Fawcett, 1956; Trans. M. Belgion), p. 71.
4. M. Singer, The Rādhā-Krishna *Bhajanas* of Madras City, in his *Krishna: Myths, rites and attitudes* (Honolulu: East-West Center Press, 1966); A. Ramanujan, Structure and anti-structure: The Virasaiva example (working paper presented at the Seminar on Aspects of Religion in South Asia, 1971).
5. L. Pirot & A. Clamer, *La sainte bible: Texte latin et traduction française avec un commentaire éxégétique et théologique* (Paris: Letouzey et Ané, 1948); vol. XI, part 2, p. 262.

6. K. Rahner & H. Vorgrimler, *Theological dictionary* (New York: Herder and Herder, 1965), p. 72.
7. *Ibid.*, p. 266.

Postface

1. M. Cole and S. Scribner, *Culture and thought: A psychological introduction* (New York: J. Wiley and Sons, 1974).
2. T. Parsons, Culture and social system revisited, *Social Science Quarterly* 52 (1972): 253–266, p. 256.
3. C. Lévi-Strauss, *Mythologiques IV: L'homme nu* (Paris: Plon, 1971), p. 596.
4. J.-M. Benoist, Structuralism: A new frontier, *Cambridge Review,* (1971):10–17, p. 15.
5. B. Glaser and A. Strauss, *The discovery of grounded theory: Strategies for qualitative research* (Chicago: Aldine, 1967).
6. C. Geertz, *The interpretation of cultures* (New York: Basic Books, 1973), p. 22.
7. A. Vidich & J. Bensman, *Small town in mass society: Class, power and religion in a rural community* (Princeton, N.J.: Princeton University Press, 1968: rev. ed.), p. xviii.

References

Bachelard, G. *The poetics of space* (Trans. M. Jolas). Boston: Beacon Press, 1969.

Barthes, R. *Mythologies*. Paris: Editions du Seuil, 1957.

Bellah, R. *Beyond belief: Essays on religion in a post-traditional world.* New York: Harper and Row, 1970.

Benoist, J.-M. Structuralism: A new frontier. *Cambridge Review,* 1971, 10–17.

Boas, F. *Race, language and culture.* New York: Free Press, 1940.

Boon, J. *From symbolism to structuralism: Lévi-Strauss in a literary tradition.* New York: Harper and Row, 1972.

Boon, J. Further operations of "culture" in anthropology: A synthesis of and for debate. *Social Science Quarterly,* 1972, *52,* 221–252.

Cole, M.; & **Scribner, S.** *Culture and thought: A psychological introduction.* New York: J. Wiley and Sons, 1974.

Condominas, G. *L'exotique est quotidien: Sar Luk, Viet-Nam central.* Paris: Plon, 1965.

Cremin, L. *Public education.* New York: Basic Books, 1976.

Dewey, J. *Democracy and education: An introduction to the philosophy of education.* New York: The Free Press, 1966.

Dumézil, G. *L'idéologie tripartite des Indo-Européens.* Bruxelles: Revue d'études latines, 1958.

Dumont, L. *Homo hierarchicus: The caste system and its implications* (Trans. M. Sainsbury). Chicago: University of Chicago Press, 1970.

Dumont, L. Religion, politics, and society in the individualistic universe. In *Proceedings of the Royal Anthropological Institute,* 1970.

Dumont, L. World renunciation in Indian religion. In his *Religion, politics and history in India: Collected papers in Indian sociology.* Paris: Mouton, 1970.

Foucault, M. *Histoire de la folie à l'age classique.* Paris: Gallimard, 1972.

Foucault, M. *Les mots et les choses: Une archéologie des sciences humaines.* Paris: Gallimard, 1966.

Franklin, B. *Autobiography: And other writings* (R. B. Nye, Ed.). Boston: Houghton Mifflin, 1958.

Gans, H. *The Levittowners: Ways of life and politics in a new suburban community.* New York: Random House, 1967.

Geertz, C. *The interpretation of cultures: Selected essays.* New York: Basic Books, 1973.

Geertz, H.; & **Geertz, G.** *Kinship in Bali.* Chicago: University of Chicago Press, 1975.

Gennep, A. *The rites of passage* (Trans. M. Vizedom & G. Gaffee). Chicago: University of Chicago Press, 1969.

Ginsberg, A. *Planet news: 1961–1967.* San Francisco: City Lights Books, 1968.

Glaser, B.; & **Strauss, A.** *The discovery of grounded theory: Strategies for qualitative research.* Chicago: Aldine, 1967.

Glazer, N.; & **Moynihan, D.** *Beyond the melting pot: The Negroes, Puerto-Ricans, Jews, Italians and Irish of New York City.* Cambridge, Mass.: Massachusetts Institute of Technology, 1963.

Grodzins, M. *The American system: A new view of government in the United States* (D. J. Elazar, Ed.). Chicago: Rand McNally, 1966.

Heidegger, M. Hölderlin and the essence of poetry Trans. D. Scott). In *Existence and being* (W. Brock, Ed.). Chicago: Henry Regnery, 1949.

James, H. *The ambassadors.* New York: W. W. Norton, 1964.

Kluckhohn, F. & **Strodtbeck, E.** *Variations in value orientation.* Evanston: Row, Peterson and Co., 1961.

Leach, E. *Rethinking anthropology.* London: Athlone Press, 1961.

Leichter, H. J. (Ed.). *The family as educator.* New York: Teachers College Press, 1974.

Lévi-Strauss, C. *Mythologics I: The raw and the cooked* (Trans. J. Weightman & D. Weightman). New York: Harper and Row, 1969.

Lévi-Strauss, C. *Mythologiques IV: L'homme nu.* Paris: Plon, 1971.

Lévi-Strauss, C. *The savage mind.* Chicago: University of Chicago Press, 1966.

Lévi-Strauss, C. The story of Asdiwal. In E. Leach (Ed.), *The structural study of myth.* ASA Monograph No. 5. London: Tavistock, 1967.

Lynd, R.; & **Lynd, H.** *Middletown: A study in modern American culture.* New York: Harcourt, Brace and World, 1929.

Mead, M. *And keep your powder dry: An anthropologist looks at America.* Exp. Ed. New York: William Morrow, 1965.

Mead, M. *Male and female: A study of the sexes in a changing world.* New York: Dell, 1968.

Merleau-Ponty M. *Sense and non-sense* (Trans. H. Dreyfus & P. Dreyfus). Evanston, Ill.: Northwestern University Press, 1964.

Novak, M. *The rise of the unmeltable ethnics: Politics and culture in the seventies.* New York: Macmillan, 1971.

Parsons, T. Culture and social system revisited. *Social Science Quarterly,* 1972, *52,* 253–266.

Piaget, J. *Le structuralisme.* Paris: Presses Universitaires de France, 1968.

Pirot, L.; & **Clamer, A.** *La sainte bible: Texte latin et traduction française avec un commentaire éxégétique et théologique.* Paris: Letouzey et Ané, 1948.

Rahner, K.; & **Vorgrimler, H.** *Theological dictionary.* New York: Herder and Herder, 1965.

Ramanujan, A. K. Structure and anti-structure: The Virasaiva example. Working paper presented at the Seminar on Aspects of Religion in South Asia, 1971.

Redfield, R. *The little community.* Chicago: University of Chicago Press, 1967.

Riesman, D. *The lonely crowd: A study of the changing American character.* New Haven: Yale University Press, 1961.

Robert, H. *Rules of order* (R. Vixman, Ed.). New York: Pyramid Books, 1967.

Rougemont, D. *Love in the western world* (Trans. M. Belgion). New York: Fawcett World Library, 1965.

Saussure, F. *Course in general linguistics* (C. Bally & A. Sechehaye, Eds.; Trans. W. Baskin). New York: Philosophical Library, 1959.

Schneider, D. *American kinship: A cultural account.* Englewood Cliffs, N.J.: Prentice-Hall, 1968.

Schneider, D. Kinship, nationality and religion in American culture: Toward a definition of kinship. In V. Turner (Ed.), *Forms of symbolic action.* Proceedings of the American Ethnological Association, 1969.

Schneider, D. What is kinship all about? In P. Reining (Ed.) *Kinship studies in the Morgan centennial year.* Washington, D.C.: Society of Anthropology, 1972.

Singer, M. (Ed.). *Krishna: myths, rites and attitudes.* Honolulu: East-West Center Press, 1966.

Sinha, S. Religion in an affluent society. *Current Anthropology,* 1966, 7, 189–194.

Slater, P. *The pursuit of loneliness: American culture at the breaking point.* Boston: Beacon Press, 1970.

Tillich, P. *The Protestant era.* Abr. Ed. Chicago: University of Chicago Press, 1957.

Tillich, P. *Systematic theology.* Vol. III. Chicago: University of Chicago Press, 1963.

Tocqueville, A. *Democracy in America* (J. P. Mayer, Ed.; Trans. G. Lawrence). Garden City, N.Y.: Doubleday, 1969.

Turner, V. *The ritual process: Structure and anti-structure.* Chicago: Aldine, 1969.

Varenne, H. From grading and freedom of choice to ranking and segregation in an American high school. *Council on Anthropology and Education Quarterly,* 1974, 5, 9–15.

Varenne, H.; & **Kelly, M.** Friendship and fairness: Ideological tensions in an American high school. *Teachers College Record,* 1976, 77, 601–614.

Vidich, A.; & **Bensman, J.** *Small town in mass society: Class, power and religion in a rural community.* Rev. Ed. Princeton, N.J.: Princeton University Press, 1968.

Warner, W. *The living and the dead: A study of the symbolic life of Americans.* New Haven, Conn.: Yale University Press, 1958.

Warner, W. *Social class in America: The evaluation of status.* New York: Harper and Row, 1949.

Warner, W. (Ed.). *Democracy in Jonesville: A study in quality and inequality.* New York: Harper and Row, 1949.

Warner, W.; & **Lunt, P.** *The social life of a modern community.* Yankee City Series Vol. I. New Haven, Conn.: Yale University Press, 1941.

Warner, W.; & **Lunt, P.** *The status system of a modern community.* Yankee City Series Vol. II. New Haven, Conn.: Yale University Press, 1942.

Weber, M. *The Protestant ethic and the spirit of capitalism* (Trans. T. Parsons). New York: Charles Scribner's Sons, 1958.

West, J. *Plainville, U.S.A.* New York: Columbia University Press, 1964.